Footloose in the Himalaya

Footloose in the Himalaya

BILL AITKEN

permanent black

Published by
PERMANENT BLACK
D-28 Oxford Apartments, 11, I.P. Extension,
Delhi 110092

In association with
RAVI DAYAL PUBLISHER
51E, Sujan Singh Park, New Delhi 110003

Distributed by
ORIENT LONGMAN LTD
Bangalore Bhopal Bhubaneshwar Chandigarh
Chennai Ernakulam Guwahati Hyderabad Jaipur Kolkata
Lucknow Mumbai New Delhi Patna

© BILL AITKEN 2003
The moral rights of the author have been asserted

Endpaper illustration by Ravi Dayal
Illustration on p. 2 by Bill Aitken
Other illustrations by Anuradha Roy

ISBN 81-7824-052-1

LONDON BOROUGH OF HACKNEY	
VENDOR	RONDO
LOC	SHD
ACC.No	03/453-121293
CLASS	915.496

by Guru T
Printe

110045
)20

To
the tough, cheerful and inspiring
women of Uttarakhand

Contents

	Preface	ix
1	The Call of the Mountains	1
2	Finding Your Level	10
3	A Bend in the Road	19
4	First Footsteps	30
5	Binsar and Beyond	41
6	Time by the Village Clock	49
7	Union of Continents and the Birth of Eternity	58
8	Burha Pinnath	67
9	Chhota Binsar	76
10	Uttar Brindaban	84
11	Bala Hissar	95
12	Gateway to God	103
13	Dev Bhumi	115
14	Ganga Maharani	125
15	The Best Little Trek	134
16	A Date with Pokhu	143
17	Choor Chandni	153

18	A Night on the Tiles	164
19	A Clean Pair of Heels	174
20	The Void Manifest	184
21	The Coppery Kingdom	192
22	Wild Rivers and a Rainbow	202
23	The Greatest Show on Earth	212
24	Cliff-Hanging Gompa	220
25	The King Over the Water	230
26	The Taste of Vintage Chang	239
27	East of the Devi	249

Preface

While a fair region round the traveller lies. . . . with Thought and Love companions of our way
  —William Wordsworth, 'The Inner Vision'

The aim of recollecting these vintage walks is to try and hint at the timeless sublimity of the Himalaya even in its lower reaches. Perhaps the Himalaya is more important for the peak experiences it delivers than the peaks themselves. My own certainly occurred low on the descent from a pass into Zanskar.

I also have to honour the ordinary hill villager on whom the success of any foray into the mountains depends. Amidst the penury of their circumstances sturdy character abounds. As for walking, it is the primary requisite for facing the twin realities of glory and grottiness. Climbing—focused on the summit—too often downplays the suffering to highlight the moment of triumph. Together the verve and energy of the cragsperson, with the softer sense of wonder pilgrims bring to their endeavour, make for good companions. Travelling by armchair need not be antithetical if the reader understands the value of sweat. Sweat guarantees the sweetest of all Himalayan rewards after the 'dignity of danger'—a sense of selfhood.

Mussoorie 2002   Bill Aitken

1
The Call of the Mountains

I knew almost nothing about the Himalaya when I set off hitch-hiking round the world in 1959. The real wonder of the world's highest range was not hinted at by the symbol of Tenzing clutching a string of flags on the summit of Everest though it did confirm my instinct that mere verticality signified little. More intriguing was the promise of inner wisdom to be found in the caves of meditating yogis. After my MA thesis on the theology of Mahatma Gandhi my external examiner presciently supplied a name and an address in India. I saw my eastward tour as a field trip in comparative religion that would provide respectability to my plans to eventually teach in Britain after my travels. Forty years have elapsed. My proposed circumambulation of the globe never got beyond a third of the distance, the obstacle that intervened being the magnetic pull of the Himalaya.

Mountains have always mattered deeply to me. I was born and brought up at the foot of the Ochil Hills in Scotland and was daily ravished by their green and craggy grandeur. I longed to live among such exalted beauty but the only option in the 'Wee Coonty' of Clackmannanshire was to become a shepherd, a rather bleak and chilly option summed up locally as 'an awfie scunner'.

En route to India the sweeping white slopes of Mount Ararat on the borders of Turkey and Iran spoke directly to my soul. The stunning sense of exaltation at seeing this mountain gave me an inkling that the outer quest of academic study was a cloak that concealed a passion as volcanic as the energy that raised Ararat.

In Delhi, I found that the mountains interpenetrated the city's buildings. The wonderful vista of Rajpath is brought alive by the red gravel edging mined from the ancient range of the Aravallis while Delhi's less exalted buildings are all plastered in a fine silvery sand washed up by the Yamuna, the river that comes down from the Himalaya. At the Okhla barrage I saw on the back of a truck lined up for a load of Yamuna sand the optimistic legend 'Dreams At Affordable Prices'. The truck owner was a building contractor who seemed to know that for most Delhiwalas the prospect of owning a house in the capital was life's chief ambition.

At the foot of Dum-y-at, the Ochil Hills

I was intrigued by the alchemy wrought on Delhi's buildings by blood-red gravel from the hoariest of ranges and the silvery motes ground down from the heights of the comparatively young Himalaya. Perhaps this alchemy of the mountains would help me find my dream. After a year teaching in Calcutta I moved to a Gandhian ashram in Kausani. My expenses, at two rupees a month, were eminently affordable. Four years on I had outlived the Gandhian dream and moved to an ashram at Mirtola also in the Kumaun hills.

Mirtola was what I had been searching for. It forced me to unlearn so much and see through the sea-level encrustations that obscured the sacred state aloof peaks symbolised to me. Love intervened at this point, and after twelve years of the simple life in Kumaun I moved to neighbouring Garhwal. For my requirements Mussoorie was perfect. It was quiet and cosmopolitan and gave access to both Delhi and Badrinath. Best of all, Oakless, the house I lived in, was set on the watershed ridge of the Ganga and Yamuna. When I walk out of Oakless's gate I see floating before me the resplendent spread of the Doon Valley (some 3000 ft below) and recall with pleasure how that childhood desire of becoming part of the Ochils has been fulfilled on a scale immeasurably grander than I dared imagine.

The price you pay for living in the mountains is having to prefer your own two feet to the wafting of a Mercedes or Maruti. But to walk in Garhwal is to breathe afresh and exult in the freedom and vigour of selfhood. It is akin to the exhilaration of being in love when all the faculties are aroused yet a calm ecstasy prevails. To walk is probably the best way to soak in the full beauty of the Himalaya because it leaves you open to the unexpected and elemental. Whether striding, strolling or slogging, the effort of legs and lungs working in harmony releases a three-pointed joy where body and soul are at one with their surroundings.

Kierkegaard found walking conducive to profound thoughts while Wordsworth and Coleridge acknowledged its contribution to poetic inspiration. Dickens affirmed that 'The best way to lengthen out our days is to walk steadily and with a purpose.' Walking has the added advantage of being open to all estates and conditions. As mankind's earliest form of locomotion it remains the most universal, since even the latest design of car cannot get you upstairs to bed.

My travels were always undertaken on a tight budget. In fact I had come to India overland on fifty pounds sterling and discovered that shoe-lace travelling has the bonus of exposing the adventurous soul to the hand of providence. Of the ten thousand miles I covered perhaps only ten were hiked. The rest were hitched by an astounding assortment of transport that included lifts by a Danish scooterist, an Austrian TV salesman, a Greek melon transporter, an American oil rig team in Turkey, a police jeep in Jordan, a petrol tanker in Iran and an Australian bus tour out of Lahore. In the no mean city of Tarsus (now called Mersin) I was even offered a lift on horseback.

I made a detour to see the Holy Land and found the hatred so palpable you could cut it with a knife. This was my baptism into the realities of the world's so-called living religions and after the six-year study I had made of them at university, like St Paul, the scales were removed from my eyes. Holiness in such a setting would be deemed an obscenity. The plain fact is that the Himalaya would turn out to be a hundred times holier than the so-called Holy Land.

When I sailed from the cliffs of Dover I was a jilted lover. The woman I was passionately in love with had made it clear the night before that she was keeping her options open. At the time her indifference seemed to be the worst cut of all: why was this ravishing creature so blind to the most beautiful sentiments I was ready to lavish on her?

It has taken forty years to realise that destiny favoured me in my mistress's cool reception. Had she wept and clung I would have postponed my journey east and like all my other friends got married and lived (as they imagine) happily ever after. Instead I was pitch-forked into becoming an unlikely founding father of the hippie overland movement. Not just that, my life yet again explodes the myth that East and West cannot meet.

When after six weeks of hitch-hiking I arrived in Calcutta I had spent the fifty pounds I had set out with. Calcutta marked the end of the hitcher's land route and to get further east I would have to find a job and save up for a freighter ticket to Penang. Destiny had been at work in the Middle East to help me find a job. A missionary in the Holy Land had provided me the address of a wealthy Scots businessman in Calcutta, and I landed a teaching job at Hindi High School. This was a school for rich Marwaris and the principal happened to be a Scotsman.

Now was to occur my very first contact with the Himalaya. On the desk of a very fat little boy lay a beautiful Tibetan pen holder. I asked Aggarwal where he had got it and he replied casually, 'Oh I went to Lhasa with my father in the holidays.' (This was 1960.) I gasped to think of this podgy little boy riding across the world's highest range in a jingling caravan of mules.

My second contact with the Himalaya would only yield fruit

after twenty years. In a Park Street bookshop I picked up the grey-backed Himalayan Club *Journal* and felt a shiver of outlandish delight, almost pornographic in its intensity, at its foldouts of Himalayan panoramas. I wrote to apply for admission but had no response. In those days expatriate businessmen still ran the club and I concluded that their criterion for membership put depth of pocket before purity of heart.

A third strand of destiny made me befriend Sukumar Misra, a colleague at Hindi High School, who shared my taste for adventurous travel. He introduced me to the Asiatic Society library where I voraciously read books on the Himalaya. I also started learning Sanskrit at night school and one evening, browsing at the pavement bookstalls on College Street, I came across Swami Pranavananda's guide book to the Kailash Mansarover pilgrimage.

My heart stood still when I started reading it. Even the mundane details of the route stages I found intoxicating. It was as though my soul had found familiar moorings and that it was among these ranges my happiness lay.

Now the skein of fate led back to a Himalayan connection I had been unaware of in Leeds. The external examiner for my thesis had been Dr Aravindu Basu and talking to him after the viva he asked what my plans were. I told him I planned to visit India and check out some ashrams I had read about. He told me to visit Sri Krishna Prem—'a retired English colonel who lived in an ice cave in the Himalayas.'

To people who live in a hot climate ice caves must make sense as the likely symbol for relief to life's problems; but to a Scotsman blasted by gales off the North Sea the last place where peace could reside would be a draughty cave. God would more likely be found in a snuggery with a wee dram.

Swami Pranavananda's guide to Kailash had a reference to Krishna Prem's Mirtola ashram and I noted that at 7000 ft east of Almora there wouldn't be much ice. But the important lesson was not the professor's unscientific description of Krishna Prem's setting but to understand why Dr Basu had been so moved by this Englishman's example. As it happens my first meeting with

Krishna Prem was a bit icy but the temperature had been brought down by my own preconceived idea of what spirituality should consist of. I assessed the yogi by his outward appearance and accent—both very English—and concluded that no exotic truths could be expected from anyone with an Anglo-Saxon background. My limited understanding of the inner path and my youthful stupidity set me back four years in my search. Luckily Krishna Prem saw through my callowness and indirectly turned my footsteps back to his ashram when he recommended I visit Sarala Devi, an English educationist who ran a Gandhian school for girls in Kausani.

In Calcutta Sukumar told me he planned to visit Badrinath in the summer holidays. If I would like to accompany him on this ultimate popular Hindu pilgrimage in Uttarakhand I would have to apply to Delhi for an Inner Line permit.

It seems strange now to look back on how restricted one's movements were in the Indian Himalaya of the 1960s. Beyond Kausani I could do a day's march up to Gwaldam while from Mirtola access only extended down to the river Sarju. Innocent of how India's friendly feudalism works I honestly thought that the government would process the application I had handed in. Needless to say no permit ever arrived.

Permitless, Sukumar and I set off for Haridwar and spent a couple of days in Rishikesh arranging supplies. What I saw of the spiritual scene there was far from spiritual, and some of the marketing tactics of the holy men seemed downright crude.

We managed to bluff the authorities at Srinagar that we did not require cholera vaccinations but at Rudraprayag the policeman manning the Inner Line demanded to see my permit. The game was up. I insisted on Sukumar continuing his yatra. Meanwhile I would make my way to Mussoorie and learn some Hindi, hoping that would enable me to travel further next time.

I must say my first views of the Himalaya were not inspiring. Crammed aboard a pilgrim bus with rustic candidates for darshan with divinity, it was hot and smelly. The halts for tea were at scruffy roadside dhabas where millions of flies attacked even the doorway. The missionaries dismissed these nature spirits as demons but another way to view them is to see in their shrines a diluted expression of divinity.

On regaining the ridge I found I had walked eastwards to emerge at Jabarkhet. Being new to the ropes I was immediately issued a ticket and made to pay four annas by the toll keeper who taxed milkmen on their way to Mussoorie. I was charged on the weight of my water bottle. (Later the toll keeper and I would share a laugh on how I should have drunk the contents to avoid the tax.)

It was a splendid afternoon in the forest and I thirsted for more. Just to walk along the ridge road east of Jabarkhet was to be full of joy. In 1960 a motor road—that did not interfere with the natural contours of the bridle path—had just been built. This end of Mussoorie's long straggling ridge (running for ten miles) saw some dramatic vertical falls and in places the slope seemed to sweep up sheer from the Doon to top out in a knife edge ridge some 5000 feet higher.

This is the first real uprise of the Himalaya, stretching all the way to the border with Nepal. To avoid regional jealousies it might have been advisable to refer to this range as the Mussoorie–Naini Tal range since the latter hill station also sits astride it; but it was reckoned to be the Mussoorie range by the British and so it is called to this day.

Mussoorie's steep southern face is fascinating for its varied mineral content and the mining of these rich deposits of limestone and phosphate would lead to much ecological and political heartburning. In 1960 the exploitation had not yet begun.

The last strand in the silken tug of destiny unravelled at the language school. Before I left for Calcutta I loaned a missionary architect some trekking gear and he suggested I visit him in his mission in Agra to see the Taj at the October full moon. Just two weeks before setting out I had a telegram changing the programme. Could I now meet him at Kathgodam railway station as he had to desultory attempts at hygiene. I spent the night back in Srinagar in a tented colony for yatris and returned to Rishikesh next morning to proceed by bus to Mussoorie.

On the bus up to the hill station was a young man whose uncle owned a hotel, so unasked for I had accommodation waiting. With such a friendly introduction I took a shine to this town that has grown stronger over the years. The site was spectacular, overlooking the snow peaks to the north and Doon ghati to the south. Everything about Mussoorie seemed wondrous.

After the months in Calcutta and the grilling heat of the pilgrim bus I now found my breathing expansive. I set off for Landour and weaved my way through the narrow bazaar of sweet shops and silversmiths. A generation later, nothing has changed in the tumbledown alignment of the shops except for the sweets being kept safe from the flies (actually wasps) in glass cases. Now the silver jewellery is also in the process of being encased by modern shop frontages.

At Wolfsburn guest house facing north and surrounded by scintillating deodar scented forests, I found a perfect base for my stay. I attended Hindi classes in the morning and explored the slopes in the afternoon. The principal of the school was the Rev. R.C. Smith, a broad-minded missionary who loved both India and the teaching of Hindi. He had no problem in allowing an outsider join his course and said he welcomed those who came voluntarily since they would benefit more from their involvement.

One afternoon I dropped down the steep footpath used by Mussoorie's suppliers of milk and made my way by precipitous shortcuts to the first village that lay in a clearing a thousand feet below the hill station. The villagers were both shy and friendly and I marvelled to see how primitive their living arrangements were. Yet there was an integrity and dignity in their simple stone houses that many of Mussoorie's grander structures lacked.

It was hot climbing back and I had to wait until I was well clear of the village before I dared fill my water bottle in a stream. On the way I passed a tiny temple dedicated to a local devta and was impressed to see how many silver rupees had been nailed around the be in Naini Tal for a meeting? This was my chance to see the English yogi in his ice cave. I agreed.

I mentioned my plan to my Sanskrit teacher, Dr Govinda Gopal Mukhopadhyaya, in Calcutta. He beamed at the mention of Sri Krishna Prem and suggested that since the holy man did not encourage visitors I could write to him before leaving telling him Dr Mukhopadhyaya had given me his address. They were old friends. My Himalayan destiny was being shaped from all sides.

2
Finding Your Level

The tonic effect of the Himalaya is as hard to define as India herself: both have the daunting prospect of size, a baffling variety of scene and a complex sociology to be assimilated. What areas I have been able to see are inadequate to allow for any certain conclusions but I can confirm that in most of them I have tasted the same rare elixir that makes ordinary trekking momentarily ecstatic.

The only way to explain this when faced with the contrasting terrain of southern and northern aspects of the Himalaya and the climatic difference between the hills of Kashmir and Arunachal is that these mountains, despite their variety, are united in expressing something locked up in the beholder. We make the effort to reach the Himalaya because it unlocks the treasures of our inner being. Our lives are touched and altered by walking among these peaks and breathing willy-nilly becomes more purposeful. In some sense as agents of the divine they are endowed with the capacity to arouse that dormant sense of nobility every human soul possesses at birth but loses in the confused process of growing up in a world of conflicting values and conditioned responses. India characteristically has regarded the Himalaya as the source of her civilisational inspiration and still venerates the timeless figures of the Rishi Munis above those who wave ephemeral flags atop Everest. Greatness in India (until very recent times) was always defined by control of inner rather than outer forces.

Another word sometimes used for the Himalaya is 'Shivalaya'. Shiva is *antaryami*, the inner ruler, no less than our conscience, the true mountain guide on our ascent to meaningful manhood. It is a geographical fluke that Shiva resides on Kailash in whose vicinity arise the two great rivers that demark the extent of the Himalaya, the Indus and Brahmaputra. It is another fluke that the river flowing through the trough created by colliding continents is the Indus, the word from which 'India' (and 'Hindu') is derived.

The power of the Himalaya lies not in any civilisational artefacts but in physical and psychic contours that awe and inspire. As an idea and expression of dynamic divinity it appeals more than any other pilgrim destination. Village pilgrims suffering the rigours of the traditional yatra undoubtedly shared the feeling of awe confronted by Himalayan ridges as they painstakingly climbed bridle paths; but now that the journey is done by bus much of the naked glory won only by sweat is missing and there is a more passive feeling of achievement in the darshan of Lord Badri.

The appeal of the Himalaya is more than cultural, mythological and religious since pilgrims from all parts of the world are alive to the special lure of this range that combines the world's highest peaks with the most extraordinarily beautiful vistas. The Himalaya represents a challenge to the universal spirit in us. I can quote as an example the strange and touching lure it had for a friend of mine, a British serviceman who had glimpsed the range once very briefly, yet felt he must breathe his last before its beneficient spread. If you visit the cemetery in Kathmandu do not smile when you see a grave marked 'Jack Spratt'. In the last days of his cancer, Jack was flown from Britain on a stretcher to die before the peaks that had stirred his soul. He made it with a day to spare.

The art of beholding the Himalaya lies in accepting the paradox of aesthetic wealth alongside economic poverty, of reconciling the glory of aliveness with the evenly poised mischance of death. In such situations only a devotee can thrive, someone who surrenders to his instinct of awe at what is manifest before him.

The hardships in retrospect are unreal. In their recall the horror of that moment is replaced with thankfulness at survival. Life is a fragile business and hanging on to it by a thread in the mountains enables us to be grateful for its continuing favours. The lover of the Himalaya has too much to contemplate with relish to allow himself ever to be a complainant. Every hill walker soon discovers his level of plenitude. Mine has always been rambling along the trails of the lesser range where leaves carpet the bridle path and you slosh through the bounty of Vallombrosia with the rustle of a hundred autumns. But just as magical is to pass silently into overhanging higher greenery where the feet pad the soft humus of last year's leaves broken down to nourish the earth from which their parent has arisen. I love the cyclical feel of my local range around Mussoorie and delight in its drastic seasonal fluctuations. In the snows branches may snap and a few trees keel over but in the rains a runaway gadera (glen) can splinter trees like matchsticks and wash out a line of massive boulders. Just as a vulture strips a carcass so do our monsoon rivulets boil over to perform the most demented acts of destruction. In the hot season too the pine forests are casualty to the most cruel of afflictions, fire that snarls at all living things. Sometimes hailstorms in spring or autumn do considerable damage and even take life. Underlying all these movements (caused ultimately by the sun) is the greatest imponderable—when the earth moves.

I have always defined earthquakes as the one sign of God that everyone, even atheists when shaken by one, believes in. Our fear overlooks what marvellous proof they give of bubbling life at the heart of things. As everyone knows earthquakes do not kill as much as our unreasoned response to them. Awareness of how to react positively to the upheavals of nature is the first lesson learned from trekking in the range. You are forced to assess the dangers of getting into a situation and then have to balance the chances of getting out again. The greatest lesson of all is to learn to be responsible for decisions and live with them when they are poor. Fate may have brought you into this world but to climb the mountain path requires cultivation of a conscience that at the crossroads in a crisis will resist the urge to take the easy downpointing path.

To walk is to become part of a poem that celebrates the body's simple graces while to climb intensifies the enjoyment by responding to a challenge. Climb too high however and a lack of oxygen affects our judgement, often leading to punishment instead of pleasure.

When I was writing this, the Doon School organised an exhibition of its ascent of Trisul in 1951, which was the first successful Indian climb, led by the evergreen Gurdial Singh. This led me to plot the graph of declining sporting motivation that characterises the climbs in the Himalaya in the last five decades. In defence of today's climbers it has to be said that the values of the entire sporting world have changed drastically and even in the most hallowed of games, cricket, gentlemanly graces are a thing of the past. Larwood and his bodyline bowling was not an aberration but the shape of things to come.

Gurdial's expedition was done with love and regard for the environment. Significantly it was Gurdial who refused to lead another expedition in 1964 to Nanda Devi to place a nuclear spying device there.

In 1976 an American expedition to Nanda Devi highlighted the change from amateur enthusiasm to professional commitment wherein the classical Mummery concept of enjoying oneself was replaced by the grim new ethic of success at any price. Ad Carter's most fatal mistake as leader was to plump for the brilliant but brash John Roskelley as lead climber. The cast for this tragedy of conflicting generations guaranteed it was doomed from the start. Roskelley had a summit fixation that drove him with evangelistic fervour. Carter had been with the successful first amateur climb in 1936 when a laid-back Anglo-American team had almost apologetically summited the peak. The 1976 climb was in the nature of a commemorative expedition and had as its co-leader the tough but maverick Willi Unsoeld. The team was a mix of romantic and ambitious climbers and Roskelley presumably had been chosen to make sure someone reached the summit. The outspoken Roskelley had opinions on everything from the first day. Heated arguments broke out over the fitness of women climbers (including Willi's daughter, named Nanda Devi after the peak). Emotions ran high, decisions were avoided and the bickering intensified so much that the gentlemanly Ad Carter, disillusioned, decided to turn back. Roskelley and a partner against the odds climbed the main peak but to spoil their moment of glory Nanda Devi Unsoeld, following in their tracks, died suddenly high on the mountain from complications arising from a hernia she had contracted in Delhi.

Roskelley waited for ten years to elapse before his book *Nanda Devi: The Tragic Expedition* was published. He makes clear his disenchantment with the motivation of several of the team. At least two couples were in—and being American, quickly out of—love, and while Willi viewed love as an aid to their endeavour Roskelley vowed it would handicap their progress.

With love thrown out of the window in 1976 the mountaineering world had to wait till 1996 when commercial guided climbs to the summit of Everest (hauling up wealthy clients each waiting his expensive moment of glory) coincided with morality being thrown out of the door. A 21-year-old Japanese climber who passed by dying Indian climbers on his way to the top refused to offer succour of any kind but had the honesty to admit the summit of the Mother Goddess is 'not a place where people can afford morality'. Whoever said mountaineering brings out the best in us forgot to add that it can also bring out the worst.

Morality had ceased to operate at base in 1953 when the British Everest committee desperate for success after a quarter of a century of failures dumped the claims of Eric Shipton to be leader in favour of Colonel John Hunt whose pragmatic attitude to a peak, 'knocking the bastard off' (as Hillary would put it), guaranteed quicker returns in the year that saw a second Elizabeth on the throne of England. Shipton was an old-fashioned Alpinist more concerned with beauty discovered than altitude gained or political prestige. He had sat out the ascent of Nanda Devi in 1936 preferring to go back to the mountain's Sanctuary for the pleasure of mapping its less known parts.

Part of the villain's role has been played by improved climbing technology. Whereas Mallory and Irvine are shown high on Everest in flannel bags, tweed coats and puttees, the clients of Rob

Hall and Scott Fisher in 1996 who were wiped out by their refusal to turn back when so near their goal, wore the latest in survival gear. This enabled them to think they could beat the odds.

They also had miracle medicines and one of the most farcical scenes in the history of mountaineering is recorded in Jon Krakauer's best-selling account of the commercial climbs, *Into Thin Air*, regarding the administration of this medicine. A Hollywood socialite was dragged up the mountain by a sherpa on a short rope, and then half-dead on the summit she had to be dumped face down and given an injection in the backside to revitalise her.

The grotesque denouement of this desperate desire for fame and money (the more who reached the summit the greater the publicity for next year's ascent) was for both guides to fall short of safety by a few feet. Rob Hall, unable to reach the rope that led downhill out of the storm, perished even as he spoke to his wife in New Zealand by mobile phone. As a final coda to how Everest dollars cause some to become suicidal, his wife was carrying their child.

Macabrely these bodies still sit guarding the approach to the summit of the Mother Goddess preserved by the very elements that conspired to rob them of their lives. Had these climbers been punished for selling the mystique of a sacred place or for demeaning it in their unseemly scrabble for a place on top?

I have always responded to the village view that we are here as *mehman*, guests of the gods, visitors on this planet, not proprietors. The need to subdue nature may be a sign of uncertainty about our place in the cosmos. Throughout the lore of modern climbing can be seen the conflict between those who climb for love (in the minority) and those who climb for gain.

It was the power of Krakauer's writing that got me started with recording my own regard for the Himalaya albeit from the unambitious angle of the trekker unconcerned with permits, flags, sponsors and press conferences. My earlier book *The Nanda Devi Affair* had described my special kinship for this mountain and her lore. Being concerned with one particular peak I could not hope to do justice to my feelings for the vibrant variety of the entire range. That book had been sparked by a rare moment in the sanctuary when I sensed the Goddess was commanding me to write of her graces. Without that level of inspiration no book can hope to get off the ground. Thanks to Krakauer the Goddess intervened again to get my thoughts on the Himalaya airborne.

It happened through a film director, Hugh Thomson, who met me in Delhi in October 2000 while returning from a visit to Nanda Devi Sanctuary. Hugh was intrigued by the story of a nuclear spying device planted on Nanda Devi and asked me where the details had been printed. I told him the story had been published in a Californian fringe magazine whose name I could not remember. As he left Hugh presented me a paperback by Jon Krakauer entitled *Into The Wild* and suggested that since I had liked *Into Thin Air* I would like this too.

After seeing him out of the gate I flipped it open and on the first page was confronted with the name of the fringe magazine in which the story of the Nanda Devi spying caper had appeared. Krakauer had been commissioned by the same magazine to write both his best-selling books.

Into The Wild deals with an idealistic and affluent young American college student, Chris McCandless, who hungers to live with nature, free from the mindless acquisitiveness that marks the American dream, and steer clear of the humbug and cant that is employed to justify it. Chris drops out of college and rehearses for a long stay in Alaska (living wild off the land) by hitch-hiking through the Mid-West, hoping to pick up hints on how to live simply, and more importantly survive on his own store of wilderness wisdom. He completes his training run, repairs to Alaska and does his thing. But the wilderness proves too tough and he dies of starvation. Such are the barebones of the story but Krakauer is too good a narrator not to flesh them out with some original observations of his own on the challenges of the wild. In doing so he retraces the hitch-hiking route of the dropout and to his amazement finds that the trail is still alive. Everybody who gave Chris McCandless a lift remembered him for his burning sincerity, and almost prophet-like incandescence of character. Cleverly the book turns the story on its head to prove that McCandless hadn't died because he was an idealistic greenhorn. His death was accidental: the instructions he had read about a particular fruit did not add that when the seeds ripened they became poisonous. He ate the ripened seeds and was paralysed. This prevented him from hunting for food that could have saved his life.

McCandless's story somehow cleanses the vulgar goings on at the top of Everest where another aspect of the American dream was being paid for in lives. What comes across strongly is the purity of motive in the Alaska expedition and its absence in the Everest nightmare. I found McCandless an absorbing subject and like Krakauer could see part of myself reflected in his youthful idealism. Chris's urge to plunge into the wilderness in order to be nearer the source of life's wonder happened to misfire because of his inexperience. He ran out of luck. My own career, threatened by similar overweaning idealism, was luckier. What saved me was the acceptance of a guru who honed down the awkward edges of my rebellion and demonstrated there need be no divide between spirit and matter nor for that matter between town and jungle. This teaching did not prevent me having to learn lessons the hard way from my own mistakes. Having survived many indiscretions I now understand that the desert, the mountains and the wilderness can also be viewed as symbols. We have to distinguish between what they are and what they stand for. The combination of Krakauer's powerful writing and the idealism of McCandless made me reflect on the mountains, viewing their overall impact instead of being summit fixated. Getting to know a peak involves more than just climbing up and down it. Dozens of books have been written detailing how the fourteen highest peaks in the Himalaya have been ascended but few of these live on in the memory for having caught the beauty and inspirational quality that differentiates one from the other. Too often big expeditions and books about them are geared to success rather than enjoyment and the reader is shortchanged by their obsession with height. The lower hills and their inhabitants are of no interest to the modern climber who pays the host government to top out, leaving the latter to clean up his mess. Worst of all, the expedition report commits the cardinal sin of making the Himalaya, the most entrancing of spectacles, sound flat and boring. Instead of the greatness of the range too often can be detected the smallness of the beholder.

Some climbers in the catastrophic 1996 expedition discerned spite and anger in Everest's behaviour: she appeared to single out individuals including sherpas for her wrath. This could be interpreted as reprisals for the cocksureness of the guides who boasted they had the route to the summit taped. The superstitious regard villagers have for the terrible forces of nature they have to live with is mocked by outsiders. But they have the last laugh over the sophisticated expeditioner who may end up dead from the hubris of refusing to acknowledge that the elements in the mountains have the upper hand most of the time. Like other trekkers who prefer the lower elevations where things grow, I am alive to the more friendly moods of nature, the sifting of the wind and the crump of a safely distant avalanche. My ears record with delight the raw cawing of the choughs, the piercing plaint of the barbet duet, the floating sound of axe on wood in the valley, while an inner organ responds to the silence behind the blackbird's ecstatic trill, against which the exquisite composition assumes its significance.

The celebration of the senses we experience on our mountain walks reaffirms the oneness of life. The mountains are not only requisite, as William Penn put it, for the growth of piety. In the garb of the Himalaya they reflect the purnananda of the soul reunited briefly with the architect of the universe.

3
A Bend in the Road

My walks in the range were a natural extension of my being. 'The ocean is there to be sailed over,' averred Joshua Slocum, the American navigator of the first small boat around the world. Likewise it seems to me the Himalaya was made to be walked on. From my Mussoorie home on the Ganga–Yamuna watershed I have an astonishing choice of walks. If I don't feel fully fit or if I've just had lunch or if the sun is very strong I will stick to the motor road to Kulri bazaar that curls up at an even gradient for a kilometre. At weekends when the vacation traffic is nose to tail with a stampede of vehicles from the plains I choose to do a similar graded route but anticlockwise to emerge at the Landour clock tower. This is a narrow almost cliff-hanging road that skirts the easternmost fringe of Mussoorie's built-up area.

If I start earlier in the day I usually take on the severely steep Palpitation Hill that rises to St Emilians Church then drops down to Kulri. Though punishing on the knees and lungs it gives rise to a minor but undeniable shout of exultation on topping the rise that the other less challenging gradients fail to generate.

This hard climb is replete with history and sociology. Mark the original bungalows of the township with tall steep roofs of tin presumably designed to deter the weight of snow. But I think their design was based on the Gujjar's hut with its steep thatching. Possibly the early British shooting lodges followed the local design and were copied by conservative mistris just as stone pillars to this day follow the lines of their timber original.

At the top of Palpitation Hill (under the church) stands the Himalaya Club (now a survey office) which in the middle of the nineteenth century hosted a rip-roaring crowd of hard-drinking card-sharpers. John Lang, considered Australia's first novelist, wrote about the unruly lifestyle of these duelling gamblers in Charles Dickens's weekly *Household Words* of March 1857. Lang is buried in Mussoorie's Camel Back cemetery but he wasn't killed in a duel. He lived to defend the Rani of Jhansi (after the so-called Mutiny) as her lawyer.

On the way to the Himalaya Club you pass two schools that reflect the social disparity common in the hills. Wynberg Allen that began as an orphanage (often a euphemism for sahibs' illegitimate children) is today a model Anglo-Indian school sought after by the affluent who would be articulate. Up the hill is the down-market Hindi-medium school which provides just enough learning to make its students resent the prospect of being second-class citizens in the almost non-existent employment market in the hills.

Palaeontology also features on any steep climb where old pushtas (retaining walls) display clean-cut stones. Look closely and you may find the fossil imprint of a fern or fish-bone stamped on the stone face, memento of the cataclysmic forces that continue to perturb the foundations of the Mussoorie Range.

If I have more time at my disposal I penetrate eastwards into thick oak jungle and work my way down to the now-disused burning ghat. Across the ravine are the thickly wooded slopes of the Woodstock School estate and, nearer to the plains, the looming bulk of Pari Tibba. In the 1960s these were virgin green in their unbroken run of growth. Now new settlements are nibbling at their roots and each year a copse of canopied forest falls to the axe of encroachment.

Mussoorie from the beginning has had a history of encroaching boundaries. Colonel George Everest, the best known of India's surveyor generals, wangled the wording of the by-laws to extend his Park Estate's boundaries. Everest's estate lies on the westernmost flank of Mussoorie's long ridge and he settled there in the early 1830s when the town was in its infancy. On the easternmost extreme where I live, as I walk down towards Barlowganj (named after a Company general) I note how a humble City Board peon has assiduously copied Everest's technique of aggrandising his holding at a (non-resident) neighbour's cost. By digging out soil from his own hillside and letting gravity do its job, the concave lie of the stream dividing the two plots has turned convex. With a series of late night surreptitious rakings, the centre of the stream will be revealed in the morning to have moved a miraculous two feet in favour of the industrious peon. Now as he hammers in his stakes to make a unilateral boundary he is already planning to add another two feet next year. For this reason the hammering is not too vigorous.

In spite of her exploitation by beavering humanity nature remains overall in charge. Looking back on the contours of the hill station after forty years of acquaintance the most remarkable fact that stands out is how unchanged the broad outlines of this mountain resort remain. If I continue my steep walk down to Barlowganj bazaar then turn sharply west to follow a beautifully wooded and prodigiously watered road to Sikander Hall everything is more or less the same as I remember it in the 1960s despite a totally unnecessary and highly wasteful metal fence that has been erected, a brainless eyesore.

It is the human component that fluctuates drastically. On my walk I pass Maplewood Lodge where Ruskin Bond wrote some of his finest nature prose. Set amidst the long-leaved maple, this magical nook built of solid stone overlooks a tumbling dell that falls in sylvan delight all the way to the Woodstock stream. From his window Ruskin could stretch and touch the overarching oaks and gaze undisturbed on the langurs as they sat stripping the acorns. Then a Mussoorie bypass was built that rudely cut off Ruskin's stone lodge from the embrace of the jungle. The road it was said had been made to allow heavy machinery to reach the Tehri Dam project. Ruskin, envisaging heavy trucks rumbling past his casement day and night, fled to the quieter heights of

Landour. In the event the trucks never appeared. The Tehri Dam was a ruse to get the road built and enable politicians and contractors to get their hands on some timber during its construction. Lower down the hill in Barlowganj as further fallout from the Tehri Dam, the Irish Brothers of St George's College sold off their distinctive 'Castle'—a residential building that held a commanding position and was connected to the college campus by a romantic suspension bridge. Unromantically it was used by the less happy citizens of Barlowganj as a place of suicide.

The building was taken over by the constructors of the Tehri Dam. Environmentalists' agitation stopped work in Tehri. So the company decided to transfer its assembled workforce to Mussoorie to build instead a five star hotel. At the time of the construction the whole of the Barlowganj hillside seemed to be bleeding irreparably but now that the hotel is in business the greenery is beginning to return. What was once a daily eyesore has now been reduced to a Saturday night earache when disco decibels shatter the decorum of resigned Nature.

On the whole it seems nature won the battle against the dam contractors. It is now fashionable to seem environmentally concerned but so absurd is the monied urge to ostentatiously love nature that several smaller hotels in Mussoorie now invite craftsmen to fashion tree trunks and bamboo plants out of cement, each done so authentically that it is difficult to tell them apart from the original. The sublime mindlessness of this operation is that the part of nature chosen for replication is a *dead* tree trunk lopped of its branches. Even the sawn-off branches are painted with immaculate regard for detail.

It was on realising that visitors to the hills actually prefer dead tree trunks in cement to the living tree with its halo of green that I gave up voicing my opinion on the environment in public. Luckily the next generation seem to have a more healthy vision of natural beauty and no doubt today's fashion of the dead log tarted up in cement will change to something less sick.

Nature's ability to bounce back is the most reassuring lesson I have learnt over the years. Take this road down to Barlowganj past the Bule Shah mazaar where Wynberg Allen School jealously guards its extensive oak slopes. One year there was drought in summer and all these hillsides appeared to be scorched, wilting and wasted. Now a year later after a prolonged season of rain that set in as early as April the oak forest is back to its healthy shade of deep chrome that switches to light purple when the wind riffles through the new leaf.

I am smitten by this green and purple colour scheme. No doubt it has something to do with my boyhood love of the kilt. I used to wear as an undergraduate my mother's McKay tartan and that has a deep green and navy sett. Obviously in pre-industrial Scotland these dyes came from the plants growing in the clan area. The hungry machine of mass production has swallowed up our share of contact with simple pleasures as in the dyeing and weaving of cloth. One of the reasons I feel so at home in the Himalaya is precisely because of the chances it still offers to practise the pleasing skills of pastoral man. Though I have made little if any spiritual progress in the ashrams I have lived in, I rejoice in the opportunity they offered to hone dormant skills. Like growing and harvesting wheat, grinding it and making rotis; nurturing fruit trees, then making jam; cutting grass for cows then making butter, cream and ghee of their milk. No food on earth can taste better than a breakfast of home-grown hot roti with hand churned butter and personally stirred marmalade.

The worst severing for industrial man is his loss of true time, his divorce from the meaningful motion of the sun. Electricity devised to extend the daylight hours for good works too often is abused for the furthering of idle entertainment. Who but the grossly depraved of ear would prefer the braying of a five star disco to the fluted duet of answering owls?

Each year confirms the walker's equation that in Mussoorie people come and go strutting and fretting while nature continues unperturbed. Ruskin has moved and next door the Gordon sisters in the main Maplewood House have been gathered unto their clan. Neither of them married and both retained a high degree of mental and social efficiency well into their old age. One of them was a water colourist of near-professional stature whose passionate views of the wild landscape around their house might have triggered off associations with the Bronte sisters. But all the passion I witnessed was to see the artist sedately accompany the ex-headmaster Mr Biggs on his evening walk chaperoned by the Gordons' cocker spaniel, all parties well into their retirement years.

A distinguished annual visitor to the Gordon house was Sir Edmund Gibson, a retired colonial civil servant who had a farm in Dehra Dun. Sir Edmund was Resident (political officer) for some Gujarat states when a young revolutionary sought to dispose of him by aiming a revolver point blank at his chest. The shots went wide despite the ample target, leaving Sir Edmund firmly convinced that God did not share the revolutionary's low opinion of his professional services. He fitted the stereotype of Colonel Blimp perfectly but was in fact very sympathetic to Indian aspirations. He would get about in a rickshaw hauled by four jampannis and every evening, without fail, sink a Patiala peg of Solan Number One whisky.

Next door on the leafy walk past Maplewood is Wayside Hall—formerly the home of Annie Powell—a lovely low built bungalow once surrounded by a beautifully maintained garden of hill flowers and still embowered by greenery. Annie shifted to a house lower on the hill to live with her sister in her old age and even then was a woman of blossoming grace and kindness.

The Powells of Saharanpur had colonised this hillside approach to Mussoorie above Barlowganj and often an indicator of a Powell property was the mention of 'oak' in its name even when the property has no oaks. Thus the house where I live is named 'Oakless'. This house is the daughter of 'Seven Oaks' where the matriarch of the Powell clan resided amidst a whole forest of oaks. Her two sons Colonel Alfred and Major Arthur were both very much part of the Mussoorie scene when I came to live here in 1972. The former had made a name for himself as a shikari while his younger brother was estate manager for Woodstock.

To show how nature can upset the imaginings of man I find that since Oakless was built in 1910 (at the same time and with the same materials and design that went into the Powells' Mussoorie town house (now the Allahabad Bank building) a single oak tree has sprouted on its land. This is something of a miracle on a dry and overgrazed southern aspect.

One can go on recalling the colourful characters who graced the now empty properties along the Barlowganj road to Sikander Hall. Time has scythed their outer husk but made no dent in their cherished idiosyncrasies. Who can forget Forster with a tottering cottage near Mossy Falls who sold the tin sheets off his roof for drink? When he was rendered roofless he took to digging up the wild pink crocuses that adorn Mussoorie's lanes and sold their bulbs to gullible visitors as Dutch tulips.

It is thanks to the largeness of these old estates that the hillside above Skinner's Hall managed to retain its integrity free from the weaseling of property dealers. The last of the Skinners to be colonel of the family regiment, Colonel Mike, loved his Mussoorie home (called Midstream) and was loved in turn by all the locals for his gentle and generous ways. His sister Lillian is the last of the elegant, life-affirming set, at home in East or West. Adventurous Anglo-Indians gave Mussoorie its pleasure-loving character and today the town still depends on them for their steadfast educational standards.

To return to Mussoorie via the motor road to Kincraig can be wearisome in view of the traffic so the walker is advised to strike uphill through the forest. Whichever path you take will converge at Brooklands, a level property with a fine selection of full grown trees. This made it the obvious choice for the Divisional Forest Officer's (DFO) headquarters when the property came to be auctioned. It had been for a few years a thermometer factory, which seemed a sensible sort of industry, suited to protect both the lush forest and the interests of the local people who were chronically short of work. Incredibly, what should have been a perfect marriage of appropriate technology and a readymade labour force turned sour. For months the forest resounded to slogans and the other paraphernalia that is deemed proper by petty political careerists who harness ideology to the work shy and make a livelihood for themselves. The result of this pointless self-defeating agitation was closure of the thermometer factory and unemployment for its local staff ever since.

Now there is a little zoo attached to the DFO's estate but so well wooded is the area that you can pass it by without noticing. This southern face (that culminates at St Emilians) is remarkable for the richness of the springs that issue from its base. They led to the founding of a brewery next to Sikander Hall and a cart road that bore away its barrels for consumption up the hill. The soil on this hillside is black and rich in humus. It is thanks to the trees protected by private estates that the rain water has been allowed to percolate and recharge these voluminous springs. Everybody states that Mussoorie has a water problem but here is water flowing abundantly and going to waste the whole year round. The walker notes that nature discharges her duties bountifully while man lacks the will—or skill—to distribute the largesse evenly.

I am now back at Burra Mor (the Big Bend) on a level with Oakless. Here development has been allowed piecemeal and the clutter of a mohalla detracts from the sylvan beauty still intact above and below the Panipat Lala's settlement. Hill people lack the capital to buy or build so it is left to the plains' moneylender to reap the harvest of debt. (The Lala is also apt to sow his seed liberally and three brothers between them in one generation can produce two cricket teams were sport ever to interfere with the dharmic duty to create wealth.) New apartments without any sanitation have come up, built by jerry builders. After the horse had bolted the Supreme Court put a lock on the stable door. I have a feeling that ultimate justice for outraging the mountain slopes will be served by nature. Just one severe earthquake will level these unsanctioned luxury apartments into a pile of rubble.

The older generation who remember the princely days of wine and roses that made the town a kind of Indian Las Vegas pronounce the gloomy verdict that the Queen of the Hills has become a trollop. Inevitably after independence Indians felt no need to imitate the lifestyle of their erstwhile British masters. Into the void created by derecognition of the princes arrived the *nouveau riche* and amongst the most populous, the tax-free farmer. They drive to Mussoorie at weekends in flashy utility vehicles to visit their offspring in the town's highly reputed schools and having little to say they say it loudly. Playing cards and scratching their crotch they contribute to the economy and the destruction of the environment by their random chucking of plastic bags.

For the discerning walker who knows where to head Mussoorie offers fine walks far from the noisy throng that clogs the Mall. From outside the cemetery gate on Camel's Back road a steep bridle path takes you up and over the Mall to descend at Christ Church at the Library end. Not a soul will be met on this diagonal which offers superb snow views outside the rainy season. In the rains the botanically inclined are agog at the largesse of Mussoorie's flora—a thousand species of plants, a hundred alone of ferns. You pass empty old houses each with its legends and note that several of them have been taken over by mahatmas from the plains who summer here along with their well-heeled disciples. What I assume to be the old Scottish kirk crowning the secondary summit to Gun Hill is deserted and dilapidated with a few struggling hydrangeas as reminders of its former glory. How transient is sponsored religion.

The spree of capitalist freebooting that followed independence peaked in the cavalier mining of limestone from the Mussoorie hills. Rated amongst the purest in the world, the local mineral caught the attention of Punjabi contractors who had moved to Dehra Dun after displacement from Pakistan. Cutting environmental and safety rules to the minimum they employed an army of Bedford trucks known as gattoos that ran up and down the hillsides frantically loading the profitable limestone. A procession of these high-powered trucks raced between Mussoorie and Dehra Dun ploughing up the roads and adding to the pall of dust and smoke that blocked out our views of the Doon. Factories to process the stone were set up near Rajpur and from there it was trucked to the Doon railhead for onward passage to Jamshedpur. To compound the greed of the private sector a large Uttar Pradesh Government mining establishment was built at Park Chungi and within the space of a few years it had almost erased the entire profile of Colonel George Everest's estate, which was set on a landmark known as Hathi Pau.

The degradation was so appalling and the involvement of prominent people so embarrassing that public complaints reached the Rajya Sabha in Delhi. It was reported that even the Commissioner of the division and his family were involved in gattoo plying. On one occasion the popular Garhwali neta H.N. Bahuguna gave a speech in Mussoorie deploring the illicit quarrying but the effect of his speech was marred when he was seen being driven away in the limousine of one of the limestone contractors he had so vehemently denounced five minutes earlier.

All this mining made it hotter and no effective reafforestation was done to compensate for the felled trees. Natural springs were severely affected by the blasting and it was only when the ordinary citizens of Mussoorie were faced with thirst that a campaign was launched to rein in the quarriers.

Some public spirited souls spearheaded by Maisie Gantzer and Princess Sita of Kapurthala not only had the plying of gattoos regulated but also petitioned the Supreme Court to intervene to save the town's environment and its future as a hill resort. They inspired a generation of schoolchildren to plant and care for trees and this has proved to be the best safeguard against the predatory business instincts of plainsmen. Later ex-army personnel were drafted in to forest afresh the damaged hillsides and though at the beginning these eco-task forces were derided as cosmetic, now that their trees have begun to grow the success of their labours cannot be denied.

As a tree planter I found it an uphill task on Mussoorie's dry southern face. After the monsoon passed the plants had no deep moisture for another eight months. Winter showers and a brushing of snow could hardly make for vigorous growth. It was heartbreaking over the years to find that only one in ten saplings survived the first year and only one in a hundred made it to adolescence. A tree has only one in 500 chances of reaching maturity owing to the limestone soil, relentless sun and free-for-all grazing by cattle and goats.

It was depressing to discover that officialdom neither at the local nor state level was serious about tree planting. The City Board put constant hurdles in my way and on one occasion fined me two hundred rupees when I removed a dead tree trunk in order to make space for new saplings. The dead trunk had been marked for clearing by the forest department but the clearance to fell from the City Board had not come even as the planting season was due to expire. The babu who fined me seemed delighted at having stopped me planting new trees. In the event I had the last laugh because Mrs Gandhi's Emergency came into force and one of its urgent programmes was the planting of trees. I complained how the babu was preventing me from greening the nation and soon received from his superior a cringing apology plus waiving of the fine.

4
First Footsteps

My first hike in the Himalaya was on a long weekend during my course at the Landour Language School ostensibly to climb Nag Tibba. This was the culminating point of the range looking north that separates Mussoorie from the higher peaks. The ranges become more involved and convoluted the nearer you get to the snows. Distances in the Himalaya are apt to be deceptive. The snows look nearer than they actually are. From Mussoorie, Bander Poonch lies some forty kilometres as the crow flies but to reach base camp will take several days of frustrating effort.

The British surveyors did an excellent job in conveying the rumpled spread of these tangled interior ranges but unfortunately the government does not allow easy access to these early contour maps. And when managing to get hold of one in London or Zurich the ordinary trekker blanches before the steep and complex layout before him. The cost of supplying an expedition to the base of these snow ramparts is the next obstacle. Add to this the red tape that officialdom still loves to ensnare explorers with, and the allure of border areas begins to wear thin even before you leave Mussoorie.

For a simple trek like the excursion to Nag Tibba neither map nor supplies is needed. Plenty of Woodstock students make the trip and the critical parts of the route can be discerned from Landour. There is a short cut by a steeper route but I chose to go the long

FIRST FOOTSTEPS

way round by Deolsari which boasted of a dak bungalow where I hoped to spend the night. Strictly speaking a permit was required but a tip to the chowkidar, I was told, would allow me to sleep in the veranda and use the bathroom.

I kept my rucksack light and packed only a sleeping bag and water bottle. For food I took Marie biscuits and some peanut butter made locally in Landour for the American School children. This was a mistake since any advantage of protein intake was nullified by my inability to swallow the sticky mass. The problem of drinking water that haunts new arrivals to India reached panic proportions in me on this trek. I was scared to draw water from any source near a village and that meant effectively going without any for most of the way.

I set out buoyantly along the ridge from Jabarkhet and passed no one save for the occasional milkman accompanying his jingling pony. I had learnt to say 'Namaste', the local greeting, and, in Calcutta had acquired the more upmarket salutation 'Namaskar'. The ten-kilometres walk to Suakholi was mainly along the crestline and gave a wonderful sense of being airborne. But in May the countryside was dull and dried out and the sun smote with a lethal intensity. I had had the good sense to wear a hat and sunglasses but lacked then the wisdom of wearing long cotton pyjamas rather than shorts. Not only do these offer cool protection, they satisfy the local code of appropriate dress. To sport shorts is often to embarrass your village host since appearing trouserless is to suggest a contempt for decency. This is twice as bad in a woman and one of the signs of having becoming part of village India is when you can understand the distress caused by visitors and their unthinking Western customs.

At Suakholi I did the expected thing by sitting down on a loose wooden plank in the thatched tea shop to order chai. The locals like to get a good look at the passing traffic and the usual salutations and exchange of information are made. It does not pay to appear overfriendly or otherwise. The villagers have their own yardstick of acceptability and a guest courteous enough to observe tea stall etiquette can expect to have his order upgraded to

At the tea stall

'speshal' chai. In those days it came served in a small silvered brass beaker, blisteringly hot and sickeningly sweet. The trick was to hold the beaker in a second looser vessel and allow some of the heat to disperse. When one is tired this chai—found the whole length of the Himalaya—is the best pick-me-up I know of. It affords instant energy and acts like an intravenous injection on the jaded bloodstream.

Nowadays the brass beaker has been replaced by cheap glass vessels and the price since 1960 has gone up from four annas to two rupees. The temperature however remains the same, as does the level of sweetness. All who host expeditions to the Himalaya know that two areas where accounting is best left to the porters is the consumption of beedis (country cigarettes) and sugar. Sugar in the hills acquires a near mystical status and anyone caught purloining it is best left to the local deity for chastisement. It is unforgivable to even notice let alone wax indignant over the fast disappearing supply of expedition sugar. The correct thing for maintenance of harmony is to take twice as much as you need. On such details the fate of an expedition can hang.

From the tea shop the path down to the Aglar river drops sheer, passing, from the mixed broad leaf species of the ridge into dense but gaunt growth of pine. The path is so steep that I have to trot to keep my balance. I always admire from above the artistic unfolding of hill footpaths for they replicate the muscular lope of a descending body and precisely follow the weight displacement of people striving to keep their balance. Here is rare evidence in the hills of egalitarianism, for the low caste make the same marks as do the footsteps of the higher born. Women do not differ much in their weaving line of descent save in their daintier stride. And since they usually carry the heavier loads they are truly responsible for pacing out the line of advance. Nothing like a load to make you choose the easiest footing.

I pass an idyllic forest bungalow tucked away under the ridge and marvel at how sensible the British were in siting their rest houses. This was near enough to the bazaar for emergency supplies but far enough to dissuade the tea shop gamblers to meet for their nightly round of card-sharping.

As always on these steep descents through broad-leaved jungles you pass a series of enchanted pools fed by a pure spring. Black boled alder trees whose wood hardens from water exposure rear out to block the sunlight and a sylvan plenitude settles on the healthy growth of dark green shrubbery. Just a mile away on the south side of the same mountain the brooks are all dry and their white stones exude the grilling heat of mid-morning. Are not shady pools and all oasis-like symbols a reflection of our search for the cool waters that the Psalmist describes? In Indian terms the Buddhist teaching that nirvana can be discovered in the midst of samsara is recalled by these limpid pools of life-giving water set amidst dry mountain ranges that cry out against the unrelenting scorch of the season.

Too soon I pass into the warmer rust pine layer and immediately my ears, attuned to the musical silence of the deeper greens, are assailed by the harsh chiming of the cicada. It is a brutal switch from nirvana to samsara but the sight of tall stately pine marching steeply down the shrubless slopes is so novel that I overlook the din. The bridle path from the forest bungalow has been replaced by a village pakdandi, a weaving shortcut that involves a few deft dancing steps to maintain an even momentum. A sign of the true highlander is his penchant for the *diretissima* route irrespective of its steepness. This holds true not just for pine jungles but snowy slopes too. The Pahari's fitness and balance on the latter glissades are something to see and hill women are just as fast and graceful in showing a clean pair of heels.

The first sight of resin tapping makes the tree lover wince. The local technique of using a heavy basula (adze) shows no mercy to the trunk. A runnel several inches deep is notched by the blade and a tin or earthen cup placed beneath to catch the semen-like sap. The British are universally blamed for these cash crop plantations that commercialised forestry and denied the locals rights to these 'reserved' areas. One benefit did accrue from governmental intervention and that was to endow the forest department with a sense of pride in their own professionalism. Rules were stringently enforced and in spite of the heavy calls for railway sleepers (to supply something like 50,000 kilometres of track) the balance between growth and felling was maintained. It was after independence that venal politicians hand in glove with rapacious contractors subverted the system.

To my mind trees are one of the chief beauties of the Himalaya and many of my favourite treks have involved pleasant days spent below the tree line, in the subalpine belt that stretches from around 5000–10,000 ft. The higher one goes the ore stately the trees grow. This has much to do with the fact that villages cannot function well above 8000 ft which is the ceiling for wheat to ripen. Also above 10,000 ft the body is prone to incur the dangerous symptoms of mountain sickness. Though I exult in the beauty of the alpine meadows (buggials) above the tree line I find living at 12,000 ft tiresome. In adjusting to the thinner air the body loses its appetite and the mind tends to freak out from the problem of breathlessness.

Descending to the infant Aglar, I cross the bridge at Thatyur and begin a climb that culminates in a dense forest of deodar sweeping up like a curtain before me to mark the barrier of the Nag Tibba range. Thatyur then boasted of no motor road and was marked by a single tea shop of planked wood. Villagers are too canny to build houses on land near rivers. Why waste good agricultural soil for a mere residence. Also floods are a possible threat in these unstable ranges. Villages are usually carefully sited away from threatening situations and with a commanding view of the fields their inhabitants cultivate. Traditionally the lowest castes were expected to keep their distance from the twice-born and a poorly sited settlement often houses those who have no choice in fixing their destinies.

The stream that flows into Thatyur from Nag Tibba drains a rising valley with villages on both flanks. The shortcut to Nag Tibba climbs on a north-westerly course but in the heat I prefer to keep to a shadier level. Straight ahead is the bulk of the mountain and at its base sits the village of Auntar with its extraordinary elongated stone temple, much like the forts you find in Lahaul. The stones at the base are huge; nowhere else in India have I seen such a solid foundation to a shrine. Another curiosity about Auntar is its timber aqueduct that brings in fresh water off the mountain by a series of wooden trestles. Had this somewhat sophisticated mode of irrigation been suggested by the American missionaries of Landour who for years have been operating clinics in these tracts around Mussoorie? The trestles looked like something out of a cowboy movie.

My goal was Deolsari which lay to the east of Auntar. I had eaten a boiled egg at Thatyur for lunch and then lain down to snooze for half an hour in the heat. The flies were a nuisance but nothing to compare with the deafening cicada on those pine slopes. Trekking in the month of May means all the brown gloss of fallen pine needles underfoot which has to be carefully negotiated. To climb is even worse since your shoes cannot get a purchase on the phirule (needles). Village women help to the extent of combing large tracts of the pine slopes to collect the needles as bedding for their cattle. On the whole phirule is a trekker's nightmare since a carelessly tossed beedi can set these slopes alight and cause a fire that might stretch all the way to the Nepal or Himachal border.

Woodstock has a strong interest in ornithology and I was encouraged to look out for partridges which skulk about in the thick undergrowth that I was now brushing my way through to reach Deolsari before dark. As I reached, the light was fading. Set amidst the deep swaying inclose of deodar was a wooden pagoda and from its dark recesses came a tom-tomming of what sounded like a sinister message by drum. It felt spooky. I was still too new to India to have shaken off the boyhood notion that the only music the Almighty's ear was attuned to was a church organ.

Nearby was the dak bungalow and when word got round that an angrez was in the vicinity a series of halloos brought forth the chowkidar—in striped pyjamas and tight fitting sweater—at a trot. I could stay the night at the prescribed fee but without the prescribed receipt. That seemed a reasonable restriction on my uninvited status and having confirmed the arrangements the chowkidar trotted off again to make the food and water bandobast. I waited, parched and hungry. He soon returned with a lantern in one hand and a large English gardener's watering can—black from age—in the other. This was my drinking water.

I looked in panic at the unscoured container. I had been advised to carry potassium permanganate granules to make water more safe to drink. I furtively opened my packet of permanganate, and managed to pour a stream of granules into the watering can. Obviously I had added several granules too many. What emerged from the can was midnight blue ink that tasted bitter and metallic. It was so horrible I couldn't touch it. The chowkidar had gone and I felt too foolish to enquire about a further supply. Meanwhile the drumming from the temple wafted eerily from the depths of the trees. Without water I couldn't swallow the rotis and potato the chowkidar had brought. I had no choice but lie down on the stringy charpoy hoping sleep would silence my scream of self-pity. The early morning sun made the dark deodar cluster around the temple seem less threatening, but the primitive lifestyle of the villagers came as a shock.

I was unaware of the cultural nuances that attach to Garhwal's interior villages then cut off from modernity by the lack of roads. This area is near the Jaunsar Bhabar region where it is common for girls to be sold for profit. If this sounds shocking to modern ears it didn't upset the British who accommodated licensed prostitutes in Landour bazaar. (They got a mention in the Mussoorie City Board by-laws published in 1957.)

Poverty and the poor yield of the land forced farmers to sell their daughters. Under the former rule of the state of Tehri there was some sanction for transactions in the flesh trade since the holy shrine of Badrinath provided devadasis for the pleasure of the gods—and consequently, men. It remains a fact that to this day, trekkers who loiter around certain villages will be assumed to be pimps on the lookout for 'mirchi', chillies, the code word used in the plains for new entrants to the brothels of Haldwani, Bareilly and Saharanpur. ('Safed [white] mirch' signifies the most alluring catch, 'kali [black] mirch' the least prepossessing.)

The village houses of Deolsari had some sparkling new planks of deodar wood in their verandas and even at a distance you could scent the powerful overhang of cedar shavings. As it turned out the deodar forest at the base of Nag Tibba would be the chief beauty of my first trek. My Hindi was non-existent so there was no question of learning about local problems. As always in a hill situation the men were apt to hunker down round a beaker of tea or hookah and philosophise about the hardship of life while their womenfolk vigorously performed all the manual work around the homestead and thereafter in the fields.

The women were voluble and screeched gossip at one another. Cutting grass on steep hillsides, this at least gave them protection from bears. Nag Tibba's virgin forests were said to host plenty of black bears and when I set off after two hot rotis and mint chutney (from the chowkidar's kitchen) I was warned to keep to the bridle path and not stray into the forest.

I returned to Auntar some two miles away and began the climb but only got a few hundred feet when I decided to call it off. The forest was huge, black and forbidding. It had the enchanted air of possessing a life of its own. All around the cedar trees swayed, breathed and seemed to mutter like Tolkien's ents. It wan't just the threat of danger that made me stop. Part of me had already been bewitched by the beauty of the seductive swaying trees, whole groves of them gyrating almost in erotic abandon. When graced with such a rare darshan who needs formal certificates of success?

Even modest Himalayan outings require energy, resolve and a realistic appraisal of the difficulties of the terrain. The first lesson I learned on the Nag Tibba trek was not to be greedy for topping out. The summit wasn't going to go away and next time round I would have the measure of what it took to complete the job. On later occasions when I did climb the peak I found my pleasure still peaked on beholding the ripple of cedar at the base. With a single sweep of viridian the hillside seemed to sing a chorus of joy as though I was looking at a petrified Welsh miners' choir whose echoes, fossilised by time, were suddenly released by the wind that moved their lips though no sound was heard except by the inner ear. The summit came as an anti-climax.

It is real happiness to be on top of Nag Tibba nonetheless because the south-facing slopes are richly endowed with trees and carpeted thick with humus. Birds and wild animals rootle happily through this wilderness and thanks to the fear of bears few villagers venture this far to lop leaves for their buffaloes. Gujjars come in the monsoon to crop the grass. Little has changed in the forty years I have known the peak. The same swish of soughing wind bends the cedar in a gentle sifting that soothes the senses, and lower down, rare, colourful partridge still skulk in the undergrowth. After all these years Nag Tibba remains a remote and intriguing destination.

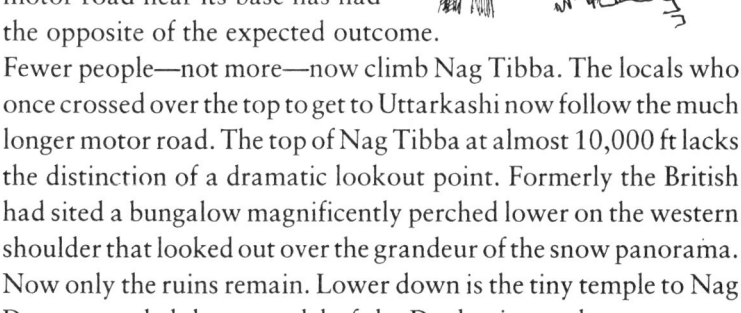

Strangely, the building of a motor road near its base has had the opposite of the expected outcome. Fewer people—not more—now climb Nag Tibba. The locals who once crossed over the top to get to Uttarkashi now follow the much longer motor road. The top of Nag Tibba at almost 10,000 ft lacks the distinction of a dramatic lookout point. Formerly the British had sited a bungalow magnificently perched lower on the western shoulder that looked out over the grandeur of the snow panorama. Now only the ruins remain. Lower down is the tiny temple to Nag Devta, a scaled down model of the Deolsari pagoda.

A lesson my first trek taught me was how bare and wretched human existence is amidst so much uplifting beauty. The most common perception about the Himalaya was exploded for me at the outset: the nobility and inspiration the great range has on our psyche is only part of the reality. The full reality includes the crude hovels where one's fellows live, little better than the cattle they labour over, feeding, milking and mucking out. The inspirational quality of the mountains is undeniable but it is only one aspect of the Himalayan experience. Expedition accounts usually start at base camp safely above the squalor of human existence that increases with the altitude. Most of us do not want to face the ignoble aspect of the Himalaya; we prefer to pick on the nice parts and pretend the less appetising areas do not exist. We rave about the scent of brahm kamal on high but evade mention of the stink of unwashed humanity in the village.

Mountaineering chronicles foster the myth that a sense of glory increases with the height achieved. But anyone who has crossed the 10,000-ft. limit knows that quite the opposite is true. Thereafter breathing becomes more difficult, eating ceases to be enjoyable and sleeping is an effort. If there's any glory in experiencing severe headaches at one extremity and the agony of protruding piles at the other then the mind is either crippled from being starved of oxygen or the climber is a born-again masochist.

The Himalaya is all about these extremes. Its weather, terrain and ecology switch drastically in a short span. Gentle slopes of inflammable pine end abruptly at a precipice on which the sun's rays hardly ever play. The cold, dank, steep northern face hosts springs in dramatic contrast to the arid southern side. Which of these two sides of the mountain is the true Himalaya? The answer is—both. Along with the glory of the shining summit we have somehow to square the squalor of the human condition lower on the mountainside.

5
Binsar and Beyond

On my next excursion I glimpsed where the key lay to resolving the extremes of glory and squalor. I had followed the silken strand of destiny to Kathgodam, the railhead station for Kumaun. There in October 1960 I collected my rucksack and caught the Kumaun Motor Owners' Union (KMOU) bus for Almora. Painted green, these local buses were privately owned and often driven by their owner, perhaps an ex-serviceman retired from the Kumaun Regiment. They drove carefully and courteously and in those days, segregated their passengers. On a bench behind the driver were padded seats of the 'upper' class and separated by a wooden partition was the space set aside for the 'lower'. You entered the lower class through a back door and found wooden benches down either side leaving an open space for the spare wheel and the passengers' luggage to be dumped. Often the well at the back would be piled with mail bags to denote the dak bus, a sedate slow service that stopped at every opportunity.

Compared to transport services in the cities the KMOU was highly personalised. The driver felt responsible for his passengers and would often drive out of his way to set them and their luggage outside their homesteads. Because of the many stops for tea and talk it was not uncommon for passengers to be left behind. In this event the conductor would check where the missing person had booked his ticket to; his luggage would be identified from the pile and entrusted to the KMOU agent at the appropriate destination. Both on road and rail India has a remarkable record of public honesty in delivering unattended baggage to its rightful owner intact.

I caught an uncrowded dak bus to Almora and was entranced by the varying scenery. We growled non-stop for an hour up to Bhowali through cleared hillsides where prosperous farms denoted settlers spilt over from Naini Tal's confined limits high on the ridge the bus was aiming for. From Bhowali with the shops selling seasonal fruits the bus engine cooled as it raced down the steep northern face to Khairna to meet the Kosi river. At Garam Pani we stopped to perform the Kumauni ritual of eating *raita* at Tiwariji's, cucumber being a hill delicacy laced with locally grown mustard seed, yoghurt and red chillies.

A new road was being blasted out of the Kosi gorge that bypassed the long detour to Ranikhet and as the bus groaned up this one-way unmade road I had my first tantalising glimpse of the snow peaks. They rose much higher in the vibrant blue sky than I had expected and seemed to be the most priceless jewels I had ever set eyes on. Without question Kumaun has the best snow views. Nepal may have higher and Himachal whiter but for sheer character and dramatic outline the panorama seen from anywhere in Kumaun beats all the other outposts from Kashmir to Arunachal that I have checked.

Once again destiny was arranging my footsteps to what is probably the best view of them all. Almora turned out to be a friendly little town with an authentic hill identity. Strangers were welcome since Swami Vivekananda had made Almora's a name synonymous with sadhana (spiritual search.) Cranks Ridge hosted a collection of colourful foreign devotees and the town's orthodox brahminical culture was so secure in its own esteem that it did not see these exotic outsiders as any threat to local dharma.

On arrival in Almora I asked at the KMOU agency how I could get to Mirtola where the English yogi lived in his ice-less cave. The agent called Mohan Babu was chubby and pock-marked and over the years I came to admire him as a karma yogi. No matter how irate the public was in complaining about the bus service, Mohan Babu was unfailingly polite. But it was not the politeness of the public relations expert or the wheedling skills of the professional diplomat. Mohan Babu was a genuinely sympathetic person and related sincerely to customers' problems. After telling me to come back at six in the morning for the bus to Panwanaula he suggested I go and meet Dr Bindu who lived just under the bus stand. He could advise me on the Himalaya, said Mohan Babu.

Bindu Joshi hailed from one of Almora's leading families and was the patriarch of a huge rambling mansion called Anand Bhavan. Such was my luck that on crossing the threshold of Dr Bindu's house my future was decided. In the space of five minutes the somewhat eccentric bachelor doctor had read my needs and provided a prescription. I was to visit the English yogi and convey Bindu's compliments as a fellow alchemist. Then I was to walk to Binsar to discover the ultimate vista of the Himalaya. After that I must walk over the mountains to Kausani where Bindu had a relation who taught Sanskrit. Halfway I would stay at Takula where Bindu's brother Devi Dutt was the principal of Gananath College.

For staying overnight in Binsar I was sent to meet 'Elisha' who owned a shop along the Mall in Almora. This turned out to be L.R. Shah, a delightful, cultivated property owner who gladly gave me a letter to his chowkidar at Binsar allowing me to spend a night in the furnitureless bungalow. The quality of these Almora characters I met that first day in the hill station was something remarkable. Never have I met such people of outer grace and inner refinement, from the bus agent to the shopkeeper.

Next morning at the Panwanaula bus stop on the newly built kutcha road stood a little boy called Chandramani Pathak who said he had been sent by Krishna Prem to guide me. Again in that instant I had made a friend for life. Chandramani would grow up, join the Kumaun Regiment and retire to a chowkidar's post in Delhi. His brother Keshav went to America to make tandoori rotis and achieve success in his family affairs. Their father Kulomani whom Krishna Prem referred to benignly as 'the scare-crow' was the best of village brahmins in maintaining his orthodoxy while being open-minded about the English yogi's worship of Radha and Krishna near his village.

My initial impression about Mirtola was that Krishna Prem and his disciple Sri Madhava Ashish seemed to be Englishmen disguised as Hindu mendicants. They both wore ochre robes but were too big-bodied and bluff-spoken to be taken seriously as conventional Hindu holy men. This proved to be a useful insight on their actual status for they turned out to be more complex than the usual run of renunciants.

Not only were they clumsy and graceless when compared to Mohan Babu and L.R. Shah, they were outspoken and highly opinionated. They also seemed to be fairly well heeled and the beautifully maintained ashram garden appeared to be better suited to the stately English home their upper-class accents evoked.

After lunch they walked me to the path that leads to Jageshwar, a sacred site that boasts of a cluster of superbly preserved tenth-century temples set amidst a magical deodar forest. From Jageshwar I set out to walk along the ridge to Binsar some ten kilometres away. By the time I reached halfway at Dhaul Chhina the sun had set so I spent the night on a charpoy outside a shopkeeper's stall. The night was silvery still after the cooking vessels had been put away and the timbers of the upstairs veranda had ceased to creak. Coyote howls broke the expansive silence followed by the sharp coughing of a barking deer. Behind these punctuations was a rhythmic duet sung by tiny owls which tinkled like a Mozart piano piece.

Daylight brought coughs and more scouring of vessels signifying morning tea. After two alu parathas (a diet that would become my staple on treks) I hefted my rucksack and set off steeply up the towering ridge to Binsar. From Dhaul Chhina the bridle path follows

BINSAR AND BEYOND

the watershed ridge open to the blinding vision of snow peaks filling the void when you glance from the path to their glare. They are so near and so inaccessible. The highest peaks are of Nanda Devi where a steep face of ice seems to make them unclimbable. Closer acquaintance would show that this view from mid-Kumaun was an illusion. The face of Nanda Devi was actually obscured by another mountain—the summit ridge of Panwali Dwar. Only if you have been near these soaring ramparts can you discern the actual lie and read the true score of this unfinished symphony.

As I toiled in the morning heat up to a shoulder of Binsar's bulky massif I learned another valuable lesson. Loathe to let go of the reassuring bridle path which now started to drop steeply I found myself torn between choosing the commonsense option of continuing upwards—in spite of the path petering out—or descending on the beaten trail in the vague hope that it might eventually regain some height. Luckily instinct won and higher up I regained a road designed for jeeps that took wide sweeps to its tryst with a forest bungalow sited right under the impressive 'flagstaff' peak.

It is rare in modern schooling for students to be taught to trust their common sense, so it is not surprising that many intelligent people in the mountains make simple errors of judgement. The point about trusting instinct is that when we fall back on our own animal cunning (a low expression no doubt), it proves more useful in a tight corner than wisdom borrowed from an alien source.

One of the real pleasures of a successful trek is to pit your native cunning against the anonymous lie of the trail. You are forced to look for clues and practise live detection to further your itinerary. And even when you choose the wrong fork you have the satisfaction of knowing that your instinct had been to follow the other alternative.

On the easy ground of the Lesser Himalaya these exercises in extricating oneself from unnecessary detours are fun but higher up where the weather can turn hostile and obliterate your path you can be in serious trouble from taking the wrong turning. Only practice in reading the signs and trust in the body's navigational instinct to find safety can extract you from these life-threatening situations.

I learned in the Himalaya that it is more important to sense real time as represented by the circling of the sun than depend on the artificial aid of a wrist watch. It took years to cultivate but there did come a time when I could predict timings by an instinctive sun dial that came within a few minutes of chronometer time. This gave me considerable confidence on a long day's trek when I needed to know how much ground I could realistically cover. Obviously this varied according to the terrain but the satisfaction lay in knowing the target you had set yourself some hours earlier was about right for making camp. Your trek was in step with the rhythm of the sun and matched the limits each season imposed on it.

From these reflections on the awareness of time and place was repeated the most valuable lesson of all: the trekker is solely responsible for his destiny. You had to develop a nose for disaster and be alerted far before the danger was upon you. This meant every part of your being had to be alive to the passing scene. You had to see what was underfoot as well as gauge what the heavens had in store for you. You had to assess your body's store of energy and estimate its rate of burn. Survival depends on how much reserve of energy you have after beating the odds.

Luckily on that climb to Binsar I did not take the down path that would have necessitated a long hot haul back and the danger of walking through bear jungle in the gloaming. I emerged near the old temple of Binsar and found the settlement deserted. A few old bungalows with overgrown gardens and one lean chowkidar hoeing a patch of yams—the only plant the langurs could not get at—was all that signified Binsar.

A hundred years earlier Sir Henry Ramsey, the uncrowned king of Kumaun, had lived here at Ghuralkot, a lodge on the shoulder of the great massif, west of the flagstaff that marked its pinnacle. Ramsey was administrator, judge and benefactor who rode daily the fourteen miles into Almora to attend office. Unlike most British officers who came and went Ramsey stayed on as a much-loved figure. To my surprise it was to Ramsey's lodge that I was directed with Elisha's letter to the chowkidar.

Ghuralkot was as near to heaven in its setting as any house I have seen. Low and solid it had been built to face the snows but not promiscuously so. It leant to the lee of the hill to gain some shelter from the wintry blasts that ferociously funnelled through the gap between Binsar and Gananath. The other sides were gloriously free of any obstruction. The spire of the cantonment church of Chaubatiya above Ranikhet could be discerned to the west but the outrider of Almora's settlement Kasar Devi blocks out the view to the south. Kasar Devi marked the end of Cranks Ridge and was then inhabited by an Austrian monk Lama Govinda and his Parsi artist wife Li Gotami. They made a very colourful and theatrical couple as they went for an evening stroll rigged out in all the gorgeous attire Tibetan Buddhism invokes to exemplify the splendour of enlightenment.

Kasar Devi had earlier been the residence of Dr Evans Wentz who had shocked the Anglican establishment at Oxford by gaining his doctorate in a study of Celtic fairy lore. He then went on to shock them more (and earn the university press many dollars) by editing a translation of the *Tibetan Book of the Dead*.

Lama Govinda was a true scholar who lived a retired life until he wrote *The Way of the White Clouds*. This best-seller on Buddhist mysticism saw him swallowed up by the hippie movement which claimed him as its own and took him off to America.

Binsar was too far for Almora's cranks to populate. Ghuralkot may have been temporarily named *Hinds Skville* by a Scandinavian owner. When Elisha's chowkidar opened it up, the sole item of furniture in Ghuralkot was a photograph of a yacht bearing this name. There was a Scandinavian link in the gaunt presence of Sunya Baba, another resident of Cranks Ridge, who came from Denmark as a landscape gardener. Sorensen (Sunya Baba) was distinguished by a piping voice, a large Arabian Nights turban and a lapdog who spoke the language of silence. Sunya too was swallowed up by the hippie wave and went to America to lecture on the silence of the dogs. Almora soon became a favoured hippie destination because of cannabis growing wild around the town. Tim Leary was an early arrival.

My Binsar chowkidar was a scarecrow in regulation torn pyjamas and frayed woollen sweater. His forage cap worn by all

Kumauni village males was disintegrating from grease and fibre fatigue. He was desperately poor and obviously underfed. I was not surprised when he regretted he could supply no food. The monkeys daily raided his vegetable patch and all he ate at night was dry roti with raw onion. In the event I was given a lump of sticky jaggery with my roti.

I had arrived at Ghuralkot in the early afternoon and was already high from the impact of the snow peaks lining my route. Now with the clouds having boiled up from condensation the peaks wore a dreamy look as though under wraps. The cloud layer covered only their middle portion leaving the base and summits clear.

To add to the spectacle of being at 8000 feet—seemingly on the same level as the peaks—was the astonishing sensory impact that the month of October in Kumaun releases. This is the hay-cutting season when village women work frenetically with their short-handled sickle to cut grass for winter fodder. Their schedule is busy at any time of the year but now with the post-monsoon drying of the land they have to harvest the rice crop (at lower elevations) and simultaneously cut whole hillsides clear of lush grass.

The overpowering scent of newly mown hay was the heady factor in making me feel Binsar was a place of pure untrammelled joy. In addition to the peaks, the pulsating blueness of sky and the wildly intoxicating tang of fresh grass was the benison of hillsides of flowering cosmos, spilling down in a riot of pink, maroon and white. Never has my soul experienced such an orgy of abandoned delight.

As I lay down on the cold bare planks of the bungalow drinking a beaker of cold water and nibbling the sticky gur I felt this was the life for me. I made there and then the decision to give up my teaching job in Calcutta and come and live in the Kumaun hills. The Kumaun had determined my choice. Those smug plans to girdle the globe that I imagined would lead to a career in respectable academia were sidetracked by this sensual Himalayan abandonment. To quote David Robinson (*North of India*), 'The region induced addiction.'

6
Time by the Village Clock

From Binsar I journeyed to Kausani where my resolve to move to the Himalaya was furthered by Sarala Behn's invitation to work at her Gandhian school as odd job man. Instead of visiting Dr Bindu's relation in Kausani I had gone to meet Sarala since her name had been recommended by Sri Krishna Prem after he heard of my interest in the Gandhian movement.

Krishna Prem had been selfless in guiding me to Sarala: he did not have a high opinion of Gandhian philosophy although he had a lot of regard for her. Destiny would backtrack however. After four years in the ashram school, Sarala recommended I return to Mirtola for Krishna Prem's advice on somehow capturing and making permanent a return of the feelings of unutterable joy I had experienced in Binsar. How had I, hungry, comfortless and tired, known such blissful communion with the wellspring of life? That maddening state of intoxicating love had hit my plexus only once before when I had been totally smitten by a woman. Then my guts had physically ached but at Binsar all of me was aquiver with an orgiastic plenitude.

Destiny smiled. I had no money to support myself in the Himalaya. Sarala's offer involved no payment but it would cover my food, homespun clothes and most importantly education into the village way of seeing and doing things. Too often alien do-gooders turn up to analyse rural poverty and devise revolutionary schemes guaranteed to snap villagers out of their backwardness. Unfortunately most of these schemes never work because outsiders rarely spend a whole year in the hills and are unaware of how drastically things can change at different seasons. The problem one day may be drought and the next, floods.

The short-sightedness of experts often lies in ignoring why the villagers do it their own way. For example Sarala was a great believer in the digging fork over the local pharua (spade) because with a fork you turn the soil and then back away over undug soil. With a pharua you advance over the soil you have dug and thus flatten it again. However on a hill diet with little energy to invest in supple digging techniques the pharua is easier on the body. It certainly is less efficient and less scientific but it suits the local reality of undernourished physiques.

The classic story of how new techniques cannot be forced on villagers is told of a British contractor who on seeing labourers carrying small headloads of earth suggested they be supplied wheelbarrows. When he checked on the innovation next day he saw the labourers dutifully carrying soil in the wheelbarrows—but carrying the wheelbarrows on their heads!

I was introduced to the village view of time one day when I suggested to Sarala that to save money on the porterage of yams from the neighbouring village of Donni I could take some of the senior girls and carry back the loads on our heads. Donni lay a few miles east past an overgrown tea estate and was isolated in the midst of enclosing pine slopes. We left at seven in the morning after a breakfast of roti and water. Sarala refused to allow tea arguing that it was anti-poor. She also refused buffalo milk, insisting on cow's milk. The problem is hill cows give a fraction of what the buffalo does so for the sake of Gandhian ideology the girls went without milk in their diet.

The village had half a dozen slate-roofed houses, each with the living quarters upstairs faced with a wooden veranda above the cowshed. The architecture of these white painted houses is very pleasing and little touches from the local shilpkar add to the display of carved wood with Ganesh always riding above the lintern

TIME BY THE VILLAGE CLOCK

to suggest the medieval settlers hailed from the plains of western India. Not a soul was at home. All the houses were shuttered (but not locked) and the girls had to shout to elicit any human presence. A girl cowherd appeared. We asked her the whereabouts of Khim Singh, the man we had agreed to buy the yams from that morning. The little girl knew nothing but lifting her voice into the wind yodelled to her big sister. After five minutes her didi arrived from the surrounding jungle all smiles. She also didn't know anything about Khim Singh but would consult her daju (big brother). Village protocol decrees that big brothers when summoned by little sisters take longer to appear than big sisters summoned by little sisters. In fact it took an hour of yodelling interlocution before daju turned up bearing an evil looking machete in his hand. When told of Khim Singh's yam transaction he agreed to help locate our missing farmer. This daju did by cupping his hands and yodelling long and melodiously up into the pine slopes. From there a faint voice answered saying that onward enquiries would be made and that when Khim Singh was finally pinpointed within hearing distance of the village communication system he would sooner or later declare himself.

At eleven a shy man with an axe in his hand turned up and admitted to being Khim Singh. Had he forgotten his appointment we asked? He smiled and said he knew we were coming in the morning. He indicated that the sun had not yet reached the meridian so that technically he could not be faulted. Having been kept waiting for three hours I almost exploded at this casual attitude. I thought it better to pack the yams in the sacks we had brought and only then allow myself the luxury of blowing him up.

Khim Singh led us to his house and opened the downstairs byre. I assumed he had stored the yams inside. Instead he took out a kutli, a primitive digging implement, smiled and nodded towards a plot where yams were still growing. Of course he wouldn't have kept them in the byre. The villagers bury their dug up yams since that way they stay fresh. But Khim Singh was not about to uncover a buried store. Instead he began digging at the roots of a huge fresh yam plant with his tiny kutli. After five minutes of herculean effort he was able to tug out the first of the yams. And we had come to collect six sackfulls!

I was now beside myself with rage. It was nearly midday and at this rate it would take the rest of the day just to dig out a sufficient quantity for our needs. In addition the earth had to be rubbed off every root otherwise when they came to be weighed we would be paying extra. Urging the girls to grab kutlis and speed up the digging, I asked Khim Singh where the kutlis were kept. Smiling as always he pointed to the open byre. Inside I picked up several broken kutlis with the iron head-piece used for digging parted from the wooden handle. Not one of the handles was serviceable. I asked him where he kept his new handles. He ordered a small boy, amongst the several who had gathered in the course of the morning, to provide new handles. The boy went upstairs and returned with a stout branch of oak and a basula. If we wanted handles we would have to fashion them ourselves.

I was seething at the wasted hours and dreading what Sarala would make of my absurd economy drive. At this rate a whole day's labour of six people would be lost to the ashram and the yams would cost twice as much as when Khim Singh delivered them by mule.

By two in the afternoon the yams were all dug and Khim Singh, still smiling, was squeezing with measured deliberation the earth from each root. Weighing should not take more than an hour and we could still be back in the ashram by four. Then to put me on the threshold of a heart attack Khim Singh calmly announced that his weighing balance was unserviceable. Last week someone had borrowed one of the pans. Also a rat had chewed through the ropes supporting the second pan. The borrowed pan could be located, however, so he sent a little boy to yodel for it. Meanwhile to make the second pan serviceable Khim Singh hunkered down and drawing out some dry strands of the cannabis plant began twisting them slowly into string.

Three o'clock passed and a yodel confirmed that the man who had borrowed the second pan last week had been contacted and was on his way back to the village as quickly as his herded livestock would allow him. By four both pans were ready and the end to our long-drawn-out drama seemed near. Khim Singh held up the scales to show them even and then placed the first yams to be weighed. For the first time that day his smile deserted him. Where were the weights? Neighbours surely would have asked if they wanted to borrow his 'do seer' lump of iron and it was too big for the rats to have made off with. A little boy whispered that maybe Khim Singh's son had kept it upstairs to keep flat the pile of school books he had covered with old newspaper the day before. Sure enough the weights were discovered and our agony was nearly over.

I was so drained of energy that I wasn't bothered what Sarala Devi would say when we turned up more than six hours late. There was a twinkle in her eye when she saw my crestfallen look. Nothing needed to be said. I had learned the lesson of how every economic situation has its local imperatives. The villagers were liberated from the rushed concerns of townspeople. They didn't lock their doors because they shared things amongst their neighbours. Khim Singh had been too canny to dig up his yams lest we did not turn up to collect them. His taking of things as they came and his utter dependence on the natural cycle made me realise that villagers for all their backwardness preserve valuable lessons a cash economy has lost. I had started out feeling superior to the inefficient rustic but ended the day realising how dependent urban people are, divorced from nature's cycle and handless compared to the self-reliant villager.

One of the hardest areas of adjustment to village life I found is the simple act of sitting on the floor. Other village refinements—like squatting to make rotis—were agonising to my knees and back muscles. The habits of a lifetime had to be changed and bodily posture totally restructured. This led to enormous physical and psychic pain. It would have been worse if I had not accepted it as the price paid for investigating a different culture.

For four years I learned the hard way how the villager coped with all the hazards the Himalaya threw at him. Your crops were sown with great labour and pain and could be mashed to pulp by storms of hail or eaten clean by obscenely fat locusts blown in from Rajasthan. Farmers had to guard their crops from monkeys, porcupine and bears but if they dropped their guard for just fifteen minutes to attend a call of nature they could find the fields devastated by just one of these cunning adversaries. It was heartbreaking. The joys were few. They came with seasonal festivals, made all the more intense by their rarity. The labouring women for one day were spared their backbreaking chores and could dress to kill in velvet crinolines and silver jewellery that declared their family's worth.

Kausani, with its mind-boggling snow view second only to that from Binsar, had become known as the place where Mahatma Gandhi was reported to have written his commentary on the *Bhagavadgita*. He had indeed written a part of it: the preface was composed as he camped in the dak bungalow. He had come to help stamp out the feudal custom of begar whereby government officers on official duty had the right to pressgang village labour without payment. The British were viewed as villains for allowing this pernicious system to continue but they had not introduced it. Slavery in economic matters has a long history in many Himalayan states. In Uttarakhand the indigenous Dom population were effectively servants of the later waves of caste Hindus who moved in from the plains. To this day hill brahmins consider it beneath their dignity to plough, though their landholding is greater than that of the Doms.

In village matters caste is of the utmost importance and identities are defined by boasts of ancient lineage backed up by fantasies of doubtful scriptural authority. A brahmin is correctly addressed as 'guru' and a Rajput as 'maharaj'. Outsiders are known by their region irrespective of caste. Thus a Nepali coolie is referred to as 'Dotiyal' (from the region of Doti) while all plains businessmen become 'Punjabi' (especially if they are conspicuously successful).

Kausani had been set aside by the British as a tea-growing ridge where ex-armymen were settled to run the new gardens. As in other parts of Uttarakhand some Chinese planters were drafted in to teach the locals the art of tea raising. Some descendants of these early growers still live in a village called Chine in the Boraau valley. Tea was not a success in Kumaun partly because of the dry, shallow soil, but mainly because the male population was by caste custom reluctant to be seen doing manual work. It could have been a highly paying crop: the Chinese variety that grows in Kumaun has a very sought-after flavour.

The negative work ethic of the Kumauni caste male is purely for local consumption. Outside his province the same person will contribute valued labour. As quaint confirmation of how caste stymies development at home but stimulates it outside, it is the custom of hill shilpkars (former untouchables who are notable craftsmen) to adopt the name 'Singh' when they go to work in the plains. Rajputs are considered more reliable workers by plains employers who are unaware of their work-shy reputation in the hills.

To add to the complications of caste pride is the poor yield of the land. There is just enough on the valley floors to keep the present generation going but each year after 1960 I watched cultivation move further up the hillside carving steeper and less cultivable plots out of the forest. As the forest retreats, the long-term problem of dwindling renewable resources grows more intense. In Garhwal where the valleys are steeper and the effort to win a crop harder the men cannot afford the luxury of whiling away their days in the tea shop. They are forced to help their womenfolk till.

How then do Pahari villagers survive on their meagre plots when the population, thanks to medical advances, is increasing? The answer is subsidy by family members who work in the plains and send a money order each month to keep the home fires burning. This source of income became a tradition with local recruitment to the hill regiments. Post-independence there was demand for various paramilitary personnel and hill recruits swelled the ranks of these central government forces that police the borders and guard vital installations.

At Sarala's Kausani school the diet was very limited and the ashram's garden was regularly raided by monkeys. To guarantee some vegetables, this gritty disciple of the guru of non-violence invested in a shotgun. It was not enough to scare away the hordes of monkeys who lived in the pine jungle that enclosed the garden. One of their number had to be killed and strung up to keep away its fellows.

I was allotted the task of executioner. It was an utterly loathesome and bizarre job. Not only did I have to shoot one, I was required to wrap a sari around myself to get nearer the target. Looking down the barrel of superior technology at a weaker but kindred species brings home to anyone with a soul that scourges like terrorism and militarism ultimately arise from our blind ignorance of life's sacredness. When I shot the monkey I felt I had shot part of myself.

Sarala Devi was no ordinary follower of Gandhiji. She ad-libbed when she wanted to and was not afraid to punish offending students with a clip round the ear. But the intensity of her ideological beliefs could bring about some terrible injustices. Two of her senior students were found to be secretly saving a few coins against the ashram code of publicly pooling pocket money. Many of the girls in the school were from disadvantaged homes and Sarala found the simplest way to make sure they all got something to spend was to pool their money. She decided to expel the errant girls as an example. To me this seemed to derive more from personal pique at the betrayal of her lofty ideals than from any considered educational judgement. Because she was harsh on herself Sarala felt she could be harsh on the children, forgetting that she chose to be there while the children had no choice.

Although Sarala was admired by the locals for her social dedication she was viewed as an exotic alien. The education she offered was better than nothing but the villagers, like the rest of India, valued modern education not Gandhiji's idealistic return to a pre-industrial regime. Their children came to her school because there was no other and consequently, had to suffer her idiosyncrasies and fads of which, as a good Gandhian, Sarala had several. One of them was dieting as a means of nature cure. The girls' daily diet of dal–bhat caused stomach-bloat. Sarala's answer to this was to invite the kids to undertake a weekly fast. Although it was an invitation, not far beneath lurked a threat of displeasure if the children did not comply. I objected to this subtle exploitation of children's minds. I argued that they needed dal daily; it was their sole source of protein and only those with serious problems of stomach gas should be encouraged to fast.

This was a mistake. Sarala viewed her role of guru as a sacred charge. Any suggestion that her methods may not have been in accord with the highest morality deeply wounded her personally as well as damaged her public image of omniscient practitioner of the Gandhian technique. Gandhiji himself had been tyrannically paternalist when he conducted his experiments with truth on his close followers. By challenging the hallowed associations that surround the status of the guru I had effectively sent in my resignation.

7
Union of Continents and the Birth of Eternity

Kausani's overgrown tea terraces overlook one of the loveliest valleys in the Himalaya. At its centre lies the superb cluster of temples of Baijnath that once marked a capital of the early medieval Katyur dynasty. With the coming of the motor road the nondescript bazaar of Garur arose to become the town's focal point, its tumbledown shacks mocking the dignity of the temples' deserted stones. These two contrasting clusters are a commentary on how the hill culture of Uttarakhand, which flourished in great style a thousand years ago, has lost its inspiration. These terraces rich in irrigated crops sustained a brilliant burst of civilisation (one of the temples' images of Parvati is the finest of its kind ever sculpted) but over the centuries farmers' creativity dwindled even as their crops continued to flourish. The hillmen who threw together the dingy shacks that make up Garur seem to belong to a different race from the creators of Baijnath's earlier structures.

The Uttarakhand hillman's apathy towards history and indeed towards anything that challenges the intellect is puzzling. Kumauni pandits are men of extraordinary learning and inner refinement; the Kshatriyas are no less proud of their heritage yet no one can face let alone come up with the reason for their spectacular decline. The answers usually trotted out are that the British, Muslims and Gurkhas have been responsible for the downwinding of glory but the rot had set in long before these foreign invaders appeared on the scene. A more likely answer lies in Kumaun's continual wars with neighbouring Garhwal, for Garhwal likewise has little to show of its earlier style.

Of the Hindu Himalayan states I have visited, Kumaun and Garhwal stand out as the poorest in terms of cultural remains. Garhwal's former capital Srinagar was devastated by a flood—which suggests that those who built it were not gifted with long-term planning insights. An earlier capital at Chandpur consists of a fine little fort (now in ruins) but too tiny to boast of any cultural influence beyond the valley it was set in. Kumaun's early capital Champawat by contrast has some superior remains and at Dwarahat too a royalty of style can be discerned. But compared with the cultural remains of other hill states these stray examples hardly add up to signs of a vibrant population.

The Kathmandu valley is clearly the richest in quality followed by the scattered erstwhile states of Himachal. Chamba and Brahmaur have fine remains. Incidentally this was as far west as the Gurkha conquest extended. In painting the Gurkha rule in black hues it is forgotten that they were Hindus (albeit of unorthodox credentials) and were concerned to be seen as protectors of the holy places of Hinduism in Uttarakhand.

Cultural growth can only arise from an overflow of patronage from the rich or royal. In other words areas where it flourished were signified by an agricultural surplus plus a stable ruler whose army was redoubtable enough to withstand any neighbour's challenges. Uttarakhand's problem seems to have been that the two provinces of Kumaun and Garhwal were more or less evenly balanced and their fate was to pull each other down over the centuries.

Now that these two feuding provinces have been brought together in a free union there is tremendous potential for development along the lines of alpine states like Austria and Switzerland. But to develop what is without doubt the world's most scenically beautiful area will require a revival of inspiration that disappeared from the hills with the collapse of the Katyur kings. Uttaranchal requires both a vision of greatness and pragmatism to achieve it through a sustainable tourist policy.

Kausani in 1960 was also known as Bhotia parav. During the heyday of trade with Tibet these Bhotia bordermen maintained a network of mule trains carrying wool and borax from Tibet in exchange for salt and manufactured items that were in demand across the divide. 'Bhot' meant Tibet and there was no mistaking in those days that the slant of Bhotia genealogy was towards a Tibetan origin. A generation later like everything else, this genealogy has undergone a drastic change. The Chinese invasion in 1962 completely severed Tibetan trade relations with India and left the Bhotias high and dry on the Indian side of the border with credentials that ill-fitted their wealth. In the pecking order of Kumaun's orthodoxy the Bhotia's mercantile lifestyle had gained him low rank. To fall in line with official 'mainstreaming' policy these erstwhile Buddhist highlanders got themselves accepted by one of the best-known brahminical stratagems of being declared 'lapsed Rajputs'. Throughout history Indian society has had to accommodate unorthodox arrivals. If they were too poor to pay their way they would be ranked accordingly. But if the candidate for upwardly mobile status could pay then warrior lineage was available at a price.

This urge to Hinduise the Buddhist population of the border areas had started with the Arya Samaj's campaign in the nineteenth century to reclaim the Doms of the foothills into the 'Aryan' fold (as it was perceived then). Many shilpkars in Kumaun use the surnames 'Arya' and 'Ram', indicating a social force at work that made caste exclusiveness a little more porous.

It is revealing to read the terminology of Atkinson's encyclopaedic *Gazetteer* of the hills and compare it with modern usage. The term 'Khas' to denote locally derived brahmins for example has now become pejorative. Similarly in the space of forty years the term 'Bhotia' has been proscribed by polite society just as 'Harijan' in the plains has been erased from the vocabulary of socially acceptable terms.

This societal turbulence and its changing signifiers intriguingly echo the geomorphic reality underfoot. The Himalaya is the opposite of what it is popularly defined to be—an unmoving mass. It is—on a cosmic time scale—comparatively mobile in its behaviour. From the forces contesting the space within our gaseous sphere, the Himalaya continues to emerge and grow, its fluidity mirroring the changes in each day's research that bring us a little nearer to understanding how the world's greatest mountain chain arose.

Hillmen are not in the least bothered about the fashioning of their homeland though they will be fascinated to listen to symbolic renderings of the conflict in the pages of popular scripture. Even sophisticated citizens find it hard to break with the popular notion that the Himalaya defines India both physically and spiritually in its impenetrable uprise. Like Hinduism the Himalaya is thought to possess eternal dimensions, and the peaks stretching from Pakistan to Tibet are mythologically united as a family.

In popular lore, these are truths gleaned by the Rishis in their ice caves at the founding of the universe. According to the strict findings of surveyors and geographers who have taken the trouble to track down the extremes of the range, the Himalaya runs between the massifs of Nanga Parvat and Namche Barwa around which poetically the two greatest rivers of the subcontinent, the Indus and Brahmaputra, bend back on themselves to deliver their waters in the direction of the plains. We shall stick to these ground realities while conceding that the Karakoram and other snowy ranges bordering the Himalaya in Pakistan and Tibet are indeed, as popular imagination decrees, its cousins. 'Brahmaputra' is one of nine names given to the waters that rise 'from the Celestial Horse's Mouth' less than a hundred kilometres from the source of the west-flowing Indus. For much of its course through Tibet it is known as the Tsangpo and after it curls round the Namche Barwa massif to enter India it is called the Siang by the tribals of upper Arunachal. To the tribals of the lower tracts it is known as the Dihang. Only when these waters from the Tibetan plateau meet those of the Lohit downstream in Assam is the usage Brahmaputra technically correct. To confound an already confused riverine geography (the merging rivers measure many miles across) the religious source of the Brahmaputra differs from its physical source; it is at Parsuram Kund—where the Lohit, flowing in from the range adjacent to the Sino-Burmese border, leaves the hills of Arunachal—that the Brahmaputra is thought to rise. Owing to the ferocity of the terrain and its tribals, not even the British were sure that the Brahmaputra in Assam was the same river as the Tsangpo in Tibet.

There are historical reasons for the confusion of names. Assam was settled in the medieval period by tribes from Indo-China. Like the Bhotias would do later these foreign settlers adopted the local form of Hinduism and became staunch Vaishnavas. They gave birth to the name Brahmaputra a thousand years after the list of Hinduism's seven sacred rivers was compiled. You don't need to be an explorer to know that the name 'Brahmaputra', son of Brahma, is a misnomer. Perhaps because of the settlers' unfamiliarity with orthodox Hinduism they did not realise that river deities were traditionally female.

Big bends can possess potent magic. While the so-called Brahmaputra's big bend was only recently made known to the world at large the big bend on the Indus is celebrated widely for the fabulous vertical fall of land it carves a path round. This is another curiosity the findings of science suggest: that the rivers of the Himalaya are antecedent—they existed before the mountains grew on either side of them.

Orogenics—the science of how mountain chains are built—is as young an academic discipline as the Himalaya is on the geomorphic time scale. Current theory suggests that our range marks a high point between the European and New Zealand Alps. Cooling crustal deposits caused continents to crack and drift away to collide with other seemingly floating (actually sliding) masses. Breaking off from a larger parent the Indian landmass drifted northeastwards roughly from the direction of Madagascar at the minuscule speed of some fifty kilometres per million years. This early

India, it is posited, had no Himalaya and the rivers flowed north to reach the sea.

When some sixty million years ago the Indian plate rammed against the bigger and better anchored Eur-Asian plate the northern edge of India buckled up (or rather down) from contact with the leading edge of Tibet which at this time had a coastal plain watered by the Sea of Tethys. As India went under, the Eur-Asian plate was pushed by slow but immense tectonic forces to raise the level of Tibet. In this mutual driving of India under Asia lies the mechanics of how the Himalaya grew. This would also explain the continuing increase in its height. However the tectonic hypothesis cannot explain why the Himalaya is a perfect quarter of an arc whose centre is near Turfan, a depression in the earth's surface.

Whatever else it is, the Himalaya is *not* the stable, eternal unmoving mass it is popularly made out to be. By restricting its meditative inspiration to Himalayan ice caves Hinduism has shortchanged its claims since another myth that modern investigations have exposed is that snow did not settle on the Himalayan peaks till fairly recent geological times, say in the order of 40,000 years when hominids began shaking a leg. If *Ramapithecus* wallowed in a swamp in the Siwaliks it does not mean that up the hill the Himalaya stood out as a snowy rampart. Fossil finds suggest that frogs from the Chinese side could hop quite happily over the range into India and presumably so could hominids. If we calculate a rise of five centimetres for 40,000 years that would put the highest peaks of the Himalaya at some 10,000 ft so the passes would be as low as 3000 ft at that period.

The slow crumpling at the meeting of continents follows the line of the Indus in its flow from Tibet north-west into India. So enormous was the constant pressure that sediment from the ocean floor was squeezed up to surface in places like Spiti and Muktinath where fossil remains of deep sea species occur. If Hindus are mistaken in attributing great age to the snowy upthrust of the Himalaya their instincts are correct in the worship of the shalagram that takes us back to the evolutionary beginnings of life. The symbolism attached to Shiva as Lord of the Snows may not satisfy the demands of science but the image of Narayan slumbering on the cosmic ocean is an accurate visualisation of earth before life forms awoke and consciousness arose.

The Christian attempt to pseudo-scientifically date the Day of Creation to 4004 BC is embarrassing evidence of the lengths to which *homo sapiens* is prepared to go to fool himself in the name of religion. But are not admirers of the Himalaya also guilty of fooling themselves about its beauty? Rumpled bedsheets are not an edifying sight and each morning are hastily smoothened out. The Himalaya in its parallel ranges represents the crumpled sheets of Mother Earth's bed. Why is it that crinkles and folds in the clothes we wear are considered scruffy and sent to be ironed out when the bigger the fold a mountain possesses the greater that range is admired?

Kalidas, thought to be a Garhwali from Kalimath by some, is always quoted for his inspiring appraisal of the Himalaya: not in a hundred ages of the gods could he describe its glories. According to Hindu cosmology a hundred ages would take us back to a time when there was no Indian subcontinent as such let alone a high range in the north. Writing in the fourth century AD what Kalidas meant was the effect of the Himalaya on the eye of the visitor. Blinded by the vision of immaculate snow peaks in a heavenly frame of pine or rhododendron amidst the awesome silence of infinite surroundings the mind is blown, the soul stirred and our faculties overwhelmed.

The Himalaya allows highly subjective connotations. To Hindus it conjures up profound collective memories and values while to Muslims and Christians it may suggest negative religious associations of demonology and oracular possession. Mountaineers rave about the tonic effect the Himalaya has on their bloodstream while others consider such addictions a dangerous death wish. Villagers who live in the Himalaya hardly notice the snow peaks and rarely spare time to seek out the best snow view. Much of the time they will curse the gods of the mountains for their cruelty. They worship these cold and distant deities out of fear lest things get worse. Confined all their lives to a single valley the vision of a villager is neither poetic nor expansive. For a woman it's even worse. Her life is a round of unending drudgery.

How can we reconcile these two extremes—of rapturous visitor and sullen resident? There is a middle path but it requires us to be ruthlessly honest with ourselves. To live in the Himalaya and maintain the harmony between the luxury of a poetic view of the surroundings and the genuine gripe of local people who are fighting a losing battle, you need a little (but not too much) economic independence, a sympathetic ear for your neighbour's problems and the determination to renew your inspiration daily.

Throughout the Himalayan chain I have found the finely sited bungalows and beautifully situated cottages of well-off admirers empty and locked up. In Rumer Godden's novel *Black Narcissus* a party of foreign nuns are invited by a Nepali prince to open a convent in his mansion placed in stunning opposition to the full glory of Kanchenjunga. Godden keeps returning to the subtle suggestion that such close viewing of nature's majesty is too much for our souls to accommodate. Kanchenjunga, it is hinted, is a portion of eternity too great for ordinary mortals to behold at length. The novel ends with the nuns bowing to this dictate of nature, accepting that for all their purity of purpose they lack the stamina to live before its blinding glory. Interestingly an old Hindu sadhu who plays no part in the plot (which revolves around sexual jealousies) and is indifferent to the physical beauty all around, remains a permanent presence on the ridge, unaffected by the loom of the mountain's bulk.

Over the years I have witnessed almost a dozen candidates for snow views who bought bungalows, moved in and then after only a few months' residence decided it was more than they could take. Often the problem is caused by simple ignorance of the terrain. Site a house on top of a ridge and it is too hot in summer and too windy in winter. But site it lower on the northern face to get the full snow panorama and you have the terrible punishment of sunless winters. Any house in the hills requires three basic checks. Drinking water is a must and should preferably come by gravity. Winter sun is essential if you plan to live all the year round and that means catching it early and keeping it for as long as you can. The third essential is security from earthquakes and forest fires. Make sure the ridge you choose is not crowned by boulders; and where inflammable species grow, create a fire line and keep it free of litter in summer.

Since our range is both moving and growing it is important likewise to stay flexible. Your water spring may disappear overnight from an earthquake so you need to have already thought of an alternative. The water shortage in the Himalaya is so alarming that you can expect to have to fight for any new claims. Finding harmony within is just as hard as living harmoniously with one's neighbours.

This is why it helps to be not too well off. If you are willing to pay a man daily to climb down the gadera to keep your storage tanks full you will avoid quarrels and provide a hillman a job. By lashing out on expensive pipes you will only add to the bitterness of locals, who might go out of their way to sabotage your line. Viewing the Himalaya does subdue sullen thoughts but not for long.

All this leads towards the realisation that the Himalaya as well as being a majestic wall of life out there intimidating the soul with its grandeur is also a reflection of something inside us, a mirror of that which is undyingly glorious in our individual being. I often sense in the empty bungalow syndrome that the disappointed owners have fled because they relied too much on looking out. Had they closed their eyes, listened to the silence and smelt the soughing cedar they would have had a fuller taste of the tonic that contact with the Himalaya provides. As food for the soul it is stimulus for meditation, not the object.

8
Burha Pinnath

Kausani commands the watershed between upper and lower Kumaun. Historically Talla Desh 'the lower region' referred to Kali Kumaun in the foothills bordering Nepal. These are (or were) thickly forested ridges where Jim Corbett shot many of his man-eaters. Kausani's strategic importance is proven by the wooden stockade the Gurkhas had built. Sited east of Sarala's ashram, it overlooks the rich paddies of the Someshwar valley which is said to produce some of the best crops in Asia.

When I lived in Kausani I often climbed up west of the parav exploring different routes on Pinnath, the great mountain that exceeds the height of Binsar by a thousand feet. This steep bulk beetled in the background over Kausani and gave birth to the Kosi river near its summit. The river wound its way south through an enclosed valley that blocked easy access to Kausani and villagers had the choice of making a detour along the motor road to gain the parav or climb a sheer mountainside for the path that linked Kausani to tea estates that are now defunct. Kausani's bungalow for visiting VIPs used to be the residence of the tea garden's owners, Englishmen who get a mention in the early British accounts of expeditions to the interior when the motor road had not yet been extended beyond Ranikhet.

One of my favourite walks was to continue past the 'state' bungalow (the 'estate' having become captive to the phonetics of

Uttar Pradesh) to Dumlot (a deserted bungalow with a great view) and then climb on to the narrow ridge that overlooked the debouching of the Kosi from the heights. If you stuck closely to the narrow track it would lead straight up the face of Pinnath to the summit.

In the monsoon villagers were in the habit of camping out with their buffaloes in clearings called khatta. These semi-nomadic seasonal settlements were a source of much vexation to the forest officers for the villagers thought nothing of axing a full-grown tree and then sawing its timber into sturdy planks from which they built their huts. They had no written rights to graze despite the fact that the same families used the same clearings for generations together. This inconvenience had a simple solution: the forest guard could easily be bribed with a seer of ghee to pretend he had found no one there on his rare round of inspection. If however some super-efficient sahib took it into his head to survey the situation then the remedy was to set the khatta ablaze for illegal occupation of forest land.

The sufferer in this game of cat and mouse was the forest's natural cover for next season more timber would be felled for a new khatta. Over the years as the population increased in the village and fodder became harder to find, habitation of the khatta became prolonged. Younger brothers or simple-minded sons began to spend a good part of the year in the high forests and this took its toll of the timber.

I was flabbergasted to see how hill buffaloes made it up the near-vertical path. They had to be coaxed and sometimes hauled to get them over roots and other obstacles but against the odds they made it to the summit of Pinnath. This was known as Burha Pinnath, the ancient site of the temple dedicated to Shiva in his bowman form. Lower down the face of Pinnath with access from the broadening stream of the Kosi is a handsome temple endowed by the medieval Kumaun rajas. Steps lead up to the lower Pinnath temple from the river. A considerable amount of labour must have gone into the siting of this temple though to what end I have not been able to work out. There is neither water nor snow view. Set in dense jungle, it appears to be a dead end, though you can climb to the old temple from here by a steep knife-edge ridge. Its logic remains obscure, unless it was chosen by its remoteness for tantric rites. I have camped overnight too and admired the solemn air of devotion that clings to this structure but the mystery of its placement continues to baffle.

Shiva as bowman is a compelling figure in my personal lore of the Himalaya. Like Cupid he fires his arrows of desire and once they lodge in a climber's heart he's hooked to the great range for life. The peaks too on occasion seem to shoot arrowlike out of their matrix hinting at the molten motion at their core. Shivling, the great white triangle of ice that crowns the source of the Ganga, I always envision as a flame of ice. Wherever you find Shiva you find the union of opposites.

Shiva as unpredictable practitioner of raw energetic outbursts seems a much more appropriate Lord of the Snows than Vishnu whose steadfastness and unflamboyant characteristics seem aligned to the kinder contours of the plains. Most Himalayan villagers do in fact subscribe to the Saivite faith and this is due in part to the difficulty in observing the ritual niceties demanded by Vaishnavism. The joke in the hills that the followers of Vishnu die from nahana (bathing) and the followers of Shiva from khana (eating) cleverly captures differences in sociology and style between the two. If you practise too much ritual bathing in the hills it can kill you. The sturdier Saivite survives on the prasad from temples but sometimes that is so inedible it can kill you as well.

Till very recent times popular Hindu practices in the hills could be extremely unorthodox particularly in the area of bali-dan (animal sacrifice.) Orthodox fashions are catching on and nowadays more and more hillmen are at pains to be seen as subscribing to Sanskritic norms since this adds to their social respectability.

On the steep ascent to Burha Pinnath I leave behind the sweltering pines with relief for a belt of broad-leaved trees. Now the narrow path becomes less slippery and safer especially in the rains when jhonk (leeches) pop up in the pine tracts to make any progress miserable and bloody. Pine forests are also notoriously dry. Only higher can you expect to find some water springs. You know you are reaching the 8000 ft mark when stately surai (cypress) begin to line the ascent. Then the echoing woof of Bhotia guard dogs announces the proximity of the khatta. At altitude sounds travel far and you may have to cover another mile before reaching camp.

The first thing the herders do is to assess how much of a threat you are to them. They thaw when assured you are not a government servant and melt when told you live at 'Sarala ashram'. Tea is offered and a blanket for the night. But only half the day has gone and getting back down to Kausani (unless you lose the path) will only take a couple of hours by the shortcuts.

I have brought my own lunch of alu paratha but am glad of the refreshing tea. I cannot touch the proferred dal–bhat which contains more pepper than dal. The camp is under the summit ridge so if I want a snow view before the clouds rise and blank out the peaks I will have to move quickly. The dividing ridge is so sharp I have to crawl carefully to get holds. Right behind the summit and some fifty feet beneath it is a forest bridle path that has wound all the way up from Ganai Chaukutiya, a whole day's march away on the western confines of Kumaun. This path will wander southwards losing height casually until it comes out at Someshwar; it is the perfect forester's walk for creeping up unexpectedly on squatters. I will follow this path some of the way home then cut steeply down to the Borarau valley through virgin forest. As a red herring for resident bears, you must lose height at a trot huffing and puffing as if you are a party of stampeding buffaloes. A stout stick will prove an asset.

One day on this path I came face to face with a ghooral (mountain goat). I was only ten yards away and he showed no fright. He simply turned off the track and made for the edge of the ridge where he sensed he would have the advantage had I followed him. It made me realise that even in the wilderness we are never alone.

The temple on the top of Pinnath was a tiny structure containing a mini-lingam with a trident in front. Two poles with wire strung between had been placed for devotees to hang their bells from. It was a sensational way to ring out the puja to the four corners of Kumaon, every bit as satisfying as walkie-talkie-ing from the top of Everest.

BURHA PINNATH

Imagine my surprise when I went a year later and found a larger temple built with mirrors in the wall to reflect the sun. A widow had endowed the temple with a new image of the god and I had arrived at his installation. I liked her imagination in seeking to spread the light of the summit all around but secretly preferred the tiny original. Still, the bells rang gloriously and echoed the ecstatic freedom of the heart I was to lose when I slithered back down to the ashram and its ideological concerns. Pinnath remains one of the treasured summits of my life for the sheer blinding beauty all around.

To the west of Pinnath but slightly south is the even higher peak of Butkot. It is connected to Pinnath by a long ridge that took off near where I bumped into the ghooral. I always planned to do that traverse but on being told it was a three mile one, kept putting it off. Unlike Pinnath, clothed in a superb mix of thickly forested slopes, Butkot rises Vesuvius-like, black and stark as though it was a burnt out-volcano. This mountain gives birth to tributaries of the Ram Ganga, a river that rises to considerable status in the plains, subsuming the Kosi.

Access to the mountain was then from the Someshwar–Dwarahat bridle path (now a motor road) and below it stood the famous Kumauni version of the Dunagiri temple dating back to AD 1029. Although no serious contender to the real Dunagiri in Garhwal in looks and presence, the fact remains that Butkot looms large in the Lesser Himalaya and arouses local regard by its eminence.

Though I never got as far as the understudy Dunagiri I did include in my walks a trek to Aira Devi, a well-wooded peak on the southern side of the Someshwar–Dwarahat road. Now a motor road from Someshwar to Ranikhet has replaced the bridle path to Aira Devi and weakened the impact of the wilderness. In those days a swami had just opened a Sanskrit pathshala at Aira Devi signifying more inroads into the cultural core of Kumaun. Aira was a famous nature god of the district. With the coming of mainstream interpretations this nature god like so many other was converted into a form of Shiva.

After the Chinese scare in 1962 the government panicked and a berserk network of roads carved out new and little-used routes in a flurry of guilt at the neglect of hill development. So much timber was felled in this spree that according to some experts Kumaun is doomed now to become a drought-prone state in the near future. The buzzword then was 'BDO' signifying the block development officer. All the villagers' problems were going to be solved by the BDO waving his magic funding wand. Like bell-bottomed trousers and long sideburns the BDO was all the rage until it was found that the wand produced neither funds nor results. Then like other revolutionary rural schemes this one too was given a quiet burial.

Without proper preparation these well-intended schemes actually made the poor villager worse off than he was before. They overlooked the need to educate the villager about his responsibility for the successful working of the scheme. Drinking water for example that lay in springs at a distance from the village was sought to be piped to save women the daily chore of lugging up pots on their head. But at least the old method made people realise what a precious resource water was. They valued it because of the sweat it cost them to bring it home. Now piped lines were casually laid on the surface open for anyone to tamper with. They led to storage tanks built of poor quality concrete and a tap that was generously left open for cattle to benefit from; the entire water resources of the hillside went speedily to waste and the springs dried up. Women henceforth had to trudge to a more distant source. The men, unaccustomed to nipping problems in the bud, watched disinterestedly as cattle broke the pipes and precious water leaked away.

The extent of the problem can be gauged by how even the most educated are not taught to take personal responsibility nor encouraged to become physically involved in solving the problem of acute water shortage. One day walking in Mussoorie I bought some bananas and found the paper bag in which they were wrapped contained instructions from the Lal Bahadur Shastri National Academy of Administration to probationers (India's trainee bureaucrats) on how to deal with a leaking tap. Instead of advising the nation's brightest young minds to grab a wrench and change the washer, in true bureaucratic style the instructions ran to a whole page, inviting preliminary intimation to the Central Public

Works Department representative to be followed up in the event of non-action by a reminder. Failing central intervention the probationer was then recommended to bring it to the notice of his hostel in charge. Should the latter emulate the PWD and do nothing the final court of appeal was to approach in person the academy director. The same lack of urgency that characterised the villages could be found in the budding administrator.

Gandhians at least did not fight shy of manual involvement. The Kausani ashram had an udyogshala (craft shed) where the girls were taught to spin and weave. They also looked after a small herd of hill cows. These were largely ornamental since their yield of milk was pathetic. But in one way they proved outstanding performers. On a steep slope or jumping down vertical terraces they proved to be as sure-footed as steeplechasers.

I learnt to wield an adze, that most primitive but useful of woodshaping implements, and became accomplished with the wrench on broken pipes. The ashram though situated on pine slopes had a copious spring that Sarala Devi had judiciously augmented and made pukka. One day as I was ticking off Lakshman Singh my assistant handyman for removing a block of stone under one sagging length of pipe to prop up a second length of sag, instead of being offended he invited me to attend his village festival in honour of Kumaun's most popular deity the mountain goddess Nanda. It was to be a devta-natch, or conjuring up of a spirit.

Sarala was opposed to what she considered the less desirable aspects of local religion, such as animal sacrifice, but for this once I was allowed to go. That was to be my last outing for a long time. At the village, having drunk contaminated water, I developed typhoid and for nearly two months had to be nursed by Sarala and her students. This was the busiest time of the year and I expected to feel helpless and frustrated at my confinement. But strangely, in the absence of solid food, my body was forgotten and an orgy of well-being overcame my soul. I was fasting before the full spread of the snow panorama. All the cosmos in the garden of Lakshmi Ashram was in glorious bloom. I filled notebooks with poetry that poured effortlessly forth and found myself free of the need to hang onto the apron strings of any religion or ideology. The upshot was

I told Sarala I was leaving. She, understanding my need, advised me to consult Krishna Prem in Mirtola.

By April I was fully fit and ready to chance my arm at rediscovering the elixir I had tasted in the bodiless state but had lost the moment normalcy reclaimed my body. In contrast to the killjoy routine that doctrinaire Gandhianism considered to be desirable, the universe had come across as a marvellous machine utterly joyous in its working. Ideas I had once considered necessary for spiritual advancement were revealed as just that—noble ideas, laughably irrelevant to the pulsating engine of conscious being. There was no way I could explain this to Sarala or to anyone who had not tasted the ecstasy that descended unbidden on me in my near-death state.

Each winter the Kausani ashram gave me a month off to visit Gandhian institutions in the plains and rather than catch the bus to the roadhead at Kathgodam I preferred to walk spending a night with interesting people along the way. On one occasion I spent the night at Sat Tal, a Christian ashram founded by the Rev. Stanley Jones a famous American Methodist. It was here that Denman the South African who roped in Tenzing to make an abortive attempt to climb Mount Everest had lived for some time in the 1960s.

Sat Tal was beautifully laid out with its seven lakes but the ashram was finding it hard to keep up any spiritual momentum. The night I was there I found the ultimate ecumenical menagerie—a Greek Orthodox nun, an American Quaker, Roman Catholic sisters, a Hindu sadhu from Mauritius and a Russian Orthodox priest with a cockney acolyte. Obviously Cranks Ridge threw a long shadow but the very fact that such an assortment of seekers sought out the Kumaun hills suggests this area undoubtedly possess unusual qualities.

Over the years I had in the wintertime passed by Mirtola and when there were no visitors had been allowed to spend the night. I had come to like Krishna Prem for his sparkling intellect and had warmed to his disciple Ashish who turned out to be gentler than he looked. Ashish Maharaj had fallen off the temple roof and broken his legs some years earlier (I happened to be at Dr Bindu's when I saw him carried by on a stretcher). The whole town showed its concern, a remarkable demonstration of how the hillman is broadminded in matters of the soul, for both Krishna Prem and his disciple were foreigners, though on independence they became naturalised citizens.

I had no inkling when I climbed up past Gurkha Kila and waved my last farewell to the girls at Kausani that I had a small part to play in the destiny of Mirtola's gurus. It had happened a winter earlier when after spending the night with Krishna Prem I had walked to Mukteshwar and stayed with an Australian couple Nelson and Flora Beresford whom I had first met at Dr Bindu's.

The Beresfords were orchardists who had originally come to India to follow the teachings of J. Krishnamurthi but then switched course to the Pondicherry ashram. Nelson asked where I was coming from and I told him I had spent the night with Krishna Prem. Nelson and Flora had never met him. They disappointedly said there was now no time as they were planning to leave India immediately to put their youngest son David into a Rudolf Steiner biodynamic farm in England. Dave was a handsome strapping young man who had grown up in Kumaun but because of dyslexia had been unable to further his formal studies.

My chance visit was momentous both for the Beresfords and Mirtola. What I told them of Mirtola made them change their minds about going to England and they visited Krishna Prem instead. I had played a minor kind of John the Baptist role in making straight the way for Dave to be eventually annointed Sri Ashishdev, both *enfant terrible* and successor to the line of gurus at Mirtola.

9
Chhota Binsar

The watershed walk that I followed from Kausani to Mirtola covers about forty miles of high ridge that runs south-west parallel to the great snow crest of the Himalaya without any intervening range to distract the eye. It is my favourite walk in the entire Himalaya especially in winter when ankle-deep leaves strew the higher trails. When I left Kausani in April I had to expect the slippery ascent through pine and put up with the furious piping of the manic cicada that never lets up until you hit the higher broad leaf jungle.

From Gurkha Kila, the path ran above the Kosi then dropped to meet a forest bridle path that linked the wool processing village of Chanouda with Lamgara, which is an isolated bungalow between the village of Donni and Chhota Binsar. Chhota Binsar as a peak could not match the major Binsar in height or bulk but it does play a part in Kumauni folklore: the famous local epic romance *Malu-Shahi* mentions this peak.

Just as to reach Almora from Kathgodam by motor road meant in the early days a laborious circling detour via Ranikhet so the bus route to Bageshwar from Someshwar was a long flanking manoeuvre via Kausani and Garur. The bridle paths made for easy hiking and from the summit of Chhota Binsar I commanded views of both the Bageshwar and Someshwar ends of the trail. Midway it was straddled by the watershed saddle of Grechhina, chhina in

Kumauni indicates a saddle that often includes a pass. Chhina Peak at the head of Naini Tal's lake caused English memsahibs to think that from the top they could view China; sadly it was just linguistic confusion that fogged the view. Such ignorance in a foreigner is understandable but what is one to make of the administrator who during the panic of 1962 decided to rename Chhina Peak 'Subhash Peak' to censor any possible Chinese claims on it? Eventually the name Naina Peak has come into popular use referring to the lake goddess who protects the town, though not always. In the great landslide of 1888 her temple was covered with debris.

I passed several 'chhina' and all were characterised by paths that used these dips as crossing places. After Grechhina the path climbs steeply to leave the pine for broader species of trees. There are some sheer drops to the eastern flank of the main Binsar and the ridge veers up to the temple of Maika before falling just as severely to the Almora–Bageshwar road near Takula. Takula is conventionally reached by following the forest path round the western end which leads to the famous limestone cave shrine at Gananath. This temple also boasts of a magnificent image of Parvati. Gananath commands the Kosi valley; here too the Gurkhas had their defensive stockade and in the wresting of Almora town from Gurkha control the British won a skirmish (aided by some bribes in high places) at Gananath.

Some experimental forest planting had been done and a few eucalyptus trees were in evidence. I also saw some opium poppies in the chowkidar's garden. Throughout the interior a modest growth of poppy is winked at. Local custom has always considered the use of a little opium a legitimate pain killer and it could be had in Almora from a government shop (along with cannabis) on a doctor's prescription. Both poppy and cannabis seed are used as flavouring agents in village food. Roasted and ground up into chutney the taste of bhang is quite pleasant and its after-effects have the mild hallucogenic symptom of making one feel relaxed enough to giggle. With cannabis growing wild local custom wisely accepted the impossibility of controlling its use. Having seen the effects of charas (the essence of the cannabis plant) hill society concluded it was better to allow it some ceremonial status (as at the festival of Holi). No stigma attaches to sadhus who flaunt the chillum filled with sulfa (the black resin from the female flower) while every village is resigned to having a 'charasiya', the local addict who cannot kick the habit. However the charasiya is usually just benignly stoned and rarely offers any threat to law and order unless he turns to marketing the weed.

The problem with cannabis is that it is a weed. It grows on waste land and is quite promiscuous in its seeding. The villagers value it for its hemp. In the plains the green leaf, ganja, is made into mildly hallucogenic drinks. Bhang is the general term to cover all the products of this tall-growing milky plant. Even when the crop has been harvested and the unwitting visitor passes through a field of head-high cannabis you get a slight high from the sap as you brush by.

Before I came to India I had been brought up to believe marijuana was as deadly as heroin but living in the hills soon exploded this superstition. Bhang is probably less harmful than alcohol and infinitely less deadly than heroin. The reason holy men smoke charas is because it relieves the pangs of hunger and gives the illusion of well-being. To some this seems a fair price to pay for watering eyes and the weakening of the will to change the world.

Preferring on this occasion to stick to the ridge I climbed up to the temple but found it locked. The sadhu who lived here was away. Sometimes sadhus stayed for years together in a place though usually they had a beat, moving on when supplying their food became a burden for the villagers. The problem with most hilltop temples was the water supply. At Maika the steep northern face yielded springs not too far from the temple. What the present incumbent was famous for was a large mirror before which he sat, a most unusual item for a holy man's kutir. The sadhu would regard his visitors through the looking glass and this novelty possibly attracted the curious villager. Some sadhus adopt a vow of silence and converse through signs or by writing with chalk on a slate. It always seemed easier to me to talk basics and avoid the contortions of expression that went with such vows. The most amusing instance of the limitations of the spiritual effect of these disciplines was when I asked a silent sadhu, Mauni Baba, his opinion of Lal Baba, a famous but irascible holy man who had pilgrims at his ashram near the source of the Ganga. Expecting a restrained appraisal it came as a surprise to read Mauni Baba's opinion which he carefully chalked upon his slate: 'Someone should break his legs!' Such crude sentiments are inevitable when unsophisticated holy men compete for limited resources and the affection of poor villagers. Those who were popular could not afford to be too aloof and were expected to join in village ceremonies even when they did not approve of the custom being celebrated. Krishna Prem, whose ashram was well funded and made no demands on the surrounding villages, made it a point to win village affections by establishing a free dispensary. But on matters of principle Krishna Prem would not compromise. He did not attend weddings or devta-natch. He did however keep aside a place for visiting holy men and fed them with due honour for the prescribed period of three days.

From Maika the path now plunged into wild terrain. Across the Takula road it climbed steeply into the open forests that marched up the huge bulk of Binsar. Animals during the day were hardly a threat. The only one I had disturbed was a barking deer when I set out in the morning. Just beyond Gurkha Kila I had almost put my foot on the dozing calf which leapt up and drummed away, our hearts fluttering in unison at this sudden collision.

The walker of wandering bridle paths learns never to take an obvious shortcut unless you can see where it debouches. Dozens of footpaths took off from the long meander up the side of Binsar and every one of them would have performed a snakes and ladder trick of taking me back to the Takula motor road. I gained height and the coolness offset the heat of the morning. At every water course—provided there is no habitation above—it is politic to refill your bottle. Frequent rests are good to tone up your awareness which can become slack from fatigue. The greatest pleasure from a Himalayan walk is to experience the soft contrasting contours of green glades that give way to brown pine-strewn paths signifying a drop in height. The sudden change is delightful especially in reverse when you toil up a hot dry hillside and pass into a cool and moist north face. Each season adds its touches of colour and fragrance. The jungles around Kausani are alive with a wild white climbing rose that runs riotously during summer. By contrast the scarlet rhododendron flowers as the snow ends in March, making for spectacularly startling effects. To sink down on such a bank of greenery after a sweat-laden climb is to experience something of the kingdom of heaven. Water that on most days is colourless and tasteless now seems like nectar and you relish every sip as you look around.

On the whole I enjoy most walking in the middle ranges above the pine level where the green canopy of alpine species has produced a silent mulch of humus. All manner of life sprouts in this damp black soil and the altitude makes no demand on the lungs. Moisture is the key to mountain delight. Take the moisture and the mulching away and confine the fluid element to the cold, powerful fast-flowing streams of the desert regions at similar heights across the great snow crest and I find a different kind of pleasure. Whereas the alpine level appeals by its soft contours, rich yield of fruit and flower and undemanding climate, the trans-Himalayan deserts astonish by their unlikely impact. In addition to a hostile spread of barren slopes you find a dreamy translucence that bewitches the eye. On the south side of the range the happiness one feels is of fulfilment whereas across the divide a mood of profound mental stillness obtains. Taken together they yield an understanding of the range's dual nature. The southern aspect seems to speak of transcendence while the northern gives intimations of immanence. The important thing is that the Himalaya provides both and in the monsoon season when there is too much moisture for comfort on the southern flanks the walker can cross over and enjoy the rarefied expanses beyond the full fury of the rains.

Familiarity with local variations will teach that you can experience some desert virtues without actually having crossed the great snow crest. Lahaul is one such example. You remain within reach of the alpine meadows should you follow the Chandrabhaga west towards the Pangi Valley. Another curious way to test the halfway ground between the inducements of Kumaun and the beckonings of Tibet is to trek up the Gori Ganga past Munsyari, squeeze past the enormous cliffs at Naharpani that signify the crest line of the great range and find yourself on the alps around Martoli. You scent here the beginnings of the Tibetan plateau days before you reach it. Though high above the tree line Martoli has the full flavour of an alpine meadow enhanced by the tumbling streams that sparkle amidst emerald glades.

Binsar's jungle gets thicker and darker the higher you climb. In April patches of snow still cling to the sunless gadera and the fall of snow is evident in the number of branches broken along the way. Although it's easy to find your way along bridle paths on a second visit the first time round can be trying if evening is closing in and there is no one to tell you which of two ways is the right one. Instinct then has to be relied upon but with caution. Stick to the broader path even if it's less used. A steep shortcut may bring you to a dead end at a herder's khatta and then you will have to climb back again.

The bridle paths were designed to link forest inspection bungalows so that in theory if you follow such a path, you will eventually end up at some human habitation. That was forty years ago and a good many bungalows have had their beams pinched for firewood and their doorframes 'borrowed' for khatta huts. Even when I was travelling, the Lamgara bungalow (near Chhota Binsar) was in a very tumbledown state and on the half dozen visits I made I never found the chowkidar on duty.

Though the visitor needed a permit to use a dak bungalow the chowkidar, as at Deolsari, was open to a little bargaining in the absence of one. Because they lived in remote surroundings chowkidars were often eccentric and unpredictable. When I first went to Mirtola the dak bungalow (now disused) was manned by two unmarried brothers who belonged to the Shah clan of Naini Tal. They were quite well read and took English newspapers when the post delivered them. (Almora had a famous English weekly called *Shakti* that started as the mouthpiece of the local independence movement under Gandhiji.) On one occasion when I was explaining some hard words to the Shahs, they showed me a list of words that puzzled them. Could I explain, for example, the meaning of the word 'iss-note' (snot!)?

After the British left, these isolated bungalows ceased to appeal to a less athletic breed of forest officer. Motor roads and the prestige of travelling by jeep also made bungalows redundant. This is true of all Himalayan areas and when I visited the upper Chandra valley where a new motor road had been carved out to link Kullu with Kaza in Spiti I saw that all the intervening bungalows had ceased to be used by officials. The local shepherds gratefully made off with the roof and doors and the hiker had to make do with their non-sarkari replacement, the dhaba.

I had timed my arrival to reach Binsar in the evening because I planned to stay with someone I knew. Vivek Dutta was a philosopher and aesthete who had married a Belgian, Marie Therese, and decided to settle in Almora. To my delight they purchased Ghuralkot and that was where I was headed.

On the way I passed a deserted bungalow belonging to a locally famous forester. On one occasion he had visited Sarala Devi's ashram and had been so popular that he had invited some of the senior girls to visit his Binsar bungalow. The girls had been too ashamed to tell Sarala of what transpired. Apparently the forester had taken a shine to the seniormost girl. 'What did he do?' I asked the strapping Bhotia girl who confided in me (and could have poleaxed any trespassing male with one punch). 'He chased me round the table,' she said.

How many times and in how many similar situations have not ladies in India been chased round the table by senior government servants in their bungalows, official or otherwise? Lovesick foresters can defend themselves citing the punishment of their postings. Penelope Chetwode in her excellent memoir *Kulu: The End of the Habitable World* describes how on one occasion after she had retired in the government bungalow for the night an apologetic forest officer entered her room and insisted on getting into bed with her. He felt he would be doing his duty: after all English women (even those approaching seventy) were known to be sexually insatiable. Hence the local Barkis was willing to sacrifice his evening and do the needful in promoting international understanding.

The sensual nature of the snow view at Binsar could raise passions too powerful for the spiritual part in humans to cope with; echoing Rumer Godden's scenario, a young English sadhu connected to the Ramakrishna Mission is believed to have had an affair with a foreign girl staying near Ghuralkot and is thought to have committed suicide in Almora as a result of his battle between flesh and spirit.

I was suffering from a similar dilemma, unable to reconcile my physical desires with my immortal longings. Luckily my fateful bout of typhoid would open my eyes to the distorted view of the cosmos my limited exposure to life had saddled me with. Sarala's attitude to sex was simply to reject it as a tiresome aberration. This caused a lot of heartburn in her growing charges none of whom suffered from her plainness. Yet it was Sarala who put me on to the man who could clear my misconceptions.

Krishna Prem had great affection for Sarala but mocked her Gandhian tendency to reduce every human activity to its economic price. His strong maternal instinct made him deplore the lack of it in others. About sex the yogi was quite forthcoming though not in the way Sarala envisaged. Summing up her no-nonsense style, Krishna Prem concluded 'Sarala is a man without a penis.'

10
Uttar Brindaban

A cold morning and a shivering encounter with the snow panorama from Ghuralkot. I had a late start on the second leg of the ridge walk from Kausani to Mirtola. It was possible to do the forty kilometres in one day but having done it once I found that to beat the clock the walk would turn into a cross-country jog. Mirtola, or 'Uttar Brindaban' as it was then called, lay only ten kilometres away and most of the way was downhill to Dhaul Chhina. Then a fairly gradual ascent of four kilometres completed the route.

Mirtola was a sixty acre estate on a high and dry west-facing ridge that concealed the temples of Jageshwar. Four pattis (revenue districts) met near this lofty setting above 7000 ft and the highest point with a superb lookout onto the snows was Jhandakot, a bald prominence that had been used by the British in their fight against the Gurkhas as a heliograph signalling station.

The temple of Uttar Brindaban was built under the ridge in a saucer of mixed forest to protect it from the wind. This was the true watershed though the Jhandakot spur ran to Burha Jageshwar set some 2000 ft above the main cluster of temples.

The ridge walk from Jhandakot to Burha Jageshwar is without question the finest angle for capturing the nobility and drama of the Uttarakhand snow peaks. Halfway along you stand on a rock overhang where the valley drops away sheer under your feet in a

5000 ft plummet. This sensation of being part of the stunning surroundings is unsurpassed along the length of the Himalaya.

One of the pleasures of walking mountain trails is to be surprised by an unexpected angle on the snows. From Takula to Gananath (in the reverse direction) a mind-blowing view occurs as you turn the corner to take the Grechhina path. The peaks hit you in the plexus and whether you prostrate instinctively in worship as I do, or not, the fact remains that the glory stops you dead in your tracks and takes your breath away.

Angles can differ according to season. Though generally in Kumaun the best months for snow views are October to March sometimes you get astonishing close-up views after a heavy storm in the monsoon. Then through the clouds the distant peaks loom vibrantly near. Winter overall is the best season because the snowline is low and the sky a deeper blue. The cloud cover that can settle as early as ten a.m. in the summer months does not build up till after lunch in winter.

The pattern of condensation so visible in the snow ranges provides good general advice for walkers at any altitude. Early starts will see you safely at camp by two p.m. when overcast conditions invariably set in. By five p.m. the clouds covering the peaks will have largely disappeared. This pattern held for all the dry months during the twelve years I lived in Kumaun.

Uttar Brindaban had been built in the 1930s by Yashoda Mai, a Bengali lady of extraordinary human qualities whose husband was the first Indian vice-chancellor of Lucknow University. Deeply interested in theosophy, the vice-chancellor and his wife were consulted by a young English lecturer at the university who had been a pilot in the Great War. In time this lecturer became a disciple of Yashoda Mai and she named him Sri Krishna Prem. Yashoda Mai then set off for Almora to build a temple to Radha Krishna accompanied by her English disciple. Mirtola began as an outwardly orthodox Vaishnava temple under Yashoda Mai and continued so under the stewardship of Sri Krishna Prem. In 1944 another British disciple appeared. Sri Madhava Ashish was an aero-engineer who had been sent to India during the war. He stayed on as Krishna Prem's understudy though formally his teacher was Moti Rani, daughter of Yashoda Mai.

After Moti Rani's death Mirtola followed a more universal path, Krishna Prem being fond of the teachings of Rumi and Ashishda an admirer of Gurdjieff. With the restrictions on orthodoxy relaxed an international range of seekers visited the ashram. The temple remained for common worship but the teaching was adapted to individual needs, Ashishda proving himself an adept at dream interpretation as well as a pioneering eco-farmer experimenting with technology appropriate to the hills. Disciples who were chosen as residents in the ashram were bound to a grinding physical routine that sought by intensive farming ostensibly to make the community self-sufficient but actually to break our attachment to the limitations of the physical body.

When I turned up in April 1965 the farm programme was just about to take off under Dave Beresford, now called Ashish Dev. To my surprise instead of going to England his parents had decided to move to Mirtola. The day after I had visited them the previous winter the family had made an unscheduled visit to Krishna Prem's ashram. The moment Sri Madhava Ashish set eyes on David he knew he had found his spiritual heir.

Perhaps because of my role in their deciding to make that fateful visit to Mirtola I found Ashishda mellower than usual. Nevertheless I was given a thorough grilling about my motives for turning to the inner path. It was evening. In Krishna Prem's room supper of home-made bread, butter and apricot jam tasted marvellous after the day's walk. I thought it was because I was hungry but I understood the real reason later when I settled into the ashram routine. Various disciples helped prepare the 'bhog', holy food, offered to the temple deities. Without fail I could tell on which day Krishna Prem had been cooking by the taste of the food. He used the same ingredients as the others but cooked with so much feeling you could taste the difference.

Both Krishna Prem and Ashishda taught by example and if they saw a disciple shun the dirty jobs they would do them themselves. On one occasion two immaculately white-khadi clad visitors from Bombay who were keen to join in the ashram chores were asked to pick up the 'cow bucket' full of slops that stood outside the kitchen. The bucket contained fermenting matter like old tea leaves and gave off a hearty smell. Even as the Bombay visitors hesitated to dirty their white clothes Krishna Prem, freshly bathed and bustling out of the kitchen, immediately summed up the situation. With a big smile he hoisted the leaking bucket onto his shoulder. 'Ah!' he cried as he strode away 'the sweet smell of champagne.'

A former professor of English literature, Krishna Prem captivated his visitors as he served supper by quoting from the poets and mystics to illustrate the point he was making. After supper he would throw another log on the fire (Mirtola was still cold in April), pull out his pipe and have a contented puff. The atmosphere in these supper sessions was charged. The bare room where we sat on the planked floor on woollen mats turned into a magical chamber: mysteries were made clear and the deepest longings of the human soul answered. Krishna Prem became the vehicle for the wisdom of the enlightened. After the last visitor retired at nine p.m. I was invited to stay on and put forward my case for becoming a sannyasi. I was ascetic enough in some obvious ways: I only possessed the cotton clothes I stood up in. But I needed some practical advice.

Was a deep knowledge of Sanskrit necessary? Krishna Prem waved my query away airily. 'It helps,' he said (he had studied the language and made commentaries on Sanskrit texts), 'but all languages lead to the source.' In his room were dictionaries of Persian and Urdu. He was learning to read Rumi in the original. Twenty years earlier he might have given a different answer. Now he was beyond conventional intellectual props and was not much bothered what people ate or wore or worshipped since his spirit sailed free of bodily or mental hangups. Nor was he concerned about what people thought of him—and would sing lustily the refrain from *The Miller of Dee*. 'I care for nobody no not I, and nobody cares for me.' In his opinion if I wanted to rediscover the harmony I had lost I would have to work hard. By becoming a wandering mendicant all my energy would be spent in worrying about the next meal. I should instead use my God-given teaching qualification and get a job. Then I could use my spare time for finding the treasure that had fleetingly been mine.

These were not the kind of solutions I had wished to hear. I wanted a more romantic option. What was the point of becoming a teacher in India when I had already jettisoned that choice in England? What saved me from walking out of Mirtola in a huff when I returned to my tiny bare room was the weather. It had begun to snow and all the covering I had was a thin cotton wrap. (I suspect Ashishda had deliberately removed the blankets to test my resolve!) It was impossible to lie down so I had to sit up, shivering the whole night, forced to reconsider Sri Krishna Prem's advice. Demoralised by its logic and stunned by the cold the more I thought it through the more it seemed to add up. From being stubbornly opposed to his suggestions I now began to value them. Instead of striding out with a heroic gesture to prove Krishna Prem wrong about my certainties, I would calmly confront him at breakfast and say I had decided to catch the first bus to Almora to look for a job exactly as he had recommended.

In the morning I met Ashishda and confided my decision in him. He looked hard at me having expected a more aggressive response then smiled probably recognising that for the first time in my life I had based my judgement on objective fact. He softened and said there was no need to catch the first bus. I could stay a day or two and help Krishna Prem in the kitchen 'if I liked'.

Those two days extended to seven years. After Kausani's bare cupboard Mirtola seemed like an English country club. Well-heeled disciples brought goodies and though the living regime was otherwise spartan the food was nourishing. The teaching always came in unexpected situations and from the least likely angles. There was no formal doctrine. As the guru's pet Dev was encouraged to ride roughshod over the other disciples' intellectual pretensions. We were made to question everyone and everything and while this had a useful purpose in exposing frauds who posed as spiritual teachers it gave Mirtola disciples the reputation of being insufferably smug.

Because there was no time for oneself seven years sped by. I went to Mirtola expecting to find God and came away at least knowing why this would take much longer than I had bargained for. Ashrams are viewed as oases of tranquillity but Mirtola was a place of frenetic work schedules where relations with fellow disciples were fraught with conflict. The guru called this work on one's self. Most of the time we felt self-disgust at how we had let ourselves down in reacting pettily to situations we imagined we could easily cope with. It was an unmaking process and the pain was real.

There were moments of bliss without which no one would have put up with the pressure. Ashishda always led from the front never demanding any job be done that he did not do himself. By flogging himself he released a higher level of energy and through this visible grace one could sometimes glimpse the awesome realm of the inner world beckoning the brave and totally dedicated.

Up till now I had considered myself a spiritually oriented person whose lack of concern for material matters was a sign of advanced evolution. Between them Dev and Ashishda smashed this self-image. They suggested the real reason I was indifferent to material efficiency maybe was because I was a slob, too disorganised to cope with the challenges of existence. And what I fancied as my 'natural mystic' status could just as easily be a carefully cultivated self-important delusion. In retrospect I am grateful for the deflation of my posturing.

Whatever Mirtola ashram's differences from Sarala's at Kausani, in their response to the physical beauty of the Himalaya they were at one. To Sarala tourism and mountain climbing were luxury pastimes and responsible citizens avoided them. To Krishna Prem the outer beauty of the snows was a reflection of the inner attraction between Radha and Krishna. Why waste energy and money for a ticket to the cinema when you can control the projector? Look inside yourself for beauty and inspiration. I found this cold-shouldering of the ecstatic beauty all around Mirtola hard to digest. Although I found murti puja very moving and a practical means of approaching the divine it served me no better than the

monotheistic prescriptions I had been brainwashed to accept as a child in Scotland. I wanted to continue my private worship of the peaks. Luckily I could invoke other teachings of the guru that enabled me to continue.

The Mirtola teaching that love conquers everything enabled me to sneak away to my mountains without too bad a conscience. Every morning I would climb to the post office (which overlooked the snows): it was condoned because the gurus daily received correspondence that required urgent reply. So ravishing was the impact of the snow panorama from Jhandakot that I used any spare time I had to explore its northern face and even discovered a cave where I could sit and accelerate the means to my imagined self-realisation. I had obeyed the same compulsion in Kausani in the jungle above Donni and actually built a small ring of stones for furthering my meditational fantasies. Then to spoil my prospects a forest guard turned up and threatened to demolish my magic ring if he ever caught me sitting there again.

According to Ashishda and Gopalda (Sri Krishna Prem) what I was indulging in was sheer escapism. It was harmless but meant

I was marking time instead of treading the path. I needed to interface with other people who could make me confront the reasons I had to fantasise. I was a bad disciple however and felt my fantasies were exempt from the scorn that attached to other people's fantasies.

The aim of Mirtola was to keep the tension between individuals so taut that in the inevitable emotional explosion some useful lessons would emerge about why we behave the way we do. I was much too prickly to allow much of this strategy to reach me but on one occasion carried away by erotic impulses I made advances to a lady disciple that I realised would be reported to the guru. Dreading the consequences I got there first and confessed.

To my amazement Ashishda didn't take the usual line of outraged morality but told me to sit down while he read from Rumi's *Mathnawi*. The moral of the story was that love without the etiquette of tender consideration for the feelings of the beloved is a non-starter.

I apologised to the lady for my jungly proclivities and was rewarded with a week off by Ashishda to roam the hills. Perhaps Ashishda had been influenced by the experience of his mentor Ethel Merston, an English literary lady who had been a disciple of the modern Sufi Gurdjieff. It was she who introduced Ashishda—a gawky young aero-engineer newly arrived from England—to Mirtola. According to the American author Fritz Peters who grew up at Gurdjieff's French 'ashram', Miss Merston was left in charge of the students when the guru made a visit to America. On his return Gurdjieff lined up the students and asked Miss Merston to read out from her little black book the details of their delinquencies. Gurdjieff 'punished' them according to his own value system. Taking out his wallet each offender was paid solemnly: the greater the sin the bigger the bundle of francs awarded and the worse the sinner the more Mr Gurdjieff recompensed him.

On that bonus walk I followed an unexplored route south-west of Mirtola and had an extraordinary darshan of Nanda Devi's twin peaks from a ridge called Chalni Chhina. I was emotionally charged both from the wonder of the passion aroused by the peak and by the extraordinary behaviour of my guru. There seemed no difference between his greatness and that of the goddess Nanda Devi. For the first time I fully understood why the guru is defined as 'that which is great'.

On another occasion I had the forbidden pleasure of striking eastwards of Mirtola and crossing the Inner Line. This was safely in the company of a disciple who happened to be the commandant of a company of border police. The line was marked by the river Sarju and interestingly a village near the bridging point at Sheraghat had descendants of an English Tommy settler. Although the family retained garbled English names and were token Christians they had been completely absorbed by local culture.

The trip across the Inner Line went only as far as Gangolihat, a day's trek from Mirtola. In the vicinity were the famous limestone caves of Patal Bhuvaneshwar, wonderfully atmospheric with a feeling of enormous antiquity. In those days the villagers lowered you through the tiny entrance portal (a hole in the ground halfway down a steep slope of deodar) by the light of pine torches. These gave off so much soot that when you returned to the surface your face and clothes were black.

During my stay in Kausani I had encouraged the girls on their weekly day off to go for walks and on two occasions we visited Gwaldam which, though technically the start of the Inner Line, allowed visitors to spend the night there to view the mighty close-up face of Trisul. From Kausani it was a thirty kilometres walk first down steeply for fifteen kilometres then up even more steeply. The girls could easily cover these distances in a day without feeling tired such was the level of fitness induced by their unending regime of physical labour. All hill people are accomplished walkers though with the coming of the motor roads and plains fashions many nowadays pretend to be unfamiliar with such downmarket pastimes as walking.

Much of the bridle path magic disappeared with the carving out of new roads. Their alignments were artificial and did not follow the contours of the hills like the ambling six-footers. It was boring to travel in the bus from Mirtola to Almora but full of interest when walking. The last time I did this walk was in connection with my application to become a naturalised Indian citizen. I received a notice one afternoon demanding my presence at the Almora courts the next morning failing which all the paperwork would have to be done afresh. As no buses ran during the day this meant I had to walk the eighteen kilometres before nightfall. Luckily most of the route is descending. Passing through Panwanaula's collection of half a dozen shops I took the shortcut down to Bare Chhina. As luck would have it the magistrate's jeep was parked at the dak bungalow and I was able to finish my work without having to walk another twelve kilometres. I was back in the ashram by nine p.m., walking in the dark emboldened by the fact that most of the path passed through pine where bears rarely lurked.

A similar bureaucratic crisis occurred when Dev and I were to take our oaths of allegiance to the Indian constitution. If we missed the appointment with the magistrate our applications for citizenship would have to begin again and would take another seven years. The notice came in the evening and both Dev and I had to appear before the magistrate next day. But where was he? Luckily he was camping at a bungalow only two hours' walk from Mirtola and next morning we solemnly took our oaths as the magistrate's breakfast table was being laid.

Krishna Prem had encouraged us to apply for citizenship as a sign of our commitment to the inner path which he asserted was India's greatest contribution to world civilisation. By accepting the validity of spiritual enquiry as a way of life India is unique in the comity of nations. We should love and honour this greatness in Indian thinking by identifying our destinies with the nation. As it happened when, as required by law, I wrote to the British authorities announcing that I had relinquished my British citizenship I received the best of both worlds reply saying that I couldn't. Those who were born British remained British whether they liked it or not! I am tempted to give my soul a pat on its back for having the discernment to choose two wonderful civilisations in which to work out its destiny.

My life had been far too cerebral and badly needed a change of direction. This occurred when I fell in love with Prithwi, a fellow disciple. According to the gurus this was the only teaching that mattered and Ashishda encouraged me to take the plunge because Prithwi could continue the work he had started, of getting me beyond reliance on the mind.

Prithwi was an out and out bhakta who loved God and never questioned divinity. For me she was the perfect teacher. Most of my life I had been questioning—not realising that love does not question, it accepts. Ultimately I glimpsed the divine in the electrifying presence of Sri Sathya Sai Baba of Puttaparthi—and it was Prithwi who guided me to him. My wanderings searching for eternal verities had paid off.

However, the years when I could have done some serious climbing in the Himalaya were passed in the sacrificial mode trying to find myself (in Kausani) and then, having found myself in Mirtola, wishing I hadn't looked! I spent twelve years in the ashram mode when I was physically tough and accustomed to living off the land. However the existence of the Inner Line put all climbing plans on hold even if my commitment to the inner path had eased up a little to allow me the luxury of setting foot on the snows.

A few friends did make the ritual Pindari glacier trek after taking permission from the magistrate. I might have joined them but had the problem of finance. I didn't earn anything in the ashram and got my keep in exchange for labour. Everything thus conspired to confine me to the middle ranges—where I felt very much at home. But to look out onto the snows was to feel a real yearning to get a bit closer and peek under Nanda Devi's veil.

11
Bala Hissar

The arrival of Prithwi in my life coincided with the easing of restrictions in Himalayan border areas. After Mirtola I got a job proof-reading Russian Ph.D. theses which had been translated in India for the American market. The chief feature of a Russian Ph.D. thesis I was told is that Russian postgraduates were paid by the Kremlin according to the number of words they wrote. Possibly the same philosophy had seized their Indian translators for I found them all, whatever the subject, turgid, tedious and repetitive. That however was the problem of their American readers. Mine was to proof-read and thus dip my toe in the waters of literary endeavour, convinced that nothing I wrote could be as bad as this!

From this modest testing of the waters emerged my first book—*Seven Sacred Rivers*—published twenty years later. It wasn't the first book I wrote—that was on Nanda Devi, the mountain whose presence had haunted me since 1960. I was unfamiliar with the demands of publishing and the need to get professional editing advice; the book was poorly structured and repetitive as a consequence.

My move from Kumaun to Garhwal, from the enclosed life in Mirtola to the worldly air of Mussoorie was both welcome and traumatic. I wasn't getting anywhere in the ashram and was in real danger of lapsing into the rut of cultivated holiness that afflicts so many who wear the robe. Being catapulted back into polite society

I had several serious problems of adjustment. For self-esteem I had to find a job but could never hope to match Prithwi's landed status. She was now an ex-maharani: the princes had been derecognised the very month I joined her in Delhi. Prithwi's grandmother had been Romanian so there were luckily enough European genes to give her a strong sense of individuality despite her status. Many of the standard princely types were pampered beyond belief and grew up with a bizarre sense of divine rights.

I realised how lucky I had been to have grown up in a situation where you had to work for your meal ticket. Better not to have been born than become a child pensioner incapable of experiencing the immense satisfaction that comes from hard work and honest effort. It was in Mirtola that I truly understood manual labour is a divine gift rather than divine punishment. Krishna Prem bounced around the kitchen while Ashishda worked demonically on the farm and in his workshop. It was quite common for visitors on their way to have darshan of the Mirtola gurus to assume that these scurrying figures doing all the ashram chores were hired hands. They would halt outside the workshop where Ashishda was bent intently over the lathe and, assuming he was a mechanic, demand to know where they could find Sri Madhava Ashish.

It seems curious now to look back and realise that the ashram's most powerful contribution to the disciples' spiritual growth was to make them realise the joy that follows from punishing bodily labour. Most of us were of the intellectual variety unaccustomed to working with our hands. The jeer that culture is opposed to agriculture could only have been made by someone who has missed out on the unique satisfaction of performing the whole cycle of farming, from sowing to eating the produce of one's sweat. A demanding workload also guaranteed a mind too busy with its schedule to be depressed or heavily into fantasy.

Suddenly however like a prisoner freed from jail, from having no time of my own, I now had too much. How to invoke the guru within and find a balance? The early years of fitting in to a householder's routine were full of pitfalls particularly the frustration of realising that what had seemed like profound teaching in the ashram context was of no earthly use in the real world. But at least

BALA HISSAR 97

the exercise of living under constant pressure in Mirtola made any other situation seem tame in comparison.

I was familiar with Mussoorie from my visit in 1960 and had taken a shine to the town. Its cosmopolitanism and convenience made it ideal when I decided to become a freelance travel writer. Our routine was to drive up in April when the wisteria flowered in purple splendour and return in October when the marigolds began to wilt from the first frost.

From the beginning I planted dozens of saplings during the rains but hardly anything survived the long drought the south face has to endure for nine months. Looking back I realise that instead of planting five hundred trees over a period of twenty years (of which none made it to maturity) I should have dug instead just one hole each year, manured it heavily and paid someone to water it each winter. That way I would have had twenty trees to show after twenty years. Alternatively I could have fenced off small plots with pukka iron posts and barbed wire and allowed nature to grow her own trees. This latter option would not have met with local approval however. Any display of capital expenditure invites the criticism of being either anti-poor or an outsider with more money than sense.

Bhag Singh, our Mussoorie chowkidar, was a tiny personage who had come with the property when Prithwi bought it in 1950. He was silent, stubborn and totally trustworthy. Bhag Singh's dedication was a quality many Garhwali villagers display. They may argue, sulk and do things their own way but in matters of personal loyalty no power on earth can sway them. For twelve years Bhag Singh watched over Oakless single-handed during Prithwi's absence, enduring threats and inducements from encroaching neighbours and unauthorised would-be entrants. Many chowkidars in hill stations where the owner of the house does not appear for years together either let out rooms surreptitiously or simply move their family in as squatters. Bhag Singh personified dharma. He did his duty religiously and maintained a large property immaculately over the years. Sadly his last years were spoiled by a paralytic stroke which made him bedridden and deprived him of the dignity his years of service had earned.

Like so many first-generation hillmen in Mussoorie, Bhag Singh was determined his son should be educated to find better employment and he sacrificed a great deal to this end. It was a matter of status for him that his son, who went on to become a B.Com., should never be allowed to do manual work. In the hills however there are no openings—not even for Ph.D's—and the father's sacrifice went in vain. The economic realities of Uttarakhand were too harsh for his dream to come true. By contrast baniyas from the plains who settled in the hills not only adjusted successfully to local economic realities but created their own profitable businesses by adapting to the needs of visitors. In Mussoorie the best example is found in the Prakash brothers in Landour, who are grocers. Here for generations they have catered to the exacting standards of foreign missionary families and have been so good at it that the memsahibs taught them how to make the jams, cheese and peanut butter they craved far from the shores of Europe and America. So obliging and intelligent were the shopkeepers that when the Missions began to close down after independence and their properties had to be put up for sale the Prakash brothers were the obvious choice as house agents.

At least twice in the season I make the walk from Bala Hissar to Sisters' Bazaar, a rise of 2000 feet in four kilometres to buy Prakash's home-made cheese. Like all good cheddar this varies according to the ripeness of the batch. It adds to the challenge of the walk to hope for a really sharp flavour at the end.

Cheese is a luxury item and to most local tastes seems an expensive way to make your kitchen smell. At Mirtola we made a primitive form of cottage cheese and while too salty to be eaten neat it made the best stuffing for parathas I have ever tasted. One of the rare pleasures living away from the fleshpots is that you occasionally find a foreign visitor willing to carry some Danish Blue or Stilton to India. The pleasure wouldn't be the same if you had easy access to these miracles of fermentation.

On my last visit to England in 1996 I visited a Delhi friend teaching at Cambridge. He took me to a trendy restaurant for lunch. I decided to go for a dish that included a piece of Stilton.

What I got was a huge wedge of cheese it would have taken me three meals to finish. Because the restaurant was upmarket my friend would not allow me to pocket the leftovers. This instance of wilful wastage decided me to stick to the Himalaya where what little we have we thank God for.

I choose an overcast afternoon in the early monsoon for my cheese mission, hoping that the weather has kept away visitors who, unaware that Landour yields such luxuries as cheese and doughnuts, tend to snap them up. Though steep in places and at a steady gradient throughout for the two-hour walk, the road still follows the original bridle path. In fact most of the way it clings to the Ganga–Yamuna watershed and if one drew a circle to include my start and finish, Bala Hissar would stand at eight o'clock and Sisters' Bazaar at two. There is a special pleasure in covering watershed ridges where the loftiness of the view is enhanced by a shared intimacy of nature's crafting.

This trail starts way down the hill at Rajpur and dates back to the founding of Mussoorie in 1828. It was a ten-mile hike to the convalescent home for British soldiers at Landour and involved a punishing 5000 ft climb. The original hospital for recuperating Tommies today has become a hi-tech institute for top brass in the defence services. When it opened I happened to be studying at the Landour Language School. The controversial defence minister Krishna Menon (prior to the Chinese debacle and his resignation) was to do the honours and stories about his genius and arrogance were already doing the rounds. He was an intellectual giant, one of the moving spirits behind the birth of Penguin Books that revolutionised world reading habits by making paperbacks affordable to the masses. He was also a narcissistic demagogue famous for the length of his filibustering speeches in the United Nations and their hot air content.

Some officious military policemen shooed the half dozen language students away from a wall we were sitting on past which the defence minister's jeep was due to drive. The military police thought we ought to be duly respectful to the VIP and rather than lounge on a wall, we ought to stand reverentially on the road to give him a proper welcoming wave. But having been evicted from the wall all of us lay down in the lee where we would not be seen by the cavalcade, and got on with our studies. This upset the police even more and we were ordered to climb back up on the wall. To a VIP a disrespectful audience is better than no audience at all!

To illustrate the cultural tradition in the changing of baton from colonial to indigenous army there are now notice boards in Landour pointing to the officers' mess that caution against the consumption of alcohol and remind officers to 'observe decorum'. The old breed neither feared alcohol nor its fallout. Though a gentleman might get blind drunk in the mess and have to be carried home, nothing was said unless he failed to report for duty early next morning.

The notices in Landour probably issue from timid bureaucratic desks. Only the other day someone presented a friend of mine with a bottle of excellent Indian whisky which bore on its label 'specially bottled for the Indian Military Academy golden jubilee.' The rubric also suggested that possession by other than defence personnel was strictly prohibited. The answer clearly lay in destroying the evidence and my friend and I did this by taking turns to polish off the contents, keeping in mind the demands of decorum.

Mussoorie has always been a tippler's town except for a short interlude when Morarji Desai introduced (not very successfully) prohibition. What this effectively meant was the wine retail shop was closed and its stock mysteriously found its way to the local police thana. Morarji Bhai, temperamentally like Aurangzeb, was a pennypinching Gujarati whose religion lay in hating what others enjoyed. In Mussoorie we turned to ayurvedic remedies for baldness and virility that came blamelessly blended in eighty per cent solutions of alcohol. What are a few strands of hair and a limp count of hormones to the dedicated tippler?

In the early days the town was famous for its breweries that used the limestone springs around Sikander Hall. Today tourist taxis delivering residents to the five-star hotel in Barlowganj wash their cars in the spring's perennial overflow. Stronger drink than beer has always characterised Mussoorie's intake. Madhushalas dispense desi spirits and those who cannot rise to a bottle of Santara may avail of a Hogarthian swig in an atmosphere that recalls the spit and sawdust of a Fleet Street gin parlour.

Over the years respectable shops like Hamers, Diamonds and Ramchanders have all had to yield their liquor licences to avaricious politicians in league with dubious contractors. The auction price is so high that only the mafia is assumed to be able to afford it.

Despite the annually increasing price of alcohol Mussoorie remains faithful to its traditional tonic and throughout the year the only sound that breaks the night silence of our Bala Hissar area is that of the class four government servant staggering home to the accompaniment of slurred renderings of the latest Hindi movie songs. Fully tanked up on the prasad of the Devi her followers rarely fall down the khud on whose edge they continually teeter. And if they do fall little happens—the fully relaxed state of their being usually guarantees no bones are broken.

From the top of Landour bazaar to Char Dukhan there are two roads, the shorter leading to the Cantonment Board office being much steeper. From St Paul's romantic Gothic buttresses at Char Dukhan the path to Sisters' Bazaar is fairly level. Till only a few years back the combined forces of the Cantonment Board and Woodstock school kept the healthy slopes of mature oak safe but with the siting of a television tower an excuse has been found to fell the timber and the lopping of oak for fodder, unheard of on this hillside for more than a century. The offenders who supply milk to government servants know that the latter are effectively immune to the provisions of the law.

Sisters' Bazaar like the rest of Landour has kept its original unobtrusive lines. You never see anyone in this tiny bazaar because most of Landour's hidden bungalows are owned by absentee landlords who come for the occasional weekend or not at all for years at a time. Prakash's shops (for provisions and garments) are always busy nonetheless. A few foreign students still attend the language school and Woodstock parents visiting their children stay on the hillside below Prakash's.

It is obvious by walking round the various paths that circle the cantonment that the view from Landour is so powerful that house-owners, for whatever reason, cannot live with it year in and year out. We all like the idea of being confronted with eternity but balk at the prospect of being daily zapped by it.

12
Gateway to God

The sterling character of the Garhwali villager is demonstrated in the behaviour of Bacchan Singh, a humble seasonal resident of Mussoorie who meets visitors as they alight from the bus at Picture Palace and recommends the name of a particular hotel which pays him a tiny commission for successful canvassing. Locally he is referred to as a 'hotel tout' as though his usefulness was somehow tainted. But his services extend to voluntary aid for persons in distress as I found out one morning in the monsoon rain sluicing down so hard not a soul was to be seen.

There had been a death in Prithwi's family. Braving the weather I climbed to the bazaar to make arrangements for taking the body to Haridwar. Formerly Mussoorie had its own burning ghat deep in the gadera beneath Landour and Woodstock where two streams meet to form the Rispana. In the rains it was a steep and tricky descent and the wood was so wet it was a problem to light the pyre. With the advent of government-subsidised jeep taxis the local people very sensibly decided it was easier and more auspicious to strap the body onto the roof of the vehicle and take it to Dehra Dun or Haridwar for the last rites.

Bacchan Singh saw me frantically banging on the shutter of a general merchant's shop where I wished to buy some cloth and puja ingredients for the ceremonies ahead. He stepped forward under his battered umbrella and asked what the problem was. The moment I told him there had been a death in the family he asked me to return home and leave everything to him. He would knock up the appropriate shopkeepers and have all the items on my list sent to the house in the taxi that he would book to take our funeral party to Haridwar.

By this time he was as soaked as I was. I offered him money but he waved it away saying this could be settled later. It was more important to attend to the formalities occasioned by the death. I was impressed by his cool efficiency and thanked him for his help. He replied that thanks were not necessary. 'It is a Hindu's duty to help,' he stated gravely. The full impact of dharma, the ideal of religious behaviour hit me for the first time. The English word 'duty' is too simplistic to do justice to the notion of dharma that Bacchan Singh demonstrated. Here was a poor Garhwali on a cold wet morning offering to save me the chore of tramping through the bazaar in the pouring rain because it was a matter of spiritual etiquette he found perfectly natural to honour. Contrast the commercial concerns of funeral parlours in the West.

The work was done in spite of the weather and the cremation in Haridwar likewise performed with the utmost despatch and goodwill. The bier was placed on the municipal ghat and wood purchased from a store nearby. Because of the high running river the body was only a foot above the racing flow of the Ganga. In matters of last rites I find Hinduism most poetic and prefer its pyre to burial. Our graveyard in Mussoorie is a great environmental blessing however and lends the walk round Camel's Back road a peaceful interlude in a town gone berserk with building schemes. But to moulder underground cut off from the snow peaks is not my idea of meaningful darshan. My soul prefers to be free of the body and burning the body in Haridwar, the gateway to God, seems appropriate. These are personal choices; I am eclectic in choosing the best of various religions' customs.

It is interesting to note that the return to the Viking funeral in the modern West was through Madame Blavatsky's Theosophical Society. Her followers experimented with burning the carcasses of sheep in America to make cremation acceptable to polite society. According to the theosophical perspective cremation successfully severs our 'desire body' and allows the soul its freedom. Significantly this severance of the physical from the psychic level makes the appearance of confused discarnate entities like ghosts less probable. The unhappily disembodied require energy—usually blood—to quicken them. Religions that bury their dead are likely to produce more ghosts than those who cremate their physical remains.

Ghosts in the Himalaya is a topic that could fill a book. All hillmen, whatever their religion, are firm believers in the existence of ghosts and a good part of popular hill religion lies in appeasing these demonic energies. This accounts for the widespread sacrifice of animals to the local godlings: he drinks the blood while the offerant has the meat. This is a crude and distant cousin of the Christian communion service where the 'blood of the saviour' is enrolled as a powerful spiritual ally.

Tantra is the science of harnessing these magical forces of life and traditionally hill society has preferred its unorthodox doctrine to the more exacting demands of brahminical custom. In a place like Haridwar where the Ganga breaks free of the last Shivalik outrider of the Himalaya there is a merging of unorthodox custom with mainstream orthodoxy. To have one's ashes mingled in the Ganga at Haridwar is every pious Hindu's dream. As a result the town has a religious vibrancy not at all in keeping with the sombre hues of the holy places of other religions. This is due perhaps to the racing bore of the icy Ganga. She gets her name from the power of her flow. The symbolism is clear—once the body is dead and the soul purified by contact with the water—life goes on. Bacchan Singh's workmanlike disposal of my hand-wringing approach to the body's last rites is echoed by the fierce imperious run of the holy river. Pious sentiment plus efficient despatch equals dharma. To prove that this spirit of service is not confined to simple Garhwalis, Mussoorie boasts the example of Ganesh Saili, our professor of English at the local college. Ganesh is ready to help at the last rites of followers of any faith, testifying to the remarkable gift Garhwalis display of demonstrating the true meaning of religion.

With the coming of the roads activated by the Chinese invasion of 1962 Haridwar was replaced by Rishikesh as the effective starting point of pilgrimages to the char dham since the hill buses all started at Rishikesh. Both Rishikesh and Haridwar possess dozens of ashrams and other religious institutions belonging to a cross section of Hinduism's many sects and inevitably most of these are funded and managed by devotees from the plains. As a consequence there was a fierce debate about the inclusion of Haridwar in the new hill state of Uttaranchal. The fear of these plains people that the new state would allow only hill people to own land (as in Kashmir, Arunachal, Himachal and other hill states) led to an agitation for the city to be excluded from Uttaranchal. In the event the new state includes the whole district of Haridwar which encompasses plains areas that run as far as Roorkee, a vital inclusion for the viable economic future of Uttaranchal.

Roorkee was the hub in the 1830s for building the Ganga Canal that transformed not only the agricultural output of the Doab but made Haridwar into a better integrated pilgrim town. Captain Cautley, the Victorian canal planner, was not only an engineer of repute but a gifted paleontologist. His remarkable finds in the Shivaliks included the remains of *Ramapithecus*, India's oldest known hominid. He drove the canal from Har ki Pairi situated at the narrowest—and most holy—part of the enclosing Shivalik and encouraged the pandits to build a series of dharmshalas alongside it. The Ganga rides majestically past these buildings but bypasses the temple at Kankhal. Traditionally pilgrims from all over India have converged at the Kankhal temple of Raja Daksha Prajapati downstream of today's bazaar. Here Lord Shiva, insulted by his father-in-law had picked up his wife's body—Parvati had died from mortification—and flown distraught across the land. Holy places sprang up along the path of his grief. Now it is only when the river is in flood that its original course comes to life and the Kankhal temple stands on the Ganga once more.

The shadow side of building the Ganga Canal was to destroy every tree in the twenty-kilometres stretch between Haridwar and Roorkee. These were required for firing the kilns that burnt the limestone for lining the canal. Nowadays the line of the cut can be detected by the sway of poplar and eucalyptus trees, intruders to the landscape.

With so much religious endowment at Haridwar and Rishikesh a lot of phoney mendicants appeared and this has led to the settlement of property disputes by violence. As well as being a genuinely holy city Haridwar has a sleazy side to it. It is interesting to note how the Himalaya becomes a convenient prop for those holy men whose reputation is not widely recognised. Real saints like Ramana Maharishi and Sri Aurobindo were so sure of their mission they had no need of external props and lived in south India.

The popularising of Hinduism for the Westerner begun by Swami Vivekananda was later boosted by Maharishi Mahesh, renowned as the guru of the Beatles. Swami Shivananda, at whose Rishikesh ashram I stayed on my first trip to the Himalaya was another holy man well known to the West. A large-built man, originally a south Indian doctor retired from service in Malaysia, he was an extrovert with a booming laugh. His enormous body shook with mirth when he recited anecdotes to his followers. Krishna Prem told me how he had once been invited to join the Swami in nagar sankirtan (the singing of hymns while walking through the streets). As a retiring British professor Krishna Prem excused himself and watched Shivananda march to the head of the procession and begin to lead the singing vociferously. Krishna Prem had been invited to a house on the route for morning coffee and made his way there. When he arrived, much to his astonishment he found Shivananda already seated, with a cup of coffee by his side. He had only started the procession and then backtracked to the devotee's house.

Undoubtedly the Swami did popularise Vedanta and his mission had quite an impact on Europe and America. His ashram commanded the traffic that set off for the char dham and like Baba Kambliwala before him, his doors were open to all pilgrims. His successors continue the international mission. Unlike so many modern sadhus whose money comes from foreign disciples Swami Shivananda was almost entirely supported by his Indian devotees.

Prithwi and I liked to drive from Mussoorie to Haridwar and Rishikesh just to experience the pilgrim fervour that grips these places in the summer season. I invariably started my treks to the interior from Rishikesh since buses (and now jeep taxis) are easy to find. One can also join the pilgrim route higher up at Srinagar using a cross-country route via Tehri from Mussoorie. But if the bus breaks down there are few alternative services to keep up one's progress.

My first serious foray into char dham territory was in August 1979 when I decided to follow a Sikh friend's advice and do the pilgrim ascent to Hem Kund. This involved catching a bus from Rishikesh early in the morning that got you to Joshimath (300 kilometres) before four in the afternoon. This allowed your bus access to the one-way road to Badrinath (50 kilometres) whose gate closed every evening. Half way to Badrinath you alighted at Govindghat, the base gurudwara for the climb to Hem Kund, and a Sikh religious settlement that offered food and accommodation.

On that occasion I missed the Badrinath gate and had to stay overnight in Joshimath in the primitive but welcoming Nanda Devi Hotel. By eight next morning the bus set me down at Govindghat and I crossed the suspension bridge to start the climb. Steep enclosing valley walls are a sign of being confronted by the Great Himalaya. The climb is unrelenting for some three kilometres to Phulna, the first of two villages along the route. The Lakshman Ganga tumbles steeply and its ebullient roar helps divert the mind from the sweat of the zig-zag ascent. Nowadays tea shops cater to the pilgrims but earlier these were only to be found in the villages.

At the next halt, Bhyundar, a path led to Kak Bhusand Tal, a magical lake a day's journey away and sacred to crows. From the lake one could descend to Vishnuprayag by a little-used trail. After tea and pakoras our trail continued its steep haul alongside the falling torrent that was narrowing to a mill race. In twelve kilometres we had to ascend 4000 ft.

As we neared the clearing of Ghangaria (now known as Govind Dham) the slope eased and we walked past stately conifer trees. In the soft light of evening with so much humus on the trail with not a sound to be heard, there was an eerie silence except for the bells on the harness of pilgrim horses hired by those with no breath to take on the steep trail.

Alongside the forest bungalow a new dhaba had just been completed and I hired an upstairs room safe in the knowledge that bed bugs had yet to arrive in these parts. In spite of being built-up at an alarming rate—some of the huge fir trees were being felled for further accommodation—Ghangaria had a wonderfully magical feel. It was so extraordinarily silent. But this mood of wonder did not last when you went deeper into the forest and found dumped there the rubbish of the dhabas, scattered by scavenging animals.

A travel writer has the quandary of writing about pristine places knowing his words are going to sully and spoil them by attracting hordes of people. There is no point my railing at the lemming instinct in tourists. I have been guilty of the same urge myself. I had come to see Hem Kund but was not going to miss out on seeing the Valley of Flowers. Ghangaria was the base for both treks, Hem Kund being further and higher. Frank Smythe had no idea his enthusiastic description of the valley in 1938 would cause a veritable tourist stampede in the next generation, threatening to destroy the beauty of the valley he raved about. The reality is that several similar valleys exist in the same vicinity, a fact known to the local shepherds but not to the tourist planners. Had the latter been more alive to local realities trekking groups could have been spread more thinly instead of all funnelling into Smythe's fairy-tale valley which has been trampled to death.

When I reached the famous valley next morning some 2000 ft above Ghangaria, over an easy trail of four kilometres I found myself in a gently rolling meadow with flowers growing head high due to the manure deposited by the livestock the villagers leave to graze in the monsoon. It was a verdant valley akin to others I had seen and I wondered what all the fuss was about. I walked on leaving the greenery and climbed higher to the approach of the glacier. Walking out of the mist towards me was a stout tourist wrapped in a raincoat with a scarf tied round his ears. In the whistling wind he accosted me like the ancient mariner and with a faraway look kept repeating the words 'Amazing! Amazing!' Here was the best tribute to the truth of Frank Smythe's vision. It was not just the flowers but their setting in these glorious surroundings that had penetrated this visitor's soul.

The ancient mariner turned out to be Dr Ashok Kothari, a well-known urban environmental activist and keen member of the Bombay Natural History Society (BNHS). His stunned state reminded me of the words the botanist Kingdom Ward (from the *Himalayan Journal*) recorded in the Eastern Himalaya: 'I had scarcely reached the bank when I stopped suddenly in amazement. Was I dreaming? I rubbed my eyes and I looked again. No. Just above the edge of the snow it stood out vividly. So fascinating was it to stand there and gaze on this marvel in an aching pain of wonder that I felt no desire to step forward and break the spell. . . . In the face of such unsurpassed loveliness one is afraid to move. And when at last with fluttering heart one does venture forward it is on to tiptoe to wonder and to worship.' (The botanist had found a rare species of plant.)

Ashok and I would become friends. We were both committed to planting trees as the solution to shrinking forests. Ashok enrolled me as a member of the BNHS but living in north India this meant little active involvement. I did attend the centenary meeting but discovered that the early days when enthusiastic amateurs were welcome had long since gone. Now only professional scientists voiced their opinions.

Thanks to the BNHS I met Dr Salim Ali who had done so much for bringing the birds of the Himalaya alive. I cherish his advice: 'Be constructive and revel in the simple joy of life.' Also I met R.E. Hawkins, his editor, whom I always imagined to be a formidable pedant because of his Oxford University Press editorship. Instead I found a charming, eccentric and laid-back Quaker with a boundless love of the Himalaya as well as for its literature. As publisher of the *Himalayan Journal* Hawk also helped proof-read it. However he never wrote anything for the *Journal*, which seems surprising. The author Ruskin Bond has the theory that Hawkins may have been the actual writer of Jim Corbett's stories. He finds Corbett's style suspiciously innocent of any literary influences or allusions.

Hawkins complained that my style was 'somewhat prolix'. This was an indicator of his preference for the short, simple and lucid sentence. As the popular and able editor of the great shikari Corbett, Hawk compiled several works of reference on natural history and Indo-Anglian words; he also wrote the introduction to a selected edition of Corbett. Hawk did more trekking in the Sahyadri range than in the Himalaya but his unbounded curiosity and meticulous recording of natural features made him a guru figure to many. So legendary was his penchant for going off and exploring unlikely places, someone swore that in the middle of the Alaskan wilderness they had come across a lone wanderer checking the flora and fauna: it was Hawk!

Oxford University Press under Hawkins displayed a real passion for the Himalaya and one of his assistants, Ravi Dayal, now a publisher of quality himself, settled down in Ranikhet. This was fortuitous for a Garhwali gurubhai of mine, Durga Charan Kala who had also retired there after a long stint in the editorial section of *The Hindustan Times*. Although from Pauri Garhwal, Kala had been brought up in Kumaun where his father rose to become deputy commissioner. To the horror of the British this Garhwali DC was lenient in punishing Sarala Devi for leading the agitation against the government in the Quit India movement.

Sarala delighted in telling how when she had gone to call on the British commissioner, who was Kala Senior's boss, at his bungalow in Naini Tal, he had leapt up in rage from his breakfast table and rushing to the door while wiping toast and scrambled eggs off his lips shouted, 'I'll see you are put on the next boat to England where I hope you'll be hanged.' He was not amused at the burning of the resin depots, which was how the local freedom fighters chose to damage the imperial economy. Sarala laughed triumphantly and pointed out it was the commissioner and not she who was sent packing to England when independence came. Sarala's own father, a German Swiss, had been interned unfairly in London during the First World War. Hatred of British injustice as well as love for Indian freedom brought Sarala to India where she was successful in treading on a lot of British toes.

Durga Kala had researched Corbett's early life in Naini Tal and was fascinated to come across a mysterious bank account that the famous shikari bachelor used for remitting money to an Indian princess. Spurred on by this discovery Kala went on to publish a backgrounder to Corbett's early life and delved into the author's sex life (or lack of it). The book was later edited and republished by Ravi Dayal.

In the OUP's Apollo Bunder office in Bombay was the editor Adil Tyabji who was then compiling a Gujarati dictionary. Adil was a kind of role model for me since he not only trekked into the interesting parts of the Himalaya but also rode a motorbike. He was famous for smoking beedis when working on his dictionary. On the mountains on dangerous paths at night he was put in the lead. Those who followed were told to keep their eyes fixed on the red glow of Adil's beedi. If it went out they were to stop. It meant he had stepped over a precipice!

Adil, who was not overathletically endowed, was usually put in charge of base camp after the team moved up the mountain. He was told to guard the team's jerrycan of chang with his life for this would be the looked-for reward when the climbers returned from their successful ascent. Invariably when the team returned the jerrycan would be empty. Adil would greet them expansively and explain something about a leak in the jerrycan because of which he had thought it prudent not to let the contents go waste.

Adil belongs to the illustrious Tyabji clan of which Dr Salim Ali was a member. Recently in Mussoorie a shocking instance of how India's freedom struggle has been betrayed by the government came to light in the fate of Abbas Tyabji's house 'Southwood'.

Abbas Tyabji left this house, fully furnished with rare antiques, as a gift to the nation for use as a bungalow for important people visiting Mussoorie. Tyabji had been president of the Congress and was a fast friend of Gandhiji. It was Tyabji who boldly indicted General Dyer after the Jallianwala Bagh massacre.

Instead of using the house as a national memorial the Central PWD allowed it to go to rack and ruin, the priceless antiques in the meantime being quietly removed and written off as worthless. To add to this insult to the memory of the freedom fighter who passed away here in 1936, the CPWD sought to knock down the bungalow and convert the site into quarters for junior engineers. Almost as depressing as the lack of transparency in official dealings has been the apathy of the public to the fate of this heritage building.

Another ex-OUP editor who lives a lot of the time in Ranikhet is Rukun Advani, son of the well-known Lucknow bookseller, Ram Advani. A gifted writer, it always seemed to me Rukun's talents were going to waste in an academic publishing house. Then overnight in an example of the colonial paternalist attitudes that linger in many British institutions overseas, Rukun was ordered to sack his spouse Anuradha Roy, a co-editor, on the grounds of professional propriety. The fact that the same relationship obtained at the Oxford end of the business and was acceptable in the UK made it obvious that discrimination was at work. This would have been unthinkable under Hawkins but in his generation literary worth was valued as much as the sound of a ringing cash register.

I made the climb to Hem Kund next day and then went on to Badrinath for darshan. But it was Ashok Kothari's stunned expression that stood out as the highlight of my first serious excursion on high ground. I learnt on that outing to discount figures on milestones. By following the village practice of taking shortcuts you could halve the actual distance. If it took a strenuous day and a half to reach Hem Kund it was possible by running down the shortcuts to get back to Govindghat in half a day. I met one or two young Sikhs who had come from the Punjab on scooters and they delighted in clocking themselves each year to beat each other's records for going up and down in the fastest possible time. One driver claimed to have got up and down in a day. This is feasible (if dangerous) for the fully fit, but definitely not advisable for the unacclimatised.

On another occasion when I was coming back from Govindghat I found a large crowd of returning pilgrims who had waited for hours to board a bus to Joshimath. All the buses started further up the road at Badrinath and with a full complement they refused to stop at Govindghat for more passengers. What the pilgrims failed to understand was that the distance shown to Joshimath on the milestone was double the real distance by using the shortcuts. A villager demonstrated this by leading me up to the town through the fields and we arrived there in a few hours. Meanwhile the stranded party had to camp for the night and lost a whole day by believing Joshimath lay a great distance away.

A valuable rule of the road for hill travelling is never sit wringing your hands like those pilgrims at Govindghat. If you keep moving something benevolent may befall your steps. Time and again I have found this a valuable working philosophy because hidden round the next corner lies a whole new range of possibilities. Pessimism is a sedentary shortcoming; by acting positively you are willing something better to happen.

13
Dev Bhumi

Many regions of the Himalaya lay claim to the title 'Abode of the gods' but strictly speaking Uttarakhand is the only genuine claimant. It is true that Kullu at Dasehra is the abode of the gods for they all foregather at the famous annual festival. But this is their temporary abode and the gods thereafter return to their favoured sites. Garhwal in the ancient scriptures is also known as Kedarkhand. No one is agreed about the meaning of the word kedar which is the place of Shiva's meditation. However at 11,500 ft where a solid stone temple was built in his honour a clue to the word's derivation is found in the marshy meadows that characterise the site. Many small shrines have been built to enclose the numerous tiny springs (kahi dar) that bubble up and traditionally the pilgrim is invited to say 'Shiva Shambu' to which there is an immediate response in the 'bloop-bloop' of bubbling water.

These many springs may have lent a magical aura to this superb site at the base of the vast snow ramparts of the Himalaya. None of the other dhams of Uttarakhand have this scintillating backdrop. Badri the abode of Vishnu appears to have been chosen for the hot springs in attendance as does Yamnotri, the religious source of the Yamuna.

Gangotri has neither a snow panorama nor hot springs but possesses Bhagirath Sheel, the penance stone on which the meditating king influenced Ganga Maharani to flow from Shiva's Kailash down to earth. Could it be that this very ordinary stone once marked the source of the Ganga which has now receded more than nineteen kilometres to Gaumukh? The Gangotri glacier is melting at an alarming rate. When I first went there twenty years ago it was receding at the rate of 30 ft a year; today the ice is retreating at 30 metres a year. By the year 2050 the glacier may not exist.

There is no temple to mark the Gaumukh source of the Ganga because of the changing terrain. The Ganga rises south-east of Gangotri and is blocked from any passage south by the bulk of the Kedarnath massif. Gangotri is remarkable for the broad Bhagirathi river which suddenly narrows near the temple and then after crashing over a spectacularly sculpted waterfall enters a narrow gorge only a metre wide. Instead of seeing some proof of a scientific claim for this being the original source of the river, pilgrim mythology holds that King Bhagirath had built a canal to lead the Ganga round the obstructing Kedarnath.

The Yamnotri and Gangotri temples are both sited under the tree line while Kedar is above it. It is likely Badri once had tree cover that has fallen over the centuries to the demands of pilgrim fuel. At Bhojbhas a few kilometres short of Gaumukh (and higher than Kedar) twenty years ago there were slopes of bhojpatra (birch trees) which have all been cut recently thanks to the increase in pilgrim traffic caused by the building of a motorable bridge to Gangotri. When pilgrims had to walk ten kilometres to the temple fewer came and the environmental toll was bearable.

Now only Yamnotri and Kedarnath require some trekking. The day spent in walking to these shrines and the act of stretching one's legs and lungs makes for a much better mood on arrival. Usually pilgrims who alight at the bus terminals of Badri and Gangotri feel tired, dusty and bilious. The last thing they need on arrival is the noise and pollution of these seething bus stations with their crowd of porters, hotel touts and soliciting temple 'pandas' (priests). One of the first rules I learnt for visiting pilgrim shrines was from Sri Krishna Prem who had walked from Mirtola to Badrinath in the old days before the roads came: always hire a panda immediately on arrival, for he will keep the others away.

The pandas have their own extremely thorough system of allotting new arrivals, depending on the area they come from. India is divided into districts and a panda's family takes responsibility for catering to the requirements of pilgrims from their allotted area. Your panda will arrange accommodation, food and darshan in return for an offering. Furthermore he will have kept an accurate register of all in your family who have visited before and to make this more meaningful he will have got the pilgrim to personally write in his register. He will show you the authentic signature of your ancestor and the dates of his stay.

Those who belong to parts not accounted for (say from Pakistan, China or Peru) have a special panda allotted to them. These arrangements work flawlessly and the stories you hear about the greed of the pandas need to be taken with a pinch of salt. If they were so greedy no one would continue with their services. Whenever Prithwi and I have trekked on the char dham circuit the pandas have gone out of their way to show kindness. They have learned the art of good public relations and know that our friends would seek them out by name because of our recommendation.

At the end of May 1980 Prithwi decided to have darshan of Badri Vishal and we set off in her Fiat from Mussoorie taking care to pack a small spade. This was needed to dig out the back wheels from muddy patches found along the little-used road linking Tehri with Srinagar. We spent the first night at Nand Prayag and were lucky to get a room in the forest bungalow since the district forest officer was in residence and gave us permission. The bungalow lay alongside the meeting of the Alakananda and Nandakini rivers and in those days was very peacefully situated. Apart from pilgrim buses, army convoys, and government jeeps, there was no private traffic. The age of nationalised banks and government loans to buy taxis had not yet arrived.

This confluence of rivers marked the traditional site of Shakuntala's ashram in Kalidas's drama. It would be hard for Shakuntala's king to go hunting in these parts nowadays because there are so few trees left. Yet only 150 years ago according to Atkinson's *Gazetteer* tigers abounded in the forests around Karnaprayag.

A new road left Nand Prayag for the interior following the Nandakini as far as Ghat. This was a convenient junction for treks to Rup Kund and the Kuari Pass. Of all the unspoilt sylvan trails in Garhwal the climb to Kuari from Ramni (above Ghat) is amongst my favourites. This bridle path through ancient clumps of mixed forest was known as the Curzon Trail because the viceroy had chosen it for its reputed scenic beauty. However the viceregal party only got as far as the first stage when the trek had to be called off. They were attacked by wild bees, a feature of these hills.

Returning from one of my treks to the source of the Nandakini when I came to the village of Sutol I found not a single male at home. They had all gone to raid the hives of the deadly wild bee. The bees hang their large combs of honey under some inaccessible cliff safe from the wind and rain and beyond the reach of a ladder. But the enterprising villagers lower a man from the top of the cliff and as he dangles in midair he tries to smoke out the bees. Then in a desperate manoeuvre he breaks off the combs which drop to those waiting at the base of the cliff. Needless to say many are badly stung in this uneven battle and the rewards hardly seem to offset the pains incurred. But the sheer physical courage of the villager lowered almost literally into a hornet's nest is something you cannot but applaud.

Honey enjoys a high religious status in the hills and is believed to be good for every complaint. The theory that it contains the essence of many Himalayan plants is belied by the fact that much of it originates from village sweetshops where due to the paucity of flora the bees are forced to forage. Keeping domesticated bees in the hills is hard work. During the cold weather you have to feed them rather than the other way round. For the rest of the year they require a lot of protection from bears and pine martens. Perhaps their worst enemy is the wasp which comes in several sizes in the hills. The biggest species of hornet runs to two inches in body length. In swatting one of these which was attacking the Mirtola hives I accidentally put my foot on it when it was already dead, but its sting nevertheless penetrated my foot and I had a severe temperature for a week. This variety breeds in combs in the ground and have such strong poison that three stings can be fatal.

After the leafy surroundings of Nand Prayag, Badrinath came as a bit of a letdown. The sprawl of dharmshalas and the crudely painted temple in PWD pink gave the place an air more of a refugee camp than a spiritual destination. The valley hereabouts is very open and we walked up to the village of Mana. Here we experienced some true religion albeit of the local variety. A women was possessed and uttered oracular outbursts which went largely unheard since most of the men were staggering around totally drunk on locally distilled booze.

It is a curiosity of spiritual alchemy that Lord Badri, the most orthodox of Hindu icons and cared for by Namboodri brahmins, likewise commands the allegiance of these toping Marchas (as the local people were then designated). To prove the point the Rawal of the Badri temple rode up on horseback to bless the bacchanalian ceremonies afoot in Mana.

The word Badri is said to derive from the beru (wild fig) on which Lord Vishnu is believed to have survived while doing penance in the valley. The jujube tree is a claimant but does not grow above 6000 ft. A more likely candidate is *Hippophae salicifolia*, a shrub with an acid fruit that makes a palatable preserve when boiled with sugar. The hill fig—eaten as a vegetable after the latex has been boiled out—grows around Joshimath where Lord Badri descends to spend his winter. In fact Joshimath is famous for possessing what is claimed to be one of the oldest trees in India. This is a fig but of the non-fruiting variety, similar to the tree under which the Buddha sat for enlightenment in Bodh Gaya. Is there a clue here to the origins of the temple?

The insignificance of the structure at Badrinath and the attribute of 'vishal' to the deity has led some to argue that the real Badri was higher up on the Tibetan border where there are large, ancient Buddhist stone figures. This would explain the word vishal (great).

Controversy exists over the belief that Shankaracharya had rescued the image of Badri (said to have been thrown in the river by Buddhist polemical rivals) and reinstated it at the site of the present temple. Another version is that Shankaracharya's followers after the victory of their guru over the Buddhists in debate had simply taken over the temple as their legitimate spoils. A similar case has been made for other temples as at Puri, Ayodhya, Kanchipuram and Srisailem. Chinese travellers before the advent of Shankaracharya describe in detail several Buddhist shrines that mysteriously since then have found their way into brahminical custodianship. While contemporary Hindu chauvinists list temples destroyed by Muslims there is silence on Hindu takeovers of Buddhist and Jain sites. Evidence of the likely brahminical takeover of Badrinath lies in the carefully concealed fact that the image worshipped in the temple (invariably obscured by the pujari's floral offerings) is of the Buddha in the lotus posture. Hindus try to evade this awkward fact by claiming that it is as an avatar of Vishnu that Buddha is worshipped in Badri. But why then should Buddhists have thrown the image in the river? And why would Shankaracharya attack an avatar of Hinduism? The truth is many Hindus consider it bad luck to keep an image of the Buddha in their house. Likewise Hindu pilgrims studiously avoid visiting the birthplace of the Buddha and the place where he died.

The next day we walked to Vishnu-paduka to glimpse the lovely vista of Nilkantha framed at the end of the valley. What a superb peak this is and how soiled its reputation became in international mountaineering circles thanks to H.C. Sarin the president of the Indian Mountaineering Foundation (IMF). The IMF was established to put India on the world mountaineering map and keep up with the Joneses in putting Indians atop Everest. The fact that the IMF was originally housed in the defence ministry compound hints at the early departmentalising of the infant sport of climbing by the government. Its office was a tiny room in an asbestos barracks where Babu Munshi Ram sat at a desk surrounded on all sides by mounds of yellowing files. A more unmountaineering atmosphere would be hard to imagine but at least Munshi Ram hailed from the hills, which is more than could be said for many of the bureaucratic 'experts' who had never set foot in the Himalaya. Sarin's credentials for leading the IMF were based on the fact that as a student he had undertaken a bicycle tour of Norway! But he was defence secretary and effectively controlled the destinies of India's budding mountaineers. This thirst for mountaineering headlines had disastrous repercussions. Nilkantha is a peak as hard to climb as it is beautiful to look upon. The Indian team that claimed to have climbed it did so under extremely adverse conditions. Their leader was invalided back to base with serious frostbite that cost him his toes and the would-be summiters battled with hunger and blizzard conditions to reach what they assumed to be the top. Ignoring the need for cautious appraisal Sarin rushed the news to the press. What followed was a Himalayan pantomime involving a crude cover up and the unedifying spectacle of climbers wriggling out of previously stated positions.

Jagdish Nanavati of the Himalayan Club, known for his scientific exactitude in recording mountain data, happened to have undertaken a mountaineering course with Sharma, one of the summit claimants. He compared the official version with what Sharma told him. Nanavati plotted on a graph the heights of the various camps and the distances between them assuming they would tally. But there were severe contradictions in the summiters' and official accounts of the time taken to reach camps, a complication being the blizzard conditions. Another crucial factor to be reconciled was the energy levels of the summit party who were out of food and deteriorating rapidly.

Writing a monograph with calculations based on the various versions put out by the expedition Nanavati convincingly demonstrated that an exhausted summit party could not have reached the top but had probably mistaken a lower point as the summit owing to the blizzard. As honorary librarian of the Himalayan Club I discovered Nanavati's monograph in an old trunk. It was addressed to Pandit Nehru but had merited no reply.

Realising the IMF's reputation was on the line Sarin appointed a committee to scrutinise the expedition's schedule and detailed a professional surveyor to give his opinion on whether the climbers could have made it to the top in view of Nanavati's reservations.

Nanavati was not invited to join the enquiry committee and worse, it was composed of military personnel, all of whom were dependent on Mr Sarin for their promotions. Aerial photographs were taken and the military surveyor gave his verdict that Nilkantha could have been climbed. Unfazed and using the committee's own findings Nanavati now drew up a series of photometric angles to prove the top could not have been reached. The military surveyor's narrow interpretation might have been plausible but for the omission of the crucial realities of the weather and the starving condition of the climbers.

From Badri we drove down to Govindghat and set off with our dogs Puja and Chow Chow to visit the gurudwara at Hem Kund. Prithwi had been brought up in the Sikh religion and this was considered a very special pilgrimage. However it was not an old one. In 1930 Sardar Sohan Singh from Tehri, a keen student of the Granth Sahib, had come across a reference that in a former life Guru Govind Singh remembered meditating in a valley surrounded by seven peaks. Like a good pilgrim Sohan Singh checked out many valleys until at last he alighted upon Lokpal (as Hem Kund was formerly known.) Immediately he knew his quest had been rewarded by the guru's grace and he now made it his mission to tell other Sikhs about the glories that awaited them if they climbed to Lokpal. When he became too old to climb to the gurudwara his successor Sardar Mohan Singh sat at Govindghat doling out handfuls of channa to encourage pilgrims to divert from the trail to Badri.

Some students of modern religion have read Sikh triumphalism into the founding of this gurudwara at Hem Kund since it out-tops Tungnath, traditionally the highest of the shrines on the Hindu spiritual circuit of Uttarakhand. The Hem Kund building is a lavish stadium-like gurudwara funded by overseas Sikhs and took years to complete. Although its design is pleasingly modernistic its size seems out of scale for the small lake on whose shore also sits the tiny and wholly appropriate temple of Lokpal (this has also recently been enlarged). The original gurudwara had been a small structure in keeping with the size of the lake. The king-size replacement seemed grandiose and rather pointless. At this altitude pilgrims cannot linger and after a holy dip and worship they descend to Ghangaria the same day. Not even the priest stays overnight because of the lack of oxygen. Such a large building argues an impractical understanding of Himalayan conditions. Hinduism, by contrast, with its centuries of experience in coping with pilgrimage at altitudes, sensibly did not place its main shrines much above the critical 10,000 ft level at which human lungs behave normally. Anything higher and the body faces several serious health risks.

The material success of overseas Sikhs not only inspired the inflated design of the Hem Kund gurudwara but contributed to the political agitation for Khalistan, a separate state for Sikhs whose capital would be Amritsar, deemed akin to the Vatican. The more extreme believers funded by foreign dollars turned to terrorism to try and force the government's hand. To show the government took these triumphalist politics seriously the district magistrate in Chamoli on hearing of a Hem Kund devotee's plans to carry building material to Kak Bhusand Tal (to construct a gurudwara) impounded the wooden beams and tin sheets.

Just as Sardar Mohan Singh had read into the surroundings of Hem Kund the interpretation of Guru Govind Singh's memories (the seven peaks are not obvious to any but the most zealous of observers) this new attempt to convert the lake of (Hindu) crows into the site where Guru Govind Singh's hawk nested seemed another instance of spiritual oneupmanship at work. It is noticeable to any who ride a pilgrim bus to the Garhwal shrines that the Sikh pilgrims are far more active in their behaviour than Hindu pilgrims. Most of the Hindu pilgrims are peasants from the plains. At road blocks they huddle in their bus and wait apathetically for the debris to be cleared. By contrast Sikh pilgrims will immediately spring from the bus and almost joyfully start rolling boulders down the hill to clear a way. This helps explain why the Hem Kund ascent in spite of its rigour is a more vibrant pilgrim experience. All the way Sikhs greet each other with a thunderous 'Bole Sone

Hal' to which the reply echoing from above is 'Sat Sri Akal!' Natural exuberance is probably the real reason for the impressive gurudwara as a climax to the climb.

As a former Sikh maharani conscious of her history, the ascent to Hem Kund was very meaningful for Prithwi. She is a natural devotee with the gift of feeling at home in any situation where true religion is present. Our dogs being of Tibetan ancestry felt perfectly at home too in the snow and were allowed into the (unfinished) gurudwara since they had, like the other pilgrims, climbed on their own.

The way to the Valley of Flowers was likewise snowbound at the end of May and when we got there not a flower was in sight. Only a sprinkling of green and pink shoots indicated how the new life would have to sprint to perform its cycle in a brief three months' period. By the middle of August the tiny shoots underfoot would have shot up to become head high in perfume-laden flowers and then just as quickly they would dry.

Prithwi found the valley disappointing after Smythe's hype and I left her sunning with the dogs while I went to photograph the memorial stone on the grave of the lady botanist from Edinburgh who had slipped while plant-collecting and died here. As I was returning by a lower route I came across in a protected dell the first outburst of flowers in the form of crocuses. The dew on their golden petals glowed like diamonds in the cold sun and I beckoned Prithwi to descend and see how the valley had won its reputation for beauty. She grumbled at having to lose height but once in the magic dell was bewitched by the tenderness of nature's new leaf. In a way this visit was more meaningful than my earlier one during the peak season. The intensity of the beauty in its uncurled potential seemed more wonderful than the even spread of a thousand species in full blossom.

14
Ganga Maharani

On one of his few visits to north India Sathya Sai Baba had graced Prithwi's Delhi house and she asked him to bless the ice axe for my planned trek into Nanda Devi Sanctuary. Baba graciously produced vibhuti from thin air and rubbed it on the axe. It was an old-fashioned ash-handled model more used as a tent pole than for cutting steps but it had served its purpose in getting Prithwi to the Valley of Flowers when steps had to be hewn. It would also save my life in the Sanctuary.

Since my Calcutta days I had had a persistent desire to visit the Sanctuary and see for myself what Shipton had described so powerfully in his book, *Nanda Devi*. Like Pranavananda's book on Kailash Mansarover Shipton's on Nanda Devi lodged deep and almost daily a small inner voice reminded me that this was one trip I must make before I die.

Luckily Inner Line restrictions were pushed back in 1974 to Surai Tota. That meant access to the Sanctuary from Lata was now open to whoever could muster the money and energy. A stampede of foreign climbers had made a beeline to Nanda Devi's marvellous enclosure to climb the virgin peaks. I was now forty-six and did not see my physical fitness improving with age. Therefore it seemed now or never if I was to satisfy my urge to view the feet of the Devi close up. Despite the rainy season I set off on the 10th of July 1980 and much to my own amazement was able to reach my goal of the inner Sanctuary on the 27th. It was an utterly fulfilling expedition replete with the extremes of anguish and bliss. Not since childhood when I had passed my matric exam against all the odds did I feel so flooded with the satisfaction that comes from a test faced and overcome at great cost, consciously borne.

So profound was the impact of the Goddess in her sanctuary that I started writing about it the moment I got back from the encounter. I was so elated by my climb that it seemed as though some revelatory grace had seized me. I wanted to convey the immediacy of my experience with accounts of the raw sounds and smells experienced on the trail by recourse to my diary notings, but these grafted passages made for a disjointed narrative. The book that emerged perhaps showed evidence of some writerly inspiration but certainly no editorial expertise. I made a further blunder in sending the lengthy typescript to a London publisher that had turned their attention to mountaineering books. What I overlooked was that this company had earlier been notorious for furthering missionary literature. My manuscript suggesting the Christian West may have overlooked the beauties in many aspects of Hindu practice must have created quite a flutter. The ms was sent back by return of post! I tried Gollancz and had a sympathetic note of rejection. Optimistically I also sent it to Gillon Aitken, the most famous literary agent in London, and received a supercilious response. (Years later the towering figure of Aitken alongside his diminutive protege Naipaul at a Penguin literary gathering would remind me of Mutt and Jeff.) Perversely I wasn't unduly put off by the rejection of my manuscript. Since the book had been commissioned by the Goddess presumably she did not want it published by mlecchas! And I had the consolation of finding my manuscript passably entertaining even if no one else did.

This pleasantly surprised me because at school I was always being given other boys' essays to read to enable me to acquire what my teachers called style. I held a low opinion of the Fowler brothers whose handbook of English usage was considered a bible. They were only expressing their bourgeois preferences when they made the basis of a good writing style 'short, simple and Saxon sentences'. To my ears this was like suggesting that a single instrument is preferable to an orchestra. My favourite authors happen to be Johnson, Gibbon, Sir Thomas Browne, Doughty and Carlyle none of whom wrote short or simple or Saxon sentences.

My luck changed for at about this time Penguin Books opened their Indian wing. Travelogues were in vogue and I was invited to submit a manuscript. *Seven Sacred Rivers* was accepted and on the strength of its reception I submitted a revised and drastically reduced *Nanda Devi Affair*. The Devi had made a writer of me. After I got back to Mussoorie from the Sanctuary, Prithwi and I set out for the source of the Yamuna which lay only two days away. We drove the Fiat down the Aglar valley to Yamuna Bridge. With us were our trekking spaniel pups Puja and Chow Chow. That night because the last portion of the road was muddy and slow we could only get as far as Hanuman Chatti. The forest chowkidar let us stay in the run-down bungalow but for food we had to climb down to a dhaba, the only eating place nearby. When we negotiated the tricky descent in the dark we found it full of Dhotial labourers carting out baulks of timber. And it was on these freshly cut wooden beams that we sat and balanced our thalis. It was bitterly cold and the conditions villainously primitive but we relished every minute of it. For Prithwi it was an eye-opening experience. Most of her life she had been sheltered from the cruder end of society and now for the first time appreciated how good a hard-earned meal tasted.

We climbed the leafy gorge to the religious source of the river accompanied by a deaf and dumb panda who looked after our arrangements for accommodation in Yamnotri. We bathed in the sulphur springs (the ladies having to make do with the overflow from the men's tank!) and saw the pilgrims cook their rice in the scalding spurts of water that miraculously emerge from the very river-bed in which icy cold water flows. We hobnobbed with the holy men in their caves furnished with plastic sheets to keep out the draughts; I was amazed to find cockroaches in abundance around food supplies they had laid in for the winter. The bugs relished the steam as much as the pilgrims.

An easy trek, Yamnotri remains the most authentic because it is the least sought after of the char dham. Yamuna Mai is the younger sister of Ganga and her temple is one of the four recognised pilgrim shrines. The people in this remote corner of Garhwal are an easygoing lot; we were surprised to see a man and a woman kissing in a field. This is unthinkable in mainstream culture but the unorthodox nature of hill society allows for variations from the supposed norm. The district of Jaunsar Bhabar is known for the ancient custom of polyandry so prominent in the *Mahabharat* with Draupadi and her five husbands. In another reference to the Pandavas, till recently puja in village temples was performed to their enemies the Kauravas and the priest would stand with his back to the images for this ceremony.

A curiosity of the Yamuna is the Buddhist influences along its hill course. From the beautifully preserved Ashokan edict at Kalsi to the pagoda-like temple of Kharsali (where the river goddess spends her winters) it is evident the Yamuna valley hosted several important Buddhist religious sites. The Tibetan inputs in the culture of Kinnaur to the north-west of Garhwal seem to extend as far west as Deolsari at the foot of Nag Tibba where the pagoda-type temple can be found. In Himachal and Kharsali a steep roof would make sense in view of the heavy snowfall but in the lee of the Nag Tibba range its existence is due presumably to cultural rather than physical factors. It is worth a mention that Dundi, a village in the Bhagirathi valley at the foot of the northern face of the Nag Tibba range, is where former nomads from the border areas settled. They now strenuously play down their Tibetan connection. Incidentally it is from one of these families that India's famous woman climber Bachendri Pal hails.

Another curious Tibetan connection in Uttarkashi occurs in Heinrich Harrer's best-seller *Seven Years in Tibet.* Harrer was a brilliant climber whose performance on the controversial north face of the Eiger gained him a place on a German expedition to the Himalaya. When war intervened the German mountaineers were interned and Harrer's best-selling book describes how at the fag end of hostilities he had escaped from a detention camp in Dehra Dun and made his way via the Aglar valley to Nag Tibba and thence to Uttarkashi. He refers to staying with a 'friend' perhaps the only time in the book that he lets slip a clue to what he and his companions were really up to.

Towards the end of Harrer's celebrated career as climber and author the skeletons in his cupboard fell out. Long before his readers did, many in the climbing fraternity knew of Harrer's Nazi past and that, as a youthful member of Hitler's party he had climbed the Eiger to prove the superiority of the Aryan race over lesser mortals. Harrer had had his bloodline checked by the Gestapo for any impure Jewish ancestry and was duly married off to a blonde German maiden of similar uncontaminated blood. Despite Harrer's claim on entering Lhasa that his party was the first Europeans to arrive for decades the truth is the Nazis had sent a group of thirty Germans to Tibet at the same time they despatched Harrer's mountaineering team to India. That the Nazi spy network was widespread is vouched for by Krishna Prem who in the late 1930s visited Lama Govinda (an Austrian citizen like Harrer) in a Buddhist dharmshala in Benares. Keeping an eye on the Lama's visitors were several beefy Nazi party members looking ludicrous disguised as Buddhist monks with muscles rippling under their borrowed ochre robes. Because of this association with known Nazis the British authorities felt Lama Govinda should likewise be interned although he was the gentlest of genuine Buddhists. He had come to the subcontinent originally in the early 1930s, a member of the literary group sailing to Australia with D.H. Lawrence. Lama got off at Colombo to study Buddhism as did the American artists the Brewsters who moved to Almora to paint. Later Lama Govinda would join them on Cranks Ridge.

Harrer despite his own early admiration for totalitarian regimes took up a violent anti-Chinese posture over Tibet and in reprisal the Chinese raked up his Nazi past. To make matters worse for himself and his second wife Harrer claimed the Chinese had no evidence of that past. But every detail of Harrer's love affair with the Nazi youth movement—including his signature—is on record in the Berlin archives. Harrer's silence was not just that of a famous author and mountaineer concerned to hide the shame of his Nazi past. It was compounded by fear that as a spy he could have been shot.

Who was his friend in Uttarkashi? Who provided the gold with which Harrer and Aufschnaitner bought their way to Lhasa? They must have been told in Germany that gold would forward any journey on the roof of the world. It would be ludicrous for climbers in the Himalaya to burden themselves with a substance of so little use on their ascent. Just as the British had their Pandit spies who checked out the route to Lhasa it seems the Germans had recruited border people to collect information on British movements in High Asia.

Amusingly for the believers in the 'impenetrable barrier' status of the Himalaya, Harrer crossed the Nelang Pass wearing only canvas shoes. Harrer's narrative of his initiative and resolve along the way and in Lhasa shortchanges the contribution made by his gifted companion Aufschnaitner whose talents were enormous. Being of a scholarly disposition he was content to let Harrer hog the limelight and obscure the embarrassing likelihood that they were both spies. (Manohar Malgaonkar recalls how on army intelligence duty he had the task of debriefing Aufschnaitner before he left the subcontinent for Europe.) What annoyed Harrer's well-wishers and critics alike was that back in Europe the climber-author maintained an old friendship with a Nazi doctor known for having performed experimental operations in a concentration camp hospital using Jewish patients as guinea pigs.

On the subject of conflict of loyalties, it is not uncommon in the Himalayan districts to find sepoys who defected to the Indian National Army (INA) under the inspiration of Netaji Subhash Chandra Bose. When taken as British prisoners of war by the Japanese in the South Asian theatre it made sense to some that fighting for India's freedom was more dignified than languishing in detention. Most however stayed loyal to their salt as a matter of principle. They may not have liked the British but their village sense of honour would not let them be guilty of namak harami, or betrayal.

In the village of Wan I met a 'major' of the INA who spoke a smattering of German. In Arunachal I saw the grave of an INA soldier which extolled the virtues of Hitler! Perhaps because of the conflict of loyalties—aided by the lack of equipment—the INA in Burma posed only a symbolic threat to the Allied forces. It was embarrassing for men from the same hill village to meet when the victorious disarmed the losers. The real heartburn would be experienced by their families: a court martial would affect the pension which was the real reason the menfolk had joined the army in the first place.

Still, Netaji has been canonised among retired INA infantrymen to such an extent that in several hill villages the legend of him having taken sannyasa and continuing to wander at large as a siddha-mahatma continues to fire popular imagination.

In September a few years on, I visited Gangotri and Gaumukh to spy out the land for a proposed visit the following summer by Prithwi. I made friends with the irascible Lal Baba's assistant Ram Baba. This would stand me in good stead on our return visit. I also had darshan of Photo Swami (Sunderananda) who had an artistic cottage in which he kept a collection of fossil finds and driftwood. In the winter the Swami would give slide shows in the plains and being an accomplished mountaineer his angles on the less-viewed parts of the Himalaya were spectacular. The Swami was a disciple of Tapovan Maharaj, a swami from Kerala whose book on the Himalaya, *Himagiri Vihar,* made the higher trekking routes known to the public at large. Another of his disciples was Swami Chinmayananda whose mission in one generation opened the doors of orthodox Hindu philosophy to India's urban educated.

In June we set off for Gaumukh but could only get as far as Bhatwari where the motor road had collapsed. Some years earlier an earthslide had dammed the Bhagirathi and the ensuing flood from the build-up of water had erased some twenty kilometres of road. A friend in Mussoorie had given us the name of Mr Rishi the PWD engineer at Bhatwari who not only put us up for the night in his bungalow but provided us seats in one of his trucks going to Gangotri. The road was considered too rough for our small Fiat.

In those days the motor road terminated at Lanka, a clearing above the meeting of the Bhagirathi with the Jad Ganga, as beautiful a confluence as you could wish to find. Sadly with the building of a bridge no one now takes the trouble to see this ravishing sangam. You descended steeply through dark conifer stands then negotiated a rocky path above the dashing streams. Set dramatically in the middle of the joining streams is a huge split cube of rock. The gorge carrying the Jad Ganga has sheer rocky sides and it is above these that the new road bridge straddles the river. This was the site of Raja Wilson's original wooden bridge over which he galloped his charger to persuade pilgrims it was safe. Being a canny Yorkshireman Wilson had built it to collect toll taxes. It is sometimes claimed to be the highest bridge above a river in India but this is a pilgrim legend pre-dating the advent of the railway age.

To prove the enterprise of the locals when we climbed out of the gorge at Bhaironghati we were astonished to find a bus waiting to take us the final ten kilometres to the temple at Gangotri even though there was no road on which the bus could have crossed that gorge. Over the river and above the old timber foundation of Wilson's bridge two girders had been wedged. Along these were winched the heavy parts of the bus that would be reassembled on the other side. In colonial times this is how vehicles bought by the royals in Nepal were manhandled into the interior—break them down into their component parts and send them on the heads of porters. I learned about a modern variant in Kilar, the landlocked headquarters of the Pangi valley in Himachal. Jeep parts were lowered from a helicopter and then assembled to make a jeep—to give the district magistrate the status that went with owning a jeep, though the road did not connect to anywhere!

The highlight of our visits to Gangotri was the very moving puja offered to Ganga Maharani from the veranda of her temple at Gangotri. The pujari turns from the image with his candelabra of flickering lamps and faces the river as he offers the lights with great reverence to the rushing torrent below. The mood is profoundly moving. At Haridwar it is similar, but Gangotri has the towering elemental wonder of the mountains to heighten the experience. James Fraser's famous painting exactly captures the exaltation experienced at Gangotri to prove how neither Indian nor foreigner is immune to the grandeur of these Himalayan surroundings.

Soon after this I made another attempt to penetrate the north inner Sanctuary of Nanda Devi. As with the other shrines on the char dham circuit my trek to the feet of Nandi Devi was a pilgrimage and I put my trust in the local belief that if the Devi wants you to come, she will pull you to herself. This was the only way I could explain my luck in reaching her on my first attempt and my failure on the second. Now on the third attempt my sweat was rewarded. I witnessed more mysteries in the astonishing sheer drape of veiled ice that characterises the hidden northern face of the mountain, a sight of awesome beauty and sanctity.

15
The Best Little Trek

Kedarkhand represents the essence of the char dham experience. Although most pilgrims flock to Badrinath especially now that buses run almost to the temple door, arrival at Kedarnath is a more rewarding occasion. The pilgrim has to strive harder to get there and darshan tends to be less frenetic because of the absence of persistent crowds desperate for a glimpse of the jyotir linga.

Badri can be like a rugby scrum if you get caught amidst peasant parties whose members push and shove violently to achieve what is to them the most sacred moment of their lives. The probability that their parents and grandparents had been here before them heightens the occasion further into a crucial continuation of family blessings from the deity. An old lady elbowed me out of the way quite viciously on one occasion but when I glanced at her face instead of being contorted with anger it was suffused with love for the deity. I had to give way to this superior force and accept that British notions of polite queuing had never been designed for such impassioned confrontations.

The lingam at Kedar is in the shape of a tiny mountain peak, apparently an outcrop over which the garbha was built. As part of the process of mainstreaming unorthodox cults whose customs run counter to the brahminical code, the original lore of the char dham shrines appears to have been overlaid by orthodox interpretations. It seems certain that the Panch Kedar circuit, five temples to different limbs of Lord Shiva's body, ties up with the Gorakhnath cult of Nepal. In fact the climax to the Panch Kedar pilgrimage was not at Kedarnath (which worships the hind parts of Shiva in the form of a bull) but at Pashupatinath temple in Kathmandu where Shiva's head is venerated. Outward confirmation of this link is in the insignia atop both temple domes. Kedarnath displays the same symbol as the Kathmandu temple.

It is well known that the Gurkhas overran Uttarakhand in the early nineteenth century but often overlooked that in medieval times several Nepali rulers influenced events in Garhwal. The most beautiful medieval artefact in Uttarakhand, the great trisul at Barahat (modern Uttarkashi) is ascribed to an earlier Nepali overlord. Tantric teachings found a natural home in the hills where in matters of religious orthodoxy there was scope for laxity. Rulers preferred meat and alcohol as a means to salvation and this explains why in many hill temples till very recently both meat and the local wine could constitute offerings to the deity.

When control of the char dham shrines was taken away from the Maharaja of Tehri and vested in the state government a good many of the traditional tantric customs were quietly buried. When Prithwi and I went to Kedarnath we were appalled to see masons deliberately chipping away at the intertwined figures of a maithun couple on a sculpted frieze above the temple doorway. With the scrapping of the devadasi institution whereby consecrated maidens danced before the deity to afford him pleasure (and thereafter service the needs of his priests, according to Atkinson's *Gazetteer*) attempts have been made to pretend such things never existed. Hence the removal of the maithun couple. Hill society is understandably silent on many of its characteristic medieval customs such as ritual suicide at Kedarnath and human sacrifice in annual village fertility rites. The British banned the more egregiously bloodthirsty sacrifices such as the swinging of a consecrated villager to his death on a long rope to guarantee good crops from land fertilised by his bleeding body. These realities can only be found in the writings of the early colonial administrators. The famous historian of the Raj, Philip Woodruffe (who was actually Philip Mason the deputy commissioner for Garhwal), apart from his standard work *The Men Who Ruled India* has written two novels on Garhwali village life with details of these unpalatable customs. Neither book is now in print.

In defence of these village blood sacrifices some British eyewitnesses testified to the genuine mood of exaltation found in the victims. Drugged they may have been but they still believed they were performing a religious act that would benefit their village and bring themselves directly to the feet of their chosen deity.

A nice touch to the moment of arrival at Kedar when you top the last rise and behold the spread of the snow face was the presence of a village drummer who tom-tommed news of your achievement along the verduous valley leading to the temple. Our first visit had been in May just after the temple opened and snow still lay deep in the bazaar. The shops sold the charming little mementoes villagers find so entrancing but instead of copper, wood and stone they were now made of tin and plastic. The traditional images at the char dham were fashioned out of copper leaf and visitors bought flexible imprints of the various deities at whose temples they had darshan.

The Kedar temple is the most distinguished of the Uttarakhand shrines and the most solid. But it does not appear to be more than a few hundred years old. All stone, whether unhewn in the main range or extracted for religious fashioning, responds to the weathering of the centuries quite emphatically and really old temples in Uttarakhand as at Jageshwar (at half the height of Kedarnath and protected from the severity of winter snow) wear a well-worn look and all stone, whether unhewn in the main range or extracted for religious fashioning, responds to the weathering of the centuries quite emphatically.

The temple at Ukhimath across the Madhmaheshwar valley from Guptkashi is where Lord Shiva descends to spend his winters. (Gangaji descends to Mukhwa near Harsil, Yamuna Mai to Kharsali and Lord Badri to Joshimath.) Ukhimath's charming small compound features a slim temple of elegant proportions that, like the main shrine, appears to be of comparatively recent construction. Ukhi—who is the wife of Shiva in hill dress—is a junction for pilgrims moving from Kedarkhand to Badri Kshetra. At the top of the ridge dividing the waters of the Mandakini (rising from Kedarnath) from those of the Alaknanda (rising above Badri) is the third of the five temples to Lord Kedar at Tungnath. Curiously, thanks to the motor road that drives underneath it, this most spectacular of sites at 12,000 ft has the shortest approach by bridle path. The views are stunning and I had the extra bonus of going in the snow at the end of March when the rhododendrons are in bloom. The colours range from crimson to pink fading to lighter shades the higher you penetrate.

The climb from Ukhimath to Chopta (which marks the road crest) passes through some of the best jungle to be seen in Garhwal. Near the top is the fabulously sited forest bungalow of Dugalbitta sitting opposite the Kedarnath range. Wild animals can be found in these parts and so remote is the area that Mrs Gandhi incarcerated Chaudhri Charan Singh (himself to be prime minister later) here during her infamous Emergency.

Near Chopta a musk deer farm was set up for research. On my visits to Nanda Devi Sanctuary I kept bumping into Michael Green, a researcher from Cambridge, and learnt how difficult- and how important it is to study these reclusive animals. It seems they were found as low as 8000 ft till independence after which the pressure of population on the habitat drove them up to the tree line. In Pranavananda's Kailash guide, first written in 1949 (with a foreword by Pandit Nehru), the author describes musk pods as one of the chief exports of Tibet. Pilgrims are advised to buy some as a souvenir along with the pelt of the snow leopard.

The traditional traders of these rare items got richer as these became more scarce and then were banned from the market. But the trade did not stop, it only went underground. Michael Green, in the course of his work, was able to ferret out the entire chain of command from the villagers in Pithoragarh who snared the deer to the kingpin in Delhi. But even faced with the evidence the government was reluctant to prosecute. The traders apparently funded politicians who in turn granted them licences to build innocent fronts to their smuggling and poaching activities. Sarala Devi who retired from Kausani to settle on the border of Pithoragarh district told me the local magistrate had confiscated some musk pods and locked them up in a collectorate cupboard. When the cupboard was opened to present the evidence for the trial the pods were missing.

One night as I was sleeping outside on the paved angan of a shop at Ransi in 1984, I heard a party of men panting as they ran. Strangely I could see only the flickering of a flashlight as they padded by. What was this emergency in aid of? Why weren't the men talking loudly or carrying a pine torch as all hillmen do for protection against wild animals at night? In the morning I met three wildlife guards armed with guns. They were making enquiries about musk poachers. I realised I had heard the guilty men that night.

We had just returned from another visit to Hem Kund Sahib when out of the blue I received a telegram from a family in Calcutta asking for help to track the last movements of their son who had set out from the second Kedarnath shrine of Madhmaheshwar with a friend, hoping to make the first crossing of the crest of the Great Himalaya to Badrinath. They had been reported missing a month earlier. Against Prithwi's advice I decided to catch a bus to Guptkashi and make enquiries. Accidents in the mountains are common but because death is considered an inauspicious subject few are willing to volunteer information.

I knew one of the missing men to the extent of having corresponded enthusiastically over his earlier expeditions. Ranjit Lahiri seemed like a man after my own heart, forsaking the greater glory that goes with climbing peaks he took it upon himself to repeat some attractive exploratory routes done by early British climbers. He had crossed Auden's Col from Gangotri to Guttu, a scenic but by no means easy route. This crossing had inspired him to think of repeating Shipton and Tilman's traverse of the crest from Badri to Kedar in 1934.

He planned to do it in reverse, a very strenuous undertaking; he had only had one porter in support while Shipton and Tilman had several, along with three skilled sherpas who went the whole distance. At the outset the odds were against the two young Bengalis and to compound their difficulties they had to waste precious time getting permission to cross the Inner Line—something Shipton and company had been free of. Then to put their puny team in the firing line of disaster a blizzard struck soon after they set out. Details of what happened thereafter remain conflicting. All that is known is their porter returned to Madhmaheshwar temple a few days later badly frostbitten. He reported that he had got separated from the other two in the whiteout and had spent a day searching for them. When his frostbitten extremities made it impossible to continue the search he turned back down the mountain. It was all very vague and hard to piece together. I thought the least I could do was retrace their steps as far as Madhmaheshwar and hired a Nepali porter at Guptkashi.

In the temple dharmshala at Madhmaheshwar I met an old shepherd who unlike the others I questioned was unusually garrulous. He said he knew exactly what had happened. He had assisted the frostbitten porter on his return and had worked out the details of the tragedy from the porter's account. According to the shepherd the boys had got as far as Kanchini Tal, a lake a day's steep climb above Burha Madhmaheshwar. When the blizzard hit them they had climbed away from the lake and in the whiteout had unwittingly walked off the edge of the sharp ridge that beetles opposite the dramatic face of Chaukhamba, an appalling drop of several thousand feet.

No trace of the missing climbers has so far been found. Scrutiny of the boys' route and timings by the mountaineering analyst Joydeep Sircar has suggested that the porter's mention of a lake (which the shepherd mistook to be Kanchini Tal) was more probably Maindgalli Tal much higher on their route. When I did check out Kanchini Tal I was depressed to find on the climb the remains of another accident, the strewn parts of what looked like the wreckage of a jet fighter. A pea soup fog threatened to engulf our investigations but I just had time to reach the ridge and view the horrendous fall opposite Chaukhamba's terrific plummet into the gorge. Shipton and Tilman felt vexed they had chosen a poor line down from the crest. In fact it was so bad that they nearly perished from hunger in forest so thick they could hardly hack a way through. All the lines I saw from the crest seemed to share similar perpendicular options. This is why no pilgrims can go directly from Kedar to Badri (only forty kilometres as the crow flies).

Does the Kedar–Badri divide actually constitute the crest of the Great Himalaya? According to purists of the Survey of India the Kedar massif and its extension westwards is a continuation of the Dhaula Dhar. This definition is hardly meaningful. The Dhaula Dhar is typically the defining range of middle Himachal, the classical backdrop to the towns dotting the Kangra valley. To extend this range into Garhwal is a highly academic construction and flies in the face of local feelings and common sense.

In this minority colonialist view Chaukhamba is taken as the junction where the Great Himalaya subsumes the Dhaula Dhar, another twist to the bizarre nomenclature devised by the British, ignorant or contemptuous of realities that did not fit into their paramount preconceptions. Even Kenneth Mason a firm believer in the infallibility of empire felt constrained in the pages of the *Himalayan Journal* to rein in some of the unsubstantiated claims of Sir Sidney Burrard who used his position as Surveyor General to pass of opinion as fact. It was Burrard who devised the misnomer 'Kumaun Himalaya' instead of 'Uttarakhand Himalaya' either not realising or simply indifferent to the gratuitous insult this term amounted to for the people of Garhwal.

Pilgrims on the Panch Kedar circuit after visiting the main shrine had to return to Ukhimath then climb to the watershed temple of Tungnath. From this third part of the divine body of Shiva the path went down steeply to Gopeshwar. Before joining the main Badri pilgrim route a diversion from the village of Mandal climbed to Rudranath amidst dense jungle and then followed an undulating route to Kalpnath, the fifth and last of the modern list of Panch Kedar temples. In earlier days the last temple was Pashupatinath and the true devotee of Shiva would always complete the circuit with a visit to Nepal. This climax probably derived from the wandering habits of the Gorakhnath panthis known for their assiduous pilgrim culture. Throughout the hills and indeed throughout India you still find Gorakhnath akharas or ashrams for the itinerant followers of what was once considered an unorthodox sect.

Usually these were places away from the beaten track and of extreme natural beauty or of spiritual significance such as the sources of many of India's rivers or sacred flames worshipped at Muktinath and Jwala Mukhi. Gorakhnath sadhus are readily distinguished by their large earrings traditionally made of rhinoceros horn. Today after centuries of being considered unorthodox and down-market the sect is in the process of being mainstreamed. A similar process has assimilated the erstwhile unorthodox Virasaiva sect which services Madhmaheshwar. It came into existence around the same time as the Gorakhnath order and was initially hostile to brahminical dominance. With the advent of political independence Hindu sects which had looked down on one another over the centuries are now closing ranks in the expectation that under a common banner they will be able to have a say in furthering the destiny of sanatan dharma.

One little trek between Mandal and the start of the climb to Rudranath deserves mention for the electrifying beauty of its setting. It takes only a five kilometre walk through easy pine jungle to arrive at the attractive old temple of Ansuiya Devi where women pilgrims repair in the hope of conceiving a child. As with other prenatal promissory temples women who spend the night here are sometimes blessed with a dream of their impending motherhood.

Walk another two kilometres into the ascending jungle past the pine belt and you enter a magical clearing dedicated to Atri Muni one of the founding fathers of sanatan dharma. Set in a circle is a wall of climbable rock and halfway round a magnificent clear waterfall sprays out a fan of feathery runnels. The rock behind the cascade had been hollowed out by the spray and a narrow gallery encircles this poetic composition above the dell. To get up to this astonishing catwalk you find a heavy iron chain embedded in the rock at a height convenient for the hand to grasp. How this was fitted into the rock is anyone's guess but its presence adds mightily to the sense of nature's miraculous arrangements.

Swinging up on the chain the pilgrim hauls himself onto the ledge and begins a sideways shuffle towards the waterfall. But then you are brought up short by a solid rock projection that prevents further progress. Again the miraculous is evident: if you bend down you spot bored through the base of rock, a short tunnel that just allows passage for the human body. After this adventurous made-to-measure wriggle the ledge runs clear to the back of the fall. From there you can climb back down to the stream and complete what to my mind is the best little trek in Garhwal.

16
A Date with Pokhu

As a student of comparative religion I am interested in enquiring into the villagers' view of the deities in whose dev bhumi they reside. On my very first foray into the range I stayed a few days in Swami Shivananda's ashram in Rishikesh. While I could not deny the genuine atmosphere of devotion for the river goddess Ganga Mai I was irritated by all the talk of spiritual purity by people who excreted into the very river whose water they drank claiming it held magical properties, then queued up at the ashram dispensary for pills to cure their dysentery. Whatever else popular faith in the Himalaya was known for it certainly wasn't amenable to the cold logic of the mind.

Many foreigners find the preoccupation of Himalayan villagers with bhut-pret superstition to be a sign of arrested spiritual development but having grown up in a Scottish village where the belief in fairies and other psychic phenomena is very real (though never publicly acknowledged) I could detect a familiar pattern. The critics are right to suggest that superstition holds back the soul's growth but the villagers are not wrong in acknowledging the play of spirits that in practice are as much maverick energies as malevolent forces.

Travel along the length of the range and a common fatalistic perception holds about the place of the human presence in these towering surroundings. People live here on sufferance. In the easier climes of Rome, Mecca or Benaras, religious functionaries flaunt golden vessels and vestments as middlemen of the divine; the village priest in the Himalaya accepts his role as faltu, an extra with little significance before these looming altars of the gods.

Invariably when the visitor passes a wayside shrine in the hills there will be no priest on duty. You make your offering of a flower, a coin or a sweet before the crude representation of the deity confident in the belief that your prayer, if it comes from the heart, will be heard. Cynics say temples come up just to cash in on our religious sentiments but this is only partly true. Over the years on my walks round Camel's Back in Mussoorie I have seen a rock shaped roughly in the form of an elephant's trunk become part of institutional religion by annual additions motivated both by affection and the profit motive. First someone painted in eyes to make the effect of an elephant's head more realistic. This was at the level of an animist response to a prehistoric creature that impressed by its size, shagginess and power. Then after the manner of much of Hindu expansion, a pandit painted the sacred 'Om' on the elephant's head to include it in the pantheon of orthodoxy. From there 'it' soon became 'he', identified as Ganesh the lovable elephant-headed son of Shiva and Parvati. As a final touch to prove the institutional takeover, the rock was painted in lurid colours and a locked metal box placed before it for offerings. After another year the box was enclosed by metal railings with space enough between them to allow the fingers of devotees to drop offerings in the box (but not enough to allow anything to be removed!)

In this unfolding of the human urge to worship—and aggrandise—can be detected both affection and acquisitiveness. The priest who takes the offerings feels he has performed a public service by painting the idol. And how else will he cover the cost of the railings? It is in such a down-to-earth response to the requirements of both gods and man that the hillman's pragmatic approach to religion needs to be understood.

One useful social advantage that has flowed from belief in local devtas has been the low level of crime in Uttarakhand, so low in fact that outside the towns there have never been police stations.

A DATE WITH POKHU

Law and order in the villages has always been the domain of the Patwari, a civilian revenue clerk charged with transacting land matters (and therefore assumed to be open to corruption). The Maharaja of Tehri used the awe villagers felt for more famous devtas to his own advantage and when a man suspected of murder was arraigned before him the Maharaja decreed he go under escort to the court of Pokhu, the devta of Netwar on the westernmost confines of the state. It was a ten-day walk from Tehri to Netwar and all along the way the prisoner would hear people discussing his fate. Going before Pokhu implied some capital offence had been committed and no mercy would be shown to the offender, whereas in the court of the king at Tehri the punishment at least would be humane. Pokhu's reputation created the utmost dread for he dwelt in a dangerous and inaccessible valley where the people were reputed to be as wild as the animals that inhabited it. As the undertrial drew nearer to Netwar the stories of horror mounted, invariably making him collapse and confess. This way the Maharaja saved himself the expense of lawyers and a lot of time. Pokhu had proved to be a lethal legal instrument in hastening the course of justice and adept at doing what the other leading deities of the world's religions have done—instill an unholy fear in the breast of offenders.

My own trek into Pokhu's domain was fascinating, the sylvan beauty of the upper Tons valley adding to the curious religious customs of the villagers. These are now under siege from modern influences that range from television exposure (of mainstream epics) to the influx of largely urban trekkers en route to Har ki Dun.

It was Jack Gibson of the Doon School who enthused his pupils to undertake mountaineering in this area. Gibson was the godfather of Indian mountaineering which is reckoned to have taken birth in 1951 when his understudy Gurdial Singh, a housemaster at the Doon School, led a successful expedition to Mount Trisul. Significantly this early success was achieved in the old-fashioned alpine manner of approaching the mountain with aesthetic regard for its beauty and a scientific curiosity to record the natural history along its trail. The motivation was entirely sporting with little concern for macho flaunting of muscles or the political compulsion to fly a flag.

For years Gibson went back using Ruinsara Tal as a base for several attempts on Bander Poonch. Because he was an all-rounder he also took the opportunity to ski. Modern climbers have short affairs with their peak chosen for its height and saleability to a sponsor who can advertise his equipment from a successful ascent. The beauty of approach rarely gets a mention in these expeditions owing to the fixation with altitude. How can one convince the world that the trek from Netwar to Har ki Doon is infinitely more beautiful than most of the approaches to the big league peaks? Not only is the natural scenery memorable but the architecture and customs of the villagers are likewise fascinating. Gibson kept going back because he had the soul of a true mountain lover concerned with the whole scene and not just the highest point on the horizon.

Perhaps as a teacher of geography Gibson knew that this fixation with stature was not exactly scientific and that the world's actual highest peak is not Everest but (much higher) a mountain that rises from the floor of the Pacific Ocean. Nor is Everest the highest when measured from the centre of the earth, the strictly scientific way to measure all features on our planet. The winner of that contest would be Chimborazo in the Andes.

It is amusing to note that when the British surveyors were compiling the heights of the great Himalayan peaks in the nineteenth century many alpinists were convinced that the highest mountains in the world existed in the Andes. In a similar patronising gesture some climbers wished to rename the Himalaya as the 'Indian Alps'. One British surveyor recommended that Shiv Ling and the three Bhagirathi Sisters be named after the patron saints of the United Kingdom: George, Andrew, David and Patrick!

The modern motor road to Yamnotri bifurcates at Naugaon and the western fork leads to the valley of the Kamala which has more Buddhist remains. At Jarmola on the crest of Tons valley, the scenery turns sub-alpine. Dark pine forests enclose steeper valleys that hide the sun and cause the villagers to switch from cotton to woollen clothes. At Morhi, the Tons river is cold, jade and bigger than the Yamuna. The pandits in naming the Yamuna as one of the seven sacred rivers of Hinduism could hardly have been ignorant of the fact that the Yamuna is but a tributary of the Ganga and in hydrographic terms only an affluent of the Tons. Was the Tons left out of the reckoning because of its Buddhist associations just as the Mahanadi in Orissa and the Krishna in Andhra Pradesh were omitted from the sacred list? Where the Tons and Yamuna meet at Dak Pathar the flow of the former is twice that of the latter.

Perhaps another compelling reason was the religious custom around Purola which till very recently was famous for its espousing the Kaurava family who aimed to overthrow the Pandavas. The Kauravas are the designated enemy in orthodox Hinduism. Lower down the course of the Yamuna is Lakhamandal where the five brothers who represented true religion were sought to be burnt alive by their usurping Kaurava cousins. Duryodhana was the hero of the villagers around Purola till government-controlled television beamed mainstream orthodoxy exposing him as the villain of the *Mahabharata*. Overnight allegiances have changed and temples once dedicated to Duryodhana have been conveniently converted into shrines in honour of Shiva. But it is harder to conceal the reality that many village men still sport the name 'Duryodhana Singh'.

The backwardness and inaccessibility of the villages along the Tons that divides Uttarakhand from Himachal preserved social practices that offend orthodox Hinduism. Polyandry (practised by the Pandavas themselves) was an economic necessity and the farming of girls for the flesh trade in the plains another grim compulsion of these interior farmers whose produce, even had there been a surplus, could never reach a market. On top of their social backwardness is the security mantle around Chakrata, a military intelligence centre since British times, which prevents local educational development. Today the entire subdivision is officially out of bounds to visitors.

The one crop that grows wild and fetches a good return on the black market is opium and Chakrata is rumoured to be a collection centre for the surrounding villages. Unwittingly protected by the blanket security cover local students are said to smuggle out the opium on motorcycles.

The climb to Har ki Doon is at a very easy gradient and passes through the most delightful growth of chestnut I have found in the Himalaya. However with the onset of tourism the villagers who offer their services as guides need to be watched closely. It is better to choose an older man accustomed to the less acquisitive norms of portering than appoint a young layabout who may have a drug problem or the dream of quick riches by furtive examination of his clients' luggage.

I had the good luck to share the services of a tried Dehra Dun guide who works for a friend in Mussoorie. When not guiding trekking parties the guide works in a bank and it is extraordinary to witness his range of talents. He embodies authority as expedition sardar but in emergencies will cheerfully double up as coolie, cook or entertainer. One evening at Seema before the final stage to Har ki Doon I spotted our guide flirting with the lady who ran the wayside dhaba. Shortly after this the lady disappeared and the guide took over preparation of the evening meal. Later while we were enjoying the last of the meal the lady turned up, resumed her duties and as the chef's *coup de grace* served some local wine freshly distilled at the promptings of our guide.

The village of Osla above Seema is remarkable for the beauty of its domestic architecture. All the houses are built of deodar and designed to withstand the heavy snow that hits this valley situated under the Sutlej–Tons watershed. The aroma of Himalayan cedar planks is a delightful tonic to the tired trekker. Sadly the government tourist bungalows along the trail are totally inappropriate for the climate and terrain. The poverty of imagination displayed by the planners is more depressing than the poverty of the villagers. Worse is the fact that tourist managers see nothing tragic in how these cement barns constitute an environmental eyesore alongside the beautifully proportioned village houses.

Throughout Uttarakhand most tourist development has been

utterly dreary because the people who make the decisions have never trekked in their lives and have no idea how to build accommodation for those who do. As always in official matters no one is held responsible for these ugly and inappropriate constructions. The guilty officer is transferred and continues his mindless ministrations in some other department. The answer for a successful tourist policy is for the government to keep a low profile and let the locals provide the services.

Visitors to government tourist bungalows always remark on the surly and apathetic behaviour of the staff. They have no interest whatsoever in tourism nor any incentive to make the bungalows efficient. As government employees they merely have to show their faces in order to qualify for their wages.

Seema has one of these monstrous government cement barns, icily cold, with high ceilings and arctic draughts blowing through. Whereas in the old forest bungalows the chowkidar took pride in the fittings, in these faceless modern tourist extravaganzas the chowkidar has no loyalty whatsoever. There are freezing tiled bathrooms and taps with no water. If the trekker could stay the night in village homes the memory would linger.

The beauty of the setting against the mindlessness of official planners means that the sensible trekker will take his own tent. Trekkers also have to be on guard against official deviousness. All tourist trails have fixed porter rates set by the local magistrate but no one will share this information. What the visitor must remember is that these rates are for a parava, a reasonable walking distance for a heavily loaded man. Visitors who are short of time and cannot go at the rate of six kilometres a day (the average length between paravs on steeper terrain) should get their porter to agree to a daily wage. Unless you make this point clearly, at the end the porter will claim three times the amount based on his calculations of paravs. Another trick is to demand food although the cost of rations is already factored into the portering fee.

Local officials generally connive at this ripping off of the visitor. The short-sightedness of this greed that can be found at many tourist centres in the hills guarantees that the most important means of positive advertisement is lost. Word of mouth commendation is the best means of ensuring a steady flow of trekkers.

Tourists too are often to blame in seeking to shortchange the local people and many set a dismal example in littering the trail with trash. They burn bungalow quilts while smoking in bed and drop broken glass on the trail that cut the feet of sheep and cattle. Some are not averse to purchasing family heirlooms for a song playing on the ignorance of the village owner.

The most depressing interface of tourist negativity between client and government is at Har ki Doon itself. It is difficult for the visitor to keep warm without a fire here, just above the tree line. Money passed to a willing hand will see some firewood delivered and daily the beauty of the surroundings shrinks from these clandestine undertakings. Kerosene stoves could easily be organised, but are not.

The bonus of being above the tree line is that you leave the frustrations of government behind and rejoice in the contentment of the nomad. Nothing really beats a night out under the stars with the wind sifting the grass around. There is safety in numbers here and when I lie alone I am always a bit uneasy about the possible trample of bears.

One great luxury now lost to the traveller is a dead tree trunk for sitting up over, watching its embers as you cook your night meal and roast a few potatoes in the ashes for tomorrow's march. Then you settle down to sleep snugly in its glow. How I envied the sadhus who camped in the akhara at Mirtola and were supplied a tree trunk for their nightly wants along with rations. It would still be smouldering when they left next morning. Doused it would be the beginnings of another fire for the next incumbent. Fire is the most mystical of elements, and my favourite aid to meditation. The invention of electricity has all but killed our wonder at it. Rejoicing in these pleasant unforced camps we rarely stop to think what life is like for the armed forces encamped perforce on the borders where the kerosene stove is their only means to survival and the days drag on as endlessly as the nights. What punishment is greater than boredom and this must be the lot of most jawans. The only small mercy for the frozen jawan on sentry duty in a high altitude bunker is that he is not bothered with the spectre of leaping shadows and ghostly sounds that assault the ears of the trekker who camps below the tree line. On the whole ghosts (for obvious reasons) do not haunt much above the habitations of man. A ghost's favourite place, if the shikari Jim Corbett is to be believed, is the old British dak bungalow. If murders of passion were actually carried out in these edifices of the Raj I have yet to read a collected account of them. That dirty weekends regularly went on (and still do) will be disputed by no one who has marked their exquisite siting guaranteeing ultimate privacy.

Set usually on a hilltop above the village and hence incommunicado at night from the spell of intervening ghosts the sahib shikari was free to have his way with any local lass his discreet orderly vouched for, or for that matter with the orderly himself. I was amused on one occasion when I visited Mirtola in winter and passed by the Panwanaula dak bungalow (now demolished but in the early 1960s still standing). I heard voices and called out thinking it was the famous Shah brothers but then the voices stopped. I walked round to the front of the bungalow and there leaping up from a compromising position on the veranda was the son of the local political leader desperately tying the draw-string of his pyjamas while in the other direction scuttled a hill woman hitching down her voluminous skirts.

An intriguing touch to the down-to-earth role of devtas in the ordering of hill society is in the bizarre custom found in the Baspa valley. It shows how hard it is to generalise about a field so varied as that of popular religion in the Himalaya. At the Chitkul temple in Kinnaur the Buddhist villagers punish the local Devi when she misbehaves. This means when the harvests are good she is honoured and given food but when the weather turns nasty so does the attitude of the village towards her. Then she is beaten up and locked away in a tower like a naughty child! The lesson here is that this village is the most interior of all and beyond it lies the border with Tibet. Just as the lower hills display cruder aspects of plains religion so does the interior hill area reflect a progressive dilution of norms. A whole field of study awaits the researcher and just one Himalayan province could easily provide material for a lifetime's engagement.

17
Choor Chandni

When the Nanda Devi Sanctuary was closed to climbers I did not give up my affair with the Goddess. I would now probe her outer defences. I set myself the Ronti Saddle and Sunderdhunga Col as targets. The latter I knew to be an impossibility. Only with great difficulty and the route finding skills of their sherpa companions could Shipton and Tilman make this vertical and dangerous descent from the south inner Sanctuary. Several climbers have looked up at it from the other end and declared it unfeasible. (The person most likely to climb it is Martin Moran who has finished several of the routes entered into by Shipton and Tilman.)

The year I went the path had been washed away in serious floods. I was quite relieved because everything I had heard about these towering cliffs sounded grisly and uninviting. Even so it was important to see just how impossible it was.

For the Ronti exploration I used two trips to the mystery lake at Rup Kund as acclimatisation exercises. The second in 1984 enabled me to climb over into the valley at the base of Trisul. After crossing the Silli Samuder glacier (notorious for its rocking boulders) we climbed to Hom Kund, the turning back point of the Raj Yatra in honour of the Goddess. A big rock marks this shallow seasonal tarn and two streams join under it to form the Nandakini. The base camp for Trisul expeditions is slightly higher on the way to the saddle. Shipton with Ang Tharkay had exited from the outer Sanctuary by this saddle but to get in was not easy without specialised equipment, otherwise obviously the shepherds would have used it.

I wanted to have a look but the weather was uniformly cloudy. Rather than pant up just to say I had been there—a refined form of torture—I turned back hoping to return at a more favourable season. My Lata porters and in particular Nathu Singh Bhutola were behind what little I did on my Nanda Devi treks. Nathu's strength was phenomenal. To balance it his judgement was sober. We went together on six treks in and around the Sanctuary and always he was a pillar of strength. Because I could only get away in the rains our progress was restricted but ironically the only time I did get time off in October when the weather was guaranteed to stay fine it snowed on Kuari from where we attempted to penetrate to the source of the Birahi (to have a look at another angle on Ronti). Heavy rain drove us out of the area and we doubled back hoping to trek to Rudranath but there too the weather remained demoralisingly cold and wet. That expedition intended to explore the 'backside' of Nanda Ghunti ended up in Ukhimath.

It also marked the cooling of my passionate affair with Nanda Devi. With the sanctuary closed and the Goddess now distant I decided I must see other areas of the Himalaya while I had the energy and for this reason I bought a second-hand motorbike in 1986. Another factor following from this desire to see other parts of the range (or at least a sampling of its regional variations) was my concern at how few steam locomotives were left running in India. Nobody seemed bothered to record these last wheezings of the iron horse so since time was of the essence (they were all due to be scrapped in the following decade) I decided to dilute my explorations of Garhwal and chase the chugging locomotive before it steamed away altogether.

I have always shared Longstaff's high opinion of Garhwal as possessing the most beautiful scenery in the Himalaya. But unlike Longstaff who seemed to have been everywhere and so could speak as a student of comparative beauty I was only going by gut instinct. It became important to try and see as much as I could of different Himalayan regions so I could judge Garhwal's claims evenly with others.

Looking back after a fairly varied coverage of the range I still find Garhwal unsurpassed in scenic beauty of the kind I respond to. But it has to be admitted that I have not seen Sikkim, Bhutan or western Nepal. The agitation for Gorkhaland started the day I drove towards Gangtok in April 1986 and it was not safe to ride a bike there. I had reservations about Bhutan's human rights record and anyway it charged a hefty tourist entry fee which I, as a budget traveller, considered elitist. Western Nepal I have been told is not so very different from travelling through Kumaun but its inaccessibility appealed to me, especially the startling course of its great river the Karnali which describes some extraordinary loops. Few realise that this is the 'Peacock River', one of the four great streams that rise from the vicinity of Kailash Mansarover. Like the Sutlej the Karnali is a poor relation in terms of spirituality though it has in fact holier credentials than the Ganga since it rises at the feet of Kailash.

It is hard to reconcile the alpine scenery on the southern side of the Himalaya with the stark moonscape in the trans-Himalaya. Trekking across the crest is an extraordinarily satisfying experience and its landscape has a compelling quality that draws you back. Unlike Garhwal there is less of the vertical in this spacious outback and the mind is silenced by the immensity of the prospect before it. The perpendicular appeal of Garhwal is due to a more sensuous arousal where shaggy forest and shattered cliff combine in a heroic handshake against the background noise of drumming torrents. It is the difference between the void experienced by the soul and the manifest Divine felt by the heart. Wonder lurks in both and the Himalayan walker is grateful for the luxury of such contrasting beauty. Both have to be experienced to get the full measure of the range.

Of all the alpine areas I have travelled through I still find Garhwal easily the most ravishing. Kashmir's attractions are softer and Jammu's less dramatic. I find Himachal around Chamba too dry for my liking and this extends across the Pir Panjal to Pangi. Middle Himachal around Shimla is more pretty than uplifting and I have found the same to be true of Jubbal and the Pabbar valley. But once you cross back into Uttarakhand at Tiuni and climb to the Tons valley the scenery seems to soar. As a lover of forest walks I find this sylvan largesse exists right across Garhwal (if you know where to look) and in a superb climax these forests lead up to the deliriously beautiful buggials, situated in front of the glowing panorama of snow peaks. It is the combination of forest, buggial and snows that promotes Garhwal to my top spot.

Kumaun follows in second place but due to the angle of run of the Himalaya the province sees the beginning of some drought-prone areas. The foothills of western Nepal presumably share this tiredness of the soil though less since there would be little ingress of chemical fertilisers. I have covered the length of Nepal east of Nepalganj on my motorbike and found it to be teetering on the edge of aridity at least in the foothills. By contrast the lushness of Arunachal which catches the bulk of both monsoons is almost embarrassing. Here the jungles teem with growth which often seems out of control. But lacking from the tourist angle are accessible view-points facing the snow peaks. This is at present country for the anthropologist and botanist more than for the mountain aesthete. However passing through on a motorbike gives but a fleeting taste of the surroundings and a tourist's conclusions will be highly subjective.

The easiest way for me to start checking on Garhwal's claims was to move next door to Himachal. One peak visible from Mussoorie proved very intriguing. Instead of looking north you looked west for this bulky mountain. Set in the Lesser Himalaya, Choor Chandni just falls short of the 12,000 ft mark by five feet. It is visible from the plains and is supposedly called 'Silver Sweeper' because it is the Himalaya's lowest peak that holds snow for five months of the year. As a menial summit compared to the peaks of the Great Himalaya the mountain is viewed as bottom of the caste pecking order. It is recognisable from afar by the moonlight glinting on its flanks.

I was intrigued by its lowly social position in contrast to its great height. Did this freak of nature boast in Vedic times of a glacier from which sprung the favourite river of the ancient Aryans, the Saraswati? Over the centuries the Saraswati dried up and this could have been hastened by the disappearance of the glacier below Choor Chandni.

Captain White, an early British visitor to Mussoorie and the Yamuna valley, wrote a book that included a trek to the Choor (as the British referred to this mountain) illustrated with the author's own sketches, extremely well drawn. I could not follow White's route which would have taken me west of Mussoorie to Chakrata since the latter town is out of bounds to curious visitors. Instead I had to take a circuitous bus tour from Nahan in south-eastern Himachal, to Haripurdhar, a lofty road junction overlooking the Tons.

Nahan is a quiet semi-hill station once famous for its iron foundry. It was the capital of Sirmur state and has a well-laid-out plan. I would go as far as claim it is the most attractive hill town I have seen in architectural terms. A palace commands the high ground and a chaugan (polo playing field) runs alongside. The roads winding round the hilltop are lined with small but handsome houses built of cobbles since good stone is hard to find on this black gravelly first rise of the Himalaya. The town viewed from the palace falls away in several Italianate touches with formal gardens and artificial lakes now not well looked after but still with enough style to suggest what royal taste must once have obtained here. Other parts of the town wander off into bosky forest and small temples sit serenely as though undisturbed since Vedic times. The name Sirmur in British history occurs when the British, having defeated the Gurkhas near Dehra Dun, decided to recruit their defeated enemy in view of their bravery. Sirmur saw the raising of the first company of Gurkha riflemen.

Haripurdhar came into the news in recent years as a leg on a challenging Himalayan motor rally that involved international drivers. The rally soon lost its charm when politicians egged on the locals to throw stones at the windscreens as a sign of protest against elitist sports. Sadly for the reputation of Garhwal its most respected representative, Hemvati Nandan Bahuguna, stooped to these populist measures to win himself some headlines. Garhwal was projected throughout the world as a violence-prone tract, a travesty of the truth since the Garhwali is probably the most peaceable citizen in the entire Himalaya.

West from Haripurdhar runs a craggy ridge that culminates in the Choor, a rise of some 2000 ft in perhaps two kilometres. I was advised by the young man sitting next to me to get out at Baggi, a village he claimed was nearest to the bridle path that led to the summit of the Choor. My luck was in because this companion turned out to be the son of a forest guard who lived at Khanda Bana and this village possessed a forest bungalow where I could spend the night.

It was a long climb. We did not reach the bungalow till nine at night. Looking eastward my eyes were drawn to a bright spectacle of lights. What could this place be that seemed to be just across the valley? Of course it was Mussoorie, separated by the Tons–Yamuna basin. Just as I could see the Choor clearly from Landour bazaar so from Khanda Bana bungalow I could view the lights of Mussoorie. Incredibly, it had taken me three days to get this far from Mussoorie by bus.

In the morning I looked out onto the upper flanks of the Choor draped in dark conifer stands. I hadn't realised Khanda Bana was so high. Then as I looked down on the slate roofs of the village I saw a familiar temple. Where had I seen this before? It was from one of Captain White's sketches. The scene was just as it had been in the 1830s.

As I got onto the ridge and found the path leading to the temple under the summit of the Choor I looked back and had a stunning darshan of another familiar sight. Where had I seen that snow peak of such great character before? Then it clicked. This was Swargarohini, the gateway to heaven, whence the Pandavas had ascended to their promised rewards for never wavering from true dharma. The Yamuna valley as noted has both a Pandava and a Kaurava following. The Pandavas are said to have shared the local belief that from the doorway of the temple at Lakhamandal, with its statues dating from the Gupta era, you look straight onto the peak of Swargarohini. In point of fact Swargarohini has several peaks but what you see from Lakhamandal is not one of them. It is a modest but elegant outrider of the Bander Poonch massif. Swargarohini, seen close up from Har ki Dun, is a wild and unforgettable sight as it was at this distance on my climb up the Choor.

The temple priest, when I arrived at midday, invited me for a meal but I wanted to get a view from the top before the surroundings clouded over. It was April and winter weather was still to be guarded against. It was just as well I did not wait at the temple set in the lee of the northern face and almost a thousand feet below the summit. I had to scramble vigorously up large slabs and was impressed at how this peak at such an altitude could display the major league credentials of granite outcrops. I stumbled through snow to gain the top and there to crown my efforts and send the peak into the rank of 12,000 footers stood a concrete image of Shiva apparently erected by a local lala just to break the altitude barrier. It was done in the local idiom and to get the required height Lord Shiva assumed a rather elongated shape! It was a brave touch. Earlier, in 1834, Col. George Everest had raised a surveyor's pole over the summit to make it a crucial marker in his Great Trigonometrical Survey.

The weather was closing in fast and I had no chance to check the truth of the claim that you can see all four towns of Shimla, Chandigarh, Saharanpur and Mussoorie from the summit. To my surprise, my southward return route, despite facing the sunny side, was a steep slope smoothened over with two feet of snow. I wasn't dressed for glissading in fact—I was clad in jogging shoes, T-shirt and shorts.

There was nothing to be done but gingerly grope for a foot-hold on the snow. My shoes had hardly any grip and inevitably what started as a hesitant probe turned into a teetering skid. Just before I accelerated out of control I was able to grab the passing branch of a rhododendron bush. Despite my panic I was overcome by the sheer beauty of the flowers that were shaken out onto the snow by my passage. They were a magnificent mauve easily outclassing all the other shades of rhododendron I have seen. Their beauty having subdued my fear I was now able to extricate myself from the snow and alight eventually on a bridle path that wound round the summit cone presumably to take pilgrims from the village of Nahura to the temple.

I made good time noticing that the forest on the southern face was badly hacked for fodder and fuel. Westwards the valley dropped away so dense and sheer I couldn't see the bottom but I knew that across the divide lay the palace at Chail with the unusual claims of possessing the world's highest cricket pitch. This was where the Maharaja of Patiala, externed from Shimla society for his dashing way with the ladies, set up his hill seat. As well as cricket the Maharaja was a keen water sports enthusiast and is said to have invented the sport of white-water rafting in India when he experimented with an inflated rubber mattress in the Giri. Then, in the company of the Maharaja of Nalagarh, he sailed down the Giri to Dadahu in rubber dinghies, an expedition recorded by the latter Maharaja in his book *Crash, Dash and Splash*.

The Choor had certainly lived up to its reputation as a challenge not to be trifled with. When I had read Captain White's account of how hard it was to get to the top with, as he put it, 'one's breath on the eve of suspension', I thought it was poetic licence to impress the reader. In fact the Choor in bad weather could be a death trap. It is surrounded by trackless jungle and to prove that wildlife is still abundant I was told by a Gujjar I met when slightly lost in the jungle that the government was planning to keep out the graziers and convert the mountain into a musk deer reserve.

In two thrilling footnotes to my Himachal encounters I can make the unusual claim to have had both a leopard and a lion cross my path. The leopard appeared in front of my wheel as I tooled down to Solan at dusk on my motorbike. I had switched the engine off to save petrol after a long day's ride from Rampur Bashair and as I rounded a bend a leopard, full grown but lean, loped gently across the road. Though old and hungry he rippled with beauty.

He stood at the roadside unable to decide whether to climb the steep earth bank. As the bike was only ten yards away he was growling but not too ominously. Then when he concluded I wasn't much of a threat he loped back across the road, jumped the parapet and disappeared amidst the scrub on the steep slope.

The lion was met at the end of Renuka Lake, a popular tourist resort between Nahan and Dadahu. Formerly this was the Maharaja of Sirmur's fishing lodge but the government of Himachal has converted it into a wildlife park. The lion roamed free but was behind a high chain fence. Near Nahan in the Shivalik foothills the Himachal government has also created a very impressive fossil park with life-size prehistoric animals done in fibre glass. There is a small museum with some of Captain Cautley's finds for this was the area from which he dug out the remains of Asia's oldest human ancestor.

No account of Himachal would be complete without notice of the former rulers whose palaces, once so opulent, have gone to rack and ruin within a generation of republican indifference. Himachal had dozens of minor rajas most of whom could not adjust to the suddenness by which they were dethroned. Some went into politics some into business but most went into oblivion.

During the last years of the Raj, Himachali kings and princes had spent their summers in Shimla or Mussoorie dancing away the night impervious to the hostility of the new ruling Congress party. Because the British had deliberately encouraged their interest in everything useless they were ill-equipped to survive the dawn of India's new egalitarian constitution. As children they had been pampered by being sent to the best schools. If the yuvraj found Mayo too tiresome he would be sent to Doon and so on down the list. Princely logic told them it was only commoners who did everyday things like study and pass examinations. During their heyday the more important princes had the privilege of murdering their subjects secure in the knowledge they were above the law. So ingrained were these feudal attitudes that the arrival of independence was the equivalent of an atomic bomb dropped on their cloud cuckoo land.

They would now pay. Society that had publicly kow-towed to them bared its teeth and mocked the princes' vulnerability. From being honoured members of the establishment they were demoted in a socialist state to tourist attractions of curiosity value. Many of their stately homes were requisitioned by the government for offices and to keep up some of the style to which they were accustomed the princes had to turn part of their palaces into hotels. But their hearts, after a lifetime of spending, were not in earning. An exception was the Raja of Rampur Bashair, who went on to become a popular Congress chief minister of Himachal using what local affection remained for the princes to whip up support for his party. In Mandi the somewhat eccentric raja converted part of his palace into a hotel but saw it as a hobby rather than a business. When I stayed there I had the opportunity to dine at the royal table and found the old style still very much in place. A dozen solid silver bowls weighed down the heavy sterling plate with different vegetables and dals and visitors who did not believe in wastefulness had to swallow the amused assumption that only those badly brought up finished their food.

Mandi is a fascinating junction and the attractive town square is overlooked by the now run-down palace. Its royalty is believed to derive from a Bengali dynasty and this, it is said, explains the various strands of tantric culture found in the local worship. Within the medieval hill setting is a touch of Victorian pomp in the fine bridge (now too narrow to carry the traffic) that announced some jubilee of the Great White Empress.

Roads meet here for Kullu and Kangra and one survivor of the depleted culture of the princes is the corpus of hill miniatures commissioned by the hill rajas from Jammu to Garhwal. Though confined to stylised representations of the scriptures, the court painters still manage to convey the folk spirit of their region in their work. Little is known about the artists but the sheer lyricism of their lines now guarantees an appreciative audience and a demand for more information on their lives. The profession of painter traditionally fell in the category of entertainer and was equated in the public mind with singers, dancers and musicians, with the nuance of low caste that went with these occupations.

CHOOR CHANDNI

Living for many years in the (Indian) Hindu Himalaya I think the lack of a vibrant artistic culture such as is found in Buddhist regions like Zanskar, Spiti, Sikkim and Ladakh is due largely to the status of the shilpkar who for all his artistic and architectural skills was treated little better than a beast of burden.

Buddhism, free of these self-destructive societal urges, allowed every budding artist an opportunity to express his faith and an interesting demonstration of the difference can be seen on the Mall in Mussoorie where the local (mainly high caste) schoolchildren along with children from the Tibetan refugee school were invited to paint ecological slogans illustrated with paintings on the roadside parapets. The local attempts are crude and self-conscious while the Tibetan art is fluent and arresting. I noted also that the Tibetans were highly innovative using modern cultural totems like characters from *Tin Tin* to illustrate their theme. It might be added that Mussoorie has a thriving cottage industry of Muslim artists who can make world-class authentic copies of Old Masters paintings.

18
A Night on the Tiles

A brief glimpse of the Baspa valley on a motorcycling circuit of Lahaul and Spiti in 1990 decided me to go back and do a connecting trek from Sangla in Himachal Pradesh to Netwar in Uttar Pradesh. Restrictions had recently been lifted on the area but I was doubly safe having been invited by Romesh Bhattacharji to join a trekking group from St Stephen's College, Delhi. Bhattoo was an old hand at this area returning with several expeditions to try and climb peaks around Chango. Something of an expert on India's border areas he found a job best suited for his exploring talents: of excise officer deputed to investigate smuggling along the range.

Bhattoo was a great all-rounder, and with Adil Tyabji, made pioneering motorbiking trips in newly opened areas. I once accompanied him on a skiing trip to Narkanda with Chetan and Jaya, his twins. His enthusiasm for the mountains was infectious and this is what made him, long after he had left St Stephen's, organise a trek for freshers. The generation gap took its toll however. Bhattoo's innocent concern just to be there and enjoy the Himalaya received a rude jolt when the students told him quite bluntly they were only interested in achieving high altitude peaks which they could add to their *curricula vitae* to impress the boss of the company they hoped to join after graduation.

Bhattoo had two idiosyncracies. He never wore a hat in the

mountains no matter how cold and to add to the exposure level his head was permanently shaven as smooth as an egg. His other oddity was that he was the only person I met in the length of the Himalaya who never ate the staple diet of dal–bhat. This meant he went hungry on many occasions but then made up for it with gargantuan non-vegetarian meals. At Narkanda I remember he helped polish off a fifteen-egg omelette and probably would have had another but for the arrival of the sole bus of the day.

St Stephen's has a legendary reputation for voraciously hungry trekkers. Another hiking friend, Mandip Singh Soin, went with a St Stephen's group through Zanskar; when they emerged at Kargil ravenously hungry, they were invited into the officers' mess. They fell to whatever was put before them like locusts finishing all the supplies so that the commanding officer had to indent for more.

On the Sangla trip we did not have any record-breaking appetites perhaps because as a coeducational college the male students were occupied more with thoughts of flirting with the girls than eating. We got delayed by the weather and then after punctures arrived at Sangla to find that our contracted porters had all got tired of waiting and gone back home. This was the apple harvesting season and everyone was busy. It was pleasant to walk through the valley and be offered apples by the villagers as they plucked them. For once, poverty was not in evidence.

Sangla was a proud village with a fine wooden temple and our arrival coincided with the Phletch festival, the big annual event held in the spacious temple courtyard. The village houses were handsome structures built of wood with ornately carved verandas. The modern cement buildings were much less satisfactory. The houses seemed to stand on top of one another and ran down to the Baspa river where, over a small bridge, the forest bungalow lay. From the visitor's book it was noticeable that many famous names used to come here for the trout fishing but with the advent of dynamite used for road building the fish had all been blasted out of existence, a story every Himalayan region can echo.

I spent an hour having a Kinnauri cap fashioned for myself at the local tailor's. There was a tree stump last on which his natural coloured wood was stretched. He then cut some cotton material to be used as lining. Hill people are shrewd judges of the strength of textiles and will only buy a quality that matches up to their long-term expectations. It is amusing to see throughout any given district Dotiyal porters all dressed in shirts of the same violent turquoise colour. This means they had gone to the same shop in Naini Tal or Shimla where this tried and tested cloth had been sold. Normally black drill proves the most workmanlike outfit and it is a sign of a family's improved economic status if the womenfolk of the house appear in less durable fabric.

The most important part of cap making in Himachal is applying the coloured flash on the front and in Kinnaur the people take pride in theirs being traditionally of green velvet. Apparently this prized material is smuggled over from Tibet. A Kinnauri topi costs more than a Kullu topi and mine came to fifty rupees. Women as well as men wear the same hat and at the village of Pooh I heard complaints against the schoolteacher from lower Himachal who had tried to ban the wearing of the Kinnauri topi by girls; another example of the mainstreaming mindset that attempts to assert the ideal of a uniform India managed by majority values. In a border area this seems an injudicious policy and Kinnaur's balanced regard for both Hindu and Buddhist forms of worship could be put under threat. In Pooh a reaction against high caste interference had already begun and young Buddhists were being recruited for missionary work to defend their faith.

Our trek up the wooded gadera behind Sangla reminded me of my childhood climbs through the Ochil glens. But this was fairly serious mountain country where the dividing ridge between Uttar Pradesh and Himachal began to taper off in a series of passes between 18,000 and 14,000 ft. We spent the night on an open meadow with a few huts and hay lofts overlooking the ragged pinnacles of the Kinner Kailash range across the Baspa. In the full glare of the sun these smooth grey forbidding spires made me feel relieved to be on this side at Khanda Dogri where the villagers brought their cattle to graze in the monsoon.

The next day we hoped to reach the Rupin pass but soon went

astray. Every shepherd we met gave conflicting directions. This was because the ridge yielded several points of crossing and each shepherd had his own favourite. Lady Canning who had visited Lord Dalhousie in his retreat at Chini (above modern Kalpa) walked back over one of these paths from Sangla to Netwar apparently using a detour to take the slightly easier Nalgan pass east of the Rupin. This brings you out lower in the Rupin valley avoiding the rather bleak but dramatic terrain immediately across the crest under the shepherd's Rupin pass.

I went ahead with Ranu Gupta a senior student and very fit trekker but neither of our findings was conclusive. In the event because of the slow-moving main party we had to camp on a cold shoulder of mountain just below the snowline. On the third day out of Sangla we toiled up through the snow to cross the pass. It was humbling to be overtaken by a procession of sheep and goats who had found the perfect steady rhythm for this steep pull to the crest.

At the top we stopped for a group photo and found it was already one p.m. Looking south we were sobered to see not easier hills dropping into Uttar Pradesh but a cirque of wild high country snow-bound and bleak. Ranu had decided to push on ahead as he had to sit for an examination in Chandigarh and at the present rate of progress he would miss the date. I also found the going too relaxed for my tastes. I longed for a cross-country jog to put some life into my outing. Spontaneously I decided to accompany Ranu. If we set off immediately and kept up a fast clip we would be back in Mussoorie in three days. Bhattoo was an exemplary team leader always bringing up the rear and assisting the back markers. When he had no objection to my departure we packed a few biscuits, said our goodbyes, and began the descent from the pass, quite a grisly one, down a steep chute of rocks. Obviously this was used only by shepherds. It was far too dicey for the memsahib of the governor general to have negotiated. Lady Canning wrote a diary of her journey and sent it to Queen Victoria. She describes descending the pass on her 'honey pot', a rather daring expression for the humourless queen to be confronted with.

Ranu and I kept to a jogging rhythm and descended to a small lake iced over which was marked one of the sources of the Rupin. Later Bhattoo and his charges had to make camp here after a slow descent of the rock chute. To add to their discomfort their expedition stoves refused to light. Meanwhile in our dramatic retreat we passed a really magnificent waterfall fanning out into five channels. The narrow track made by the shepherds descended right in the lee of these beautiful tresses. Then we entered a ravine where snow bridges hid god knows what torrents below them. Each one had to be tested by the expedient of throwing rocks into the middle. This slowed us down. We were dismayed to see the sun begin to cloud over. Outjumping the ravines and zigzagging down the snow bridges we at last broke out into a broad valley with a forest at the far end of it. The river now free of the snow was flowing fast and fairly broad. We had no idea which side of the valley to take. This meant crossing back and forth to find easy ground but the water was freezing and came up to our knees. We saw a shepherd and yelled but he didn't register our presence above the roar of the river.

Just as the light faded we reached the first fringes of the forest. The river had carved a deep bed and again it was a problem to make headway because of the terrain. It was now quite dark and we were groping our way by the outline of the trees and the whiteness of the water. Sometimes it was easier to cling to the edge of the rushing river and risk scrambling over the snow bridges that extended down the bank. Where the river had gouged out the bank we had to climb up to forest level and pick a way over the boulders and litter of undergrowth. We were labouring under the unrealistic plan of reaching the first village before we packed in our jog for the night.

Common sense ought to have told us we were taking undue risks in unknown country and should bed down for the night. We had brought our sleeping bags and I had a rubber mat. Obstinately we continued to push our luck ferreting out a path above and along the riverbank. Eventually it became too dark to make out the way.

All we had was a pencil torch which we were loathe to use lest it be required for an emergency. Still we would not quit. In our minds we had convinced ourselves the forest must soon yield a path to the first village. Once we located it we could let our feet find their own way and continue to midnight if necessary. The moon was nearing full and our dark gropings would perhaps turn into a triumphal procession as the moon lighted our way. This was the classic recipe for disaster. To snap us back to reality came the worst moment I have ever experienced on a trek. Ranu was trying to find a way down to the water's edge and I was behind vainly trying to make out whether what I saw ahead was solid snow or running white water. The roar of the river was phenomenal and the wind off it viciously cold but we hardly noticed because of our intense concentration. Ranu peered down, shone the torch briefly then shuffled his way to the edge of a sloping boulder. Too late I saw from over his shoulder what I had taken to be a frozen bridge of snow was actually a violent stream of water rushing under the boulder.

There was a snow bridge jutting out midstream but between it and us roared a horrendous maelstrom. Ranu alerted himself just in time to the danger and his immediate reaction was to step back. But his balance was already in the forward mode as he peered ahead. This sudden change of stance put my heart into my mouth. Ranu began an agonising bodily conflict between willpower and gravity. I felt I was losing him to the racing river and dreaded what I would say to his family if he lost his footing as it seemed he must. But because of his splendid athleticism somehow his body righted itself and instead of sliding forward to certain death in the fury of the white water he began to inch back to safety.

By the time he retrieved himself I was drained of all energy. We had hopelessly misread the signs. We agreed it was suicidal to walk any more: we would have to find a camp. But the forest rose sheer from the riverbank in a steady sweep of conifer. I could make out the species because the moon was just beginning to light up the top of the ridge. We could find no flat land and had to struggle up through dense shaggy undergrowth. Ranu felt we might run into more danger if we continued higher but I wanted a site where our bodies would be wedged in by trees should we roll over in sleep or from exhaustion.

We compromised and stopped at the roots of the first big tree that offered us some protection from rolling down the slope. But there was no level space for two sleeping bags side by side. Being rammed one higher than the other on shelves only one foot wide offered little protection. For the rest of the night we huddled, stretched, agonised and groaned at what we had let ourselves in for. Two people and one rubber mat meant effectively we took turns at trying to sleep. Some sleep did come because after a six-hour jog our bodies cried out for rest. I dozed off flat on my back on the narrow shelf and woke to find myself bent round the tree trunk, my body having been wedged in by the weight of Ranu who, sleeping on a slightly higher shelf, had rolled down on top of me.

Strangely when I opened my eyes I was unconcerned with the inconvenience of our situation. The moon had risen and made the valley an exquisite masterpiece of back lighting. The splendour of the serried slopes of conifer marching up from the booming confines of the river and the glimpse of melting snow amidst the boulders made this a sight so ennobling I was stunned. The scene was like a recapitulation of Fraser's exalted painting of Gangotri albeit with moon instead of sun. Nature was telling us what we would have missed if we had been cautious and camped before entering the forest. Our rashness had been rewarded with a rare glimpse of mountain grandeur, and with a mind filled with these thoughts the night rolled away without any further regrets. As luck would have it I was carrying a nip of whisky and doubtless this enabled us to admire our surroundings.

When we looked down in the morning the irony of our situation was so blatant we had to laugh. Only a few feet beyond the place Ranu had been striving to reach, the river gave way to a regular path. We had missed our goal by a matter of a few feet. We set off after biscuits and water and within a few hundred yards downstream came across the second irony of our situation. Camped amidst their flocks were the shepherds who had overtaken us the day before as we had toiled up to the Rupin pass. Had we been able to reach their camp last night we would have had some food.

According to the shepherds' optimistic calculations the first village lay 'a few' kilometres ahead. We reached four hours later, at ten a.m. hoping for breakfast. But the village did not boast of a tea shop though there were offers to provide us vessels if we made our own tea. Rather than hang around we decided to continue to the next village which did not appear till noon. Strangely neither of these villages would allow us to open our solitary can of sardines. They had been indoctrinated by a missionary Hindu sect to eschew meat.

Generally caste in the hills has a lot to do with one's diet. Even amongst brahmins, distinctions are made between those who are merely vegetarian and those who even forego the use of onions. Some claim onions make a man overpassionate but it is just as likely that because onions flavour much of Mussalman khana they are looked down upon. Interestingly hill brahmins eat jumbu, the wild shallot that grows on the buggials, arguing that its leaves are less passion-producing than roots. The shastras were designed for Hindus of the Gangetic plains unfamiliar with life at high altitude. Only this can explain why the object used in Hindu temples to climax the worship of the deity—the chamar whisk also waved above the head of royalty—is a brush derived from the rear end of the shaggy nomadic yak.

The Rupin valley, joined now by the trail off the Nalgin, was a picture-postcard sight in October with the yellow stalks and red coxcombs of high altitude grains ripening. Buck wheat and millet are all that ripen at these elevations and lower down too the soil is too lean to support good crops of wheat. The river was a sparkling jade as it tumbled down the unrelenting fall of the valley and all afternoon we pounded down losing height, stopping only where a tea shop beckoned. The beauty of the Rupin and the character of the wooden-housed villages made the going pleasant and by four p.m. we seemed to be off the steeper slopes. As we settled down to chai at the first tea shop on even ground after a week of steep terrain the owner handed us a letter to read out. It was from a trader in Netwar stating the prices he was offering for charas (marijuana) and ophim (opium) both of which grew spontaneously hereabouts.

Ranu as a city-bred student was fascinated to be at the inception of the international drug chain. Pretending to be a seasoned operator he asked the old shopkeeper to show him the local quality. Immediately the old man provided a lump of black sulpha and another brown sliver of raw opium. Because of the poor soil the only crop the locals can raise is the poppy. Marijuana needs no cultivation: it grows wild.

That night as darkness descended we had to suffer for Ranu's curiosity. We could see the outline of a village in the dark across a stream but could not locate the bridge by which to get to it. We shouted for nearly half an hour before a woman came out and showed us to the tea shop where travellers could stay for the night. No one was answering our calls because they thought we were government inspectors raiding the opium growers.

We were now on the borders of Uttar Pradesh and next morning passed through its first village. We were greeted by two remarkable sights. One was of a huge spanking new temple of freshly sawn deodar beams with a notice above its entrance 'Harijans Not Allowed'. The other was a cricket match in progress where the local neta dressed in white kurta pyjama had lined up a dozen little children to bowl to him. Every ball was smashed away for an imaginary boundary. This scene of blissful rural contentment and massive outlay on timber derived from the profits of the opium business.

Netwar lay a few hours away by a path that followed the river. It was strange to be walking on level ground after so many days of climbing or descending. To change the rhythm we hitched a ride on a train of mules going to Netwar empty. The roadhead lay some distance above the river and in the heat of the day we had to sweat to reach it. But omelettes were available and so was an afternoon bus to Naugaon, the junction on the main Yamuna valley highway.

A NIGHT ON THE TILES

If we reached there before dark we could probably catch a truck or jeep going to Mussoorie or Dehra Dun.

Our luck was in. As we arrived at Naugaon I spotted a taxi driver I knew from Mussoorie who was returning from Hanumanchatti empty. Sardarji had stopped at Naugaon for his evening peg and with this inside him drove like the clappers to get us to Mussoorie by seven p.m. On the climb up we passed a crowd gathered around a broken parapet. A truck had disappeared over the edge killing its occupants. Unlike Sardarji its driver had had one peg too many.

19
A Clean Pair of Heels

On my third trekking foray into Himachal I tried out a more distant objective beyond the hill station of Dalhousie. In June 1993 I caught a bus to Paonta Sahib. When I first came to live in Mussoorie, this gurudwara where Guru Govind Singh grew up as boy on the bank of the Yamuna as it leaves the hills, was a tiny structure and the river so wide that the only way across was by cable and winch in a trolley. This was neither an elegant nor safe way to travel and with the erection of a large and architecturally ugly barrage a bridge was deemed necessary.

In the wake of the ensuing traffic the gurudwara was rebuilt and decked out in the latest glitzy style of the Sikh South East Asian diaspora. (The Sikh cloth merchants of Malaysia and Thailand send their children to Mussoorie schools.) Paonta remains amongst Himachal's only flat land and has developed rapidly. Northwards along the banks of the Yamuna are gurudwaras commemorating Guru Govind Singh's first victories on the battlefield.

My revised plan was to cross the Pir Panjal range to the north via the Sach pass into the Pangi valley. For this I had to go from Chandigarh to Chamba. My original plan had been over-ambitious: I wished to do a preliminary trek from Brahmaur to Manimahesh, south-east of Chamba, the sacred lake of Shiva. But the rains had set in and if the expedition proved too testing this would affect my greater aim of crossing the Sach pass. So I contented myself with admiring the remarkable medieval remains in the temple compound at Brahmaur.

After Kathmandu the Chamba region is probably the richest in Himalayan architectural and artistic expression. In spite of its princely layout and style I did not feel comfortable in Chamba. The terrain did not appeal and I detected an aridity that surprised me. The Ravi valley leading to Brahmaur was remarkably steep and bleak. Maybe these sheer slopes explained why the soil yielded little lush growth.

Returning to Chamba in the bus on a clear afternoon, rain clouds billowed up and then suddenly in a deluge the hillside above the road in front of us crashed down in a torrent of liquid chocolate. This mud slide was so powerful it blocked the road completely and when the rain stopped after half an hour the passengers had no option but to get out and leg it to Chamba. Luckily the road went downhill so with a judicious use of shortcuts we were able to arrive by nightfall.

I found myself strangely indifferent to the cultural artefacts on show in Chamba. Unlike in Garhwal where I would ask about every item that intrigued me, here I felt as a stranger it was none of my concern. I had to accept that having lived for twenty years in Uttarakhand I had become part of the region's culture and judged other cultures accordingly.

One thing that intrigued me about Chamba was why it did not boast of a regional hat that characterised the other valleys of Himachal. From the green flash of Kinnaur to the red of Rampur Bashair and from the maroon of Lahaul to the white of the Gaddis why did not this proud former state wear any distinguishing headgear? Was it tied up with the fact that Chamba marked the western limit of the Gurkha advance? Across the Pir Panjal divide the men of Pangi traditionally wore a white conical pointed cotton cap remarkably akin to the headgear still worn by Macedonians, the mountaineers of erstwhile Greece. To add to the mystery some have argued that the Pangi villagers with their fertility cults are descendants of Alexander the Great's army. Alexander was of course a man from Macedonia.

Dispirited by my ride in an overcrowded bus, and the unhelpful locals, I hired a guide to lead me to the Sach pass but had to wait an hour while he went to collect his gear. He demanded an advance of two hundred rupees to buy a pair of shoes with (as he put it) 'a sole'. I failed to understand the significance of this precaution and as a result destroyed any chance of emerging from this trek with fond memories. My own footwear was a pair of light trekking shoes hardly designed for icy slopes. The guide was a simple person eager to please and as always with a hillman his idea of distance was what he could do comfortably before nightfall, in other words, twice as much as outsiders bargained for.

We left at one p.m. and I was led to understand we had some eight kilometres to climb to Satrundi at the base of the pass, a height gain of five hundred feet per kilometre which seemed reasonable given the pleasant broad-leaved jungle through which the track wound. This was still very much the official bridle path over the Pir Panjal crest into Pangi for there was no other access to Kilar, the headquarters village. Either you could go all the way round via the Kangra and Kullu valleys to Lahaul to approach it along the Chandrabhaga valley (where a road had got to within some thirty kilometres of Kilar) or make an even greater detour through Jammu and approach from Kishtwar though there too the approach was by foot.

It was this isolated situation of Kilar that appealed to me. To walk along trails where the motor road had yet to intrude was an idea I responded to. I was also keen to verify the astonishing perpendicular fall of the Pir Panjal into the Chandrabhaga, a peculiarity of the eastern end of the range where the shepherds from Kangra having taken their flocks into the Ravi catchment led them over the Pir Panjal by a series of fearsomely steep passes, the paths so vertical even sure-footed animals can be jostled to their death.

We made good progress since my light pack was being carried by the long striding porter. By four I guessed we were long past the eight p.m. mark but oddly we seemed nowhere near the top nor indeed anywhere near the required height. By six I was beginning to get alarmed for we had covered some twelve kilometres by my reckoning and were still to break free of the tree belt. Our goal was the bungalow at Satrundi, claimed to be the highest in the Himalaya according to one tourist guidebook. What this translated into was the highest PWD bungalow in a habitable condition. Across the valley I was shown a jeep road that led to the bungalow and it seemed to spiral up forever.

As the day darkened there was a violent percussive storm followed by such a demented downpour that the paths underfoot were converted instantly into rivers of mud, freezing in their rush. To add to the misery we now emerged from the thick canopy of forest to take the full force of the rain. At least the cold drove us to walk faster to keep alive. The slushy hills began to grow bald suggesting these violent storms were the norm. Tugging dispiritedly up a series of mushy slopes we emerged at last on a rocky plateau against which the gleaming snows of the Sach pass stood out. The bungalow was perched against a huge cube of stone but to reach it we had to cross a full-scale river boiling down the ravine at furious bore. Fifteen minutes earlier the ravine had been dry.

What a way to end one's day—washed away in an arctic torrent. It was dark now and I wished I had never set foot in Himachal with its penchant to climax the day's trek with a cloudburst. But to save the reputation of the state my porter bundled me under his arm and with a kicking, struggling client he straddled the roaring stream in several desperate lunges. I was home if not dry and felt enormous relief at not having received a comprehensive ducking.

There was a crowd of villagers already in a dhaba behind the huge cube of rock and arrangements for bedding of sorts were available. The government had to maintain this formidable route as it was the sole lifeline for the villagers who lived across the Sach. Staying in the bungalow cost hundred rupees and I gladly paid, thinking how nice it would be to sleep with a fire in the grate. Stupidly I overlooked the deadly dangers of this luxury at 3350 metres where oxygen is in short supply.

Food was ordered from the dhaba and the storm cleared to reveal a splendid moonlit view of the fresh snow draping the range over which we would stamp out a path tomorrow. I got into my sleeping bag on a charpoy but found sleep would not come. So I sat up, lit a candle and wrote up my notes. It was the guttering of the candle flame that made me realise why I couldn't sleep—the fire was stealing what little oxygen there was and my mind was getting panicky from the shortage.

Getting up I strode over to the door and threw it open. With the surge of cold air my mind was immediately calmed, but now it was the turn of the porter, lying wrapped up in front of the fire, to complain.

Just when the sweet tendrils of sleep began to cling, the dhaba owner crashed in with glasses of tea. It was four a.m. and official practice demanded all users of the Sach get up for an early start. The porter and I set off up the steep snow slope with me trying to fit my footsteps into his long stride. At four-thirty I glanced back and to my surprise beheld strung out in a line behind me a dozen villagers, men and women, returning home after work in Chamba. They climbed effortlessly chatting as they went and passed within a matter of minutes, never losing the economic pace of their ascent.

Because of my poor choice of footwear and the forgotten ice axe, I was struggling and sweating to make headway and this was before the sun had made its appearance. Now I realised the wisdom of the early start and steady pace. It enabled people to be atop the pass by ten and have a meal in the well-provided dhaba. If the weather stayed fine the villagers could catch up on some sleep. The fact that everyone travelled together was another practical safety measure. That way though it slowed down the pace of the main party it meant no one lagged too far behind.

Next in my line of vision was a man bent double with what looked like a Father Christmas sack on his back. He too despite his load greeted us and passed through to follow the main party's path. The porter explained he was the daily postman who would dump his load at the top. This would be collected by the halkara from the other side of the pass. The large sack signified the day's post for the whole of the Pangi valley.

The snow got progressively softer as the morning warmed up.

I got in last but managed to reach the dhaba before the sun really bogged down the climb. Like everyone else I tucked into a huge steaming plate of dal–bhat and listened to the consensus on the weather. It was definitely going to snow according to the regulars and I was advised to discharge my porter and pay one of the villagers' for the descent to Pangi. My porter had been hired to see me over the pass and off the worst of the snow but I accepted the verdict of the main party. One of them would now carry my rucksack and agreed to be responsible for seeing me down to the tree line. In spite of the weather warning we all drowsed till midday then set off down the even deeper snow slopes to the north. Luckily the sun had not played upon them and the top crust bore the weight of a fleet-footed traveller, provided he kept up a springy momentum. If too slow he crashed through up to his thigh. To demonstrate the smart movement required, a village woman in the Pangi shawl of black and white checks strode briskly down the slope and with a clockwork high-kicking motion skipped effortlessly over the snow surface, each step performed in perfect balance so that her heel bit in to get a footing but with enough spring to bounce her out again. What was most remarkable about this precise and effective snow craft was that the woman was wearing the local grass slippers. I saw them close up at the dhaba and wondered how these loosely woven twine sandals stood up to such heavy use. They were brilliantly adapted to the conditions, acting as a snow shoe with a broad platform for a sole. Surprisingly in spite of their flimsy and chilly appearance no snow got into them but this no doubt was due to the woman's skill in her 'Knees-Up-Mother-Brown' routine.

My own descent fell miserably short of local requirements and it became embarrassing to pick my way down at a crawl with the others charging swiftly past. On one icy slope where I was stuck, leaning back with knees bent in a poor man's skiless glissade, an old man waltzed past with the greatest of ease, balancing on two bamboo canes to brake his descent. What superb mountaineers these villagers were and what a complete ass I was making of myself. First on my bottom and then on my knees I scrabbled a way down, last man in to the next dhaba which stood perilously perched on a snow-draped cliff.

Everyone laughed sympathetically as I woefully dragged myself in. With all the effort I was ready for an omelette with my tea. To my dismay I was told we were only half-way off the pass and two more hours of snow lay ahead on less steep but more tricky terrain because of crevasses. However my confidence improved on hearing this for I could keep up on less precipitous ground. Besides it is those at the front who tend to fall into crevasses. I was safe bringing up the rear!

One of the party was a government official who I later learnt was a plainclothes police officer. He was very solicitous and keen to help but in the process kept trying to ferret out information on my plans. The fact that I didn't have any offended his official mind. How could anyone just want to cross the Sach to Pangi without a specific motive? I was obviously up to no good. Luckily I was headed for Kilar and had no plans to turn west and enter the Kishtwar region, where rumblings of terrorism were spilling over from Kashmir into an area almost impossible to police, the high regions of Jammu.

My inept performance on the snowy descent must have reassured the policeman that even if I was a threat, the only damage I was likely to do was to myself. But I did pick up slightly on the more even lower slopes though this meant negotiating some hair-raising passages along melt streams that had formed under the ice. At last we saw some stately fir and dropped down off the moraine to the delightfully sylvan bungalow at Brindabani. This was at a more sensible height than Satrundi and was accordingly much more comfortable. I paid off my assistant and adjourned to the dhaba where my arrival raised a cheer from the main party who had already rested for an hour and were ready to do the last stint to Kilar.

This meant dropping down steeply to the Chandrabhaga and then toiling up to their goal at 9000 ft, to complete sixteen hours on the go.

They were inured to the hazards and punishing schedule of the Pir Panjal crossing. With a jeep road only a few months away they would soon have an alternative way out of their valley but obviously to get to Chamba it would still be cheaper and quicker to put on their grass sandals and glissade.

A brilliant alpine setting greeted me next morning as I started on the last leg to Kilar. The path dropped through some really superb forest and at last I was confronted with the great steepness of the north face of the Pir Panjal. The path zigzagged down to the river where a friendly Nepali invited me into his dhaba and refused to accept any money because I spoke so highly of his country. The stuffed paratha and rajma dal tasted good after the walk in the fresh air but now the sun was in the ascendant and across the river I could see the tin roofs of Kilar high on a bare hill, reached by a long winding path that first went down steeply on this bank then up sheer on the other.

For these few kilometres I was able to enjoy the last of the undisturbed bridle path but then near the river a new alignment was being dug for a proposed motor road that would eventually link up Lahaul with Kishtwar. Nepali labour gangs were at work cheerful and industrious despite the steepness of the terrain along which the road was being pushed. In the old days travellers along the Chandrabhaga valley would talk of traversing cliff faces clinging grimly to whatever holds they could find.

Luckily I met an unloaded muleteer returning to Kilar and so was able to cut down on the sweat to reach Kilar's lofty perch. The tiny township had a lot of character but was woefully backward otherwise. I couldn't find a chemist shop to buy even aspirin; the government hospital didn't have any either. The whole valley was similarly bereft of any modern conveniences. There were no vegetables to be had anywhere and the few dhabas run by the locals were miserably provided. The old British dak bungalow however was built like a Scottish castle with a massive staircase and big rooms that looked out onto the stunning snows of the Pir Panjal. Obviously this is a hill station waiting to be discovered though its proximity to the Jammu border must make its attractions seem risky. The new motor road from Lahaul while bringing the promise of an easier life for the deprived villagers of Pangi will also bring the risk of trouble makers.

The beautiful walk up the Pangi valley passed through splendid forests all of which bore the brunt of road making. What a magnificent walk this must have been before the bulldozers and the contractors came with their labour gangs. The road was literally being carved out of the cliffside, pneumatic drills piercing the silent trail.

I stayed in delightfully preserved forest bungalows and visited primitive fertility temples whose crude sexual imagery has been censored by fussy government officers blocking in the original wood carving with alien black marble. For the villagers the prospect of being brahminised is probably better than languishing without basic amenities. But it seems insensitive of the twice-born do-gooders to destroy the local cultural touches in their zeal to show India as uniformly orthodox. What they will achieve is an India poorer by the loss of this unique cultural *cul-de-sac*.

I only saw one Macedonian hat worn by an old villager working in a road gang but just as interesting was the beautifully embroidered headpiece women used to cover their topknots. Known as joji they were unique to Pangi and a lot of work went into their crafting.

After the idyllic forest bungalow at Cheri the bridle path rapidly merged with the works for the new motor road. The forest was taking a beating but still retained great beauty as it mantled the feet of the towering range above it. I met an old shepherd sitting tired at the roadside and stopped to chat. He had come from Kangra over the crest, with a flock, because his sons, taking advantage of the Gaddis' scheduled caste status, were studying to be professionals in more paying fields. It had been a tiring trip for the old man and he was waiting for a replacement who would come the long way round from Kangra by bus.

I spent the night in Purthi where the road began. To leave the jungle path was like stepping out of a romantic era to an ugly present. Instead of elegant wooden village pagodas you were greeted by hideous cement temples raised perhaps by some contractor to appease the outraged forest spirits. A voluble Nepali ran a log cabin dormitory for the bus passengers who gathered here overnight. The volubility increased as the night wore on. There was a liquor distilling unit attached to the dormitory.

Early on a freezing morning a small short-chassis bus arrived to take us to the bigger bus waiting on the main road higher (though it seemed lower) in the valley. The bus then delivered us to Udaipur in Lahaul and from the icy chill of the Chandrabhaga river it was clear we were now climbing. In fact the bus would climb all the way to the Rohtang pass and by evening had delivered me back to Manali. The first thing I did was go to a chemist and try and buy aspirin for my aches and pains. But not a single shop was open. There was an apple growers' strike and for all they cared I could suffer indefinitely. Once more Garhwal scored. During strikes one can always go round to the back of the chemist's shop to buy medicines!

20
The Void Manifest

My first physical contact with Ladakh had occurred on a ride out of Drass in August 1986. I was on the last leg of my motorcycle traverse of the Himalaya from Darjeeling to the Khardung La. Most people encounter Ladakh the moment they climb the Zoji La, a curious snaking pass that goes through rather than over the Great Range. Although only 11,500 ft high this pass can be a death trap and in winter snow piles up to more than twenty feet. Added to this is the anxiety of the one-way convoy system since traffic can be held up for days at a time.

The road was open between July and October and daily there was a farcical weighing of trucks at Sonmarg as the convoy was formed. Every truck thanks to bribed officials was carrying double its sanctioned load and several stalled on the poorly aligned climb. These had to be hauled out by military cranes which could not reach the spot because of the chaos resulting from trucks overtaking.

Crossing the Zoji La revealed the mindlessness of officialdom with civilian and military authorities at odds with one another and both clueless as to what was actually happening on top. VIPs overfly the problem in their helicopters. Visitors get the feeling after a whole day's wait without information that nobody is in charge. A typical scene was of a military policeman in a flapping booth who kept cranking up an old-fashioned field telephone to try and get through to his superiors. The entire day all he said was, 'Allo! Allo!

Sharmaji?' Sharmaji never answered. Never mind getting through to the top of the pass the operator couldn't even get through to his colleague ten miles up the road!

The day before I had had an easy and enjoyable ride from the Dal lake to Sonmarg, rejoicing in getting clear of the fleecing houseboat owners. There may be some disagreement about who are the kindest people in the Himalaya but none whatsoever over who are the greediest and most shameless. To move to Ladakh from the Kashmir valley is to experience the transition from hell to heaven. It was one of the most tantalising puzzles of my Himalayan traverse why Kashmir with its fabulous scenery and talented people should want to foul its tourist reputation so cavalierly. The worst sharks I have met anywhere in the world operated on the Dal lake.

The most outstanding example of kindness a stranger experienced was at the other extreme of the Himalaya. When I got a puncture in thick jungle on the 'Brahmaputra' before it leaves the hills of Arunachal Pradesh I had to abandon the bike and hitch a lift on a scooter to the nearest town (Pasighat). A young Adi tribal called Noni immediately volunteered aid and spent the whole morning arranging to solve the problem. He took me back to the jungle on his own scooter with a spare wheel. After extricating my bike from the jungle he entertained me in his village. Unlike the Kashmiri who wants to take your pants off, as a parting gift Noni gave me one of the colourful home-spun jackets worn by his tribe. I keep this memento as a symbol of how compassionate tribal society is to strangers in their land. City residents can learn a lot from the spontaneous response of nomads and tribals who do not fix a cash price for every transaction. What irony that the selfish culture of urban India considers tribal custom to be in need of 'civilising'.

My ride over the Zoji La was a nightmare at the back of a military convoy. To compound my misery the bag containing all my money, papers and camera fell off the bike. Luckily an ASC havildar bringing up the rear of the convoy spotted it and rescued my expedition. Three thousand rupees were in the bag and Havildar Harbans Singh of Una in Himachal could easily have driven on to

Leh without telling anyone he had found it. I was so impressed by this jawan's character—he refused to accept any monetary reward—that after a lot of perseverance I was able to convince the defence authorities that the havildar's exemplary behaviour deserved recognition. Eventually the authorities gave the havildar not one but two awards for his honesty.

I left Drass in the morning after bidding farewell to the havildar and his convoy and at once blinked as I took in the classic features of the trans-Himalayan scene—khaki slopes below sweeping snow peaks that ran down to slicing rivers along which poplars and apricot trees provided occasional green oases. It was icy cold even in the sunny air and from that moment I was hooked to the strange allure of these bare slopes that shimmered magically like shot-silk. Their khaki cover on closer inspection was a tantalising backdrop to a whole series of unlikely shades—purple, orange, pink, green and rust, an unbelievable mix of life-affirming tones arrestingly prismatic amidst the monochrome overlay.

On the southern side of the Himalaya the approaches always seem steeper and to get to the top is a moment of intense relief. In Ladakh however the approach seems less dramatic and when you arrive at the top you experience not relief but fulfilment as though the soul has found its own level. The skies have a lot to do with this mood of exhilaration. In Ladakh the mind sails serene under an unchanging vast canopy of blue. Even when clouds do intrude they are usually of the high-veined cirrus variety that do not dilute the overwhelming blue radiance. The blueness seems to be the colour of the Creator, rich in hue and vibrant in benevolence. How strange that the Buddha born within sight of the south-facing Dhaulagiri range should have spun out his doctrine of the Void a thousand years before it came home to its natural setting in Ladakh.

Those who describe Ladakh as a moonscape overlook the poetic reality that this landscape is more alive than dead. Uniquely in the Himalaya the visitor to Ladakh is under a constant physical spell created by the texture of the landscape. The light on the roof of the world explains why everything seems so pristine and surrealistic. There is a tingle of expectancy in viewing the landscape:

enlightenment seems at hand. And curiously this rubs off on to the people of Ladakh. Why do they seem so content when their lot is so trying? Why do they smile and greet the complete stranger with a hearty 'Julley'? Living in Ladakh is in many ways an ordeal, especially in winter. Tourism has helped the locals eke out their days but has also led to the younger generation chaffing at their elders' acceptance of a primitive economy. Buddhism seems ideally adapted to the needs of upper Ladakh with the monastic life taking care of the balance between land and population. Perhaps this is why the Islamic areas to the west find their solutions less workable and turn to violent mercenary alternatives.

An extraordinary feature of my traverse was to pass from the Shia confines of Kargil to the Buddhist interior and suddenly be confronted with a cultural change so drastic it seemed inconceivable in such a short distance. The dress, manners and mien of the people in the vicinity of Kargil and along the Suru valley had been, certainly in the case of the women, awkward, shy and forbidding. Reach Shergol (or Rangdum) and the contrast is so stunning that you feel you are in a culture warp. Buddhist women are feminine, outgoing and free of the submissiveness that the subcontinent's males have conveniently determined to be a desirable trait in women.

I stayed in a Ladakhi home converted into a guest house for budget travellers and marvelled at the uncomplaining nature of the Ladakhis. In Leh all the lights go off suddenly at ten p.m. but everybody accepts it and you hear laughs rather than moans when it happens. The Ladakhi kitchen is a pleasure to be in for the array of highly polished brass and copper ware. The diet is restricted especially if you are a vegetarian though in recent years Leh has begun to harvest phenomenal crops thanks to research done by the Vivekananda Laboratories of Almora. This lab was set up by the plant scientist Dr Boshi Sen, an eminent disciple of Professor Jagadish Bose and Swami Vivekananda.

For trekking in Ladakh the easiest route is via Stok palace across the Indus and thence into the Zanskar range. While in the kitchen one evening drinking endless cups of camomile tea (a perpetual rehydrator kept ready in large Chinese-made flasks in all Leh households) I overheard an Australian visitor say he had just climbed Stok Kangri, a handsome peak standing 6121 metres, which we could see out of the kitchen window. The Australian also admitted to having climbed Nun on the sly, since according to the rules all foreigners are obliged to pay fees for peaks above 6000 metres. The problem is that in Ladakh there are few to check on who is climbing what and, to make matters easier for the peak poachers, ascents are along comparatively straightforward snowless routes. Thus dozens of young foreigners made routine ascents of Stok Kangri; it would take the authorities years to accept this reality and introduce the concept of 'trekking peaks' where the summiter paid a token fee.

To keep the conscience of the unauthorised clear was the common knowledge that the authorities themselves bent the rules. Nanda Devi had apparently hosted American and Indian climbers trained by the CIA. In the Suru valley I met Israeli students returning from Nun-Kun whose passports at the check post were exempted from examination. Winking at the law was a sport two could play.

One very good reason why I prefer trekking is that I do not acclimatise well at altitude. Anything above 12,000 ft and I have breathing discomfort. By 18,000 ft the symptoms are much worse and I have a splitting headache at one extremity and painful piles at the other. However it is important to reach an altitude of 6000 metres (20,000 ft) if you wish to be taken seriously as a commentator on mountaineering matters and the lure of Stok Kangri which stood above that magical macho figure seemed like a sound investment. The mountain was by all accounts a straightforward climb, a trekking peak in fact where only the last thousand feet involved some minor snow craft.

Sitting alongside me was an Austrian medical student from Vienna whom I called Wienerschnitzel. VS was an alpinist on holiday in Ladakh and keen to impress his friends back home with a 6000-metre peak tucked beneath his belt. He heard me tell the Australian I planned to visit Stok Kangri to photograph the blue sheep and asked if he could join me. His unfamiliarity with the Himalaya was more than compensated for by his enthusiasm and youth but neither of us had any climbing gear. That however was easily solved. The Ladakh tourist office hired out boots and other trekking equipment at extremely cheap rates. Our boots cost only two rupees a day. VS had a bivouac sheet of aluminium foil along with a stove and other camping kit so we deemed ourselves ready.

Next morning we set out on my motorbike to cross the Indus to Stok. We began the fairly easy trek along the gorge of the river Stok passing the yurt encampment run by Tiger Tops. The rock formations are in turn beautiful, crazy and spell-binding. The trail climbs to a low pass then descends to a meadow with a herdsman's corral. This junction marked the route to Stok Kangri base situated at the head of a side valley. The herdsman had been told to tell all visitors that it was against the rules to climb without a permit and we assured him we had no gear for climbing. During the afternoon we had passed at least a dozen foreign trekkers who had been on the surrounding peaks. It was rather like being in the Alps to hear the yodels of successful non-climbing trekkers celebrating arrival atop a spire or pillar.

In the morning we plodded up the green open valley noting on the way herds of bharal looking much less glossy than those found on the southern side of the Himalaya. VS had the bad habit of all hillmen of forever taking the direct route over any avoidable obstacle. This meant on occasion scrabbling up dirt walls and getting our hired boots (which were a size too big) filled with rubble. By early afternoon we reached our objective, a fine camping site that overlooked Stok Kangri, springing up like a white sentinel. But it lay across a dicey-looking snow field. I looked forward to setting up camp and enjoying the aesthetics of the situation but VS being a yuppie had other ideas.

It was only four p.m. and if we crossed the by-now hardening snow field we could get up the side of the mountain and bivouac a thousand feet above the glacier making the conclusion of our 'trek' but a three-hour bid in the morning. If we left the glacier traverse to the morning the climb would become soggy and instead of reaching our destination at nine it would take us till noon. The VS logic was irrefutable but it didn't take into account my idiosyncratic feelings for Stok Kangri. I wanted to enjoy the foreplay of drinking in her beauty and beholding at leisure all her shapely allure. Besides I was tired and needed some sleep before the hard work of tackling the upper snow slopes.

VS vetoed my softness and said the weather might not hold. We must snatch the prize and a high bivouac with breakfast would guarantee success with the least possible trouble. Because of the guarantee of breakfast I gave in and he led the way over the tricky snow field. It was getting dark when we finally managed to outwit its treacherous surface and began a more easy scramble up the rocky side of Stok Kangri. VS was all set to get as high as he could but as darkness settled I insisted we must choose a reasonably flat bivvy site out of the wind. Reluctantly he agreed to stop but all we could find was a miserable rocky dip at some 18,000 ft. Unfortunately the cold was not severe enough to freeze the trickle of melting snow that dripped all around our cranny. It was utterly miserable, the only saving grace from the sleepless torture of this hellish perch being the astounding effect of the moonlight on the surrounding cirque, yielding a peerless white bridal beauty. We seemed to be on another planet so surreal was the drape of fluted snow.

In the bitterly cold dawn the final agony was for VS to announce that the petrol stove was out of fuel. The prospect of no breakfast was all it needed for my self-pity to spill over into disgust. Instead of enjoying the intimate beauties of Stok Kangri I was hating every minute of being there. Breakfast for me has always been the one meal that matters. Without something inside I feel irritable and unfulfilled. I can miss either or both lunch and dinner for several days together and feel perfectly happy with snacks in between. But with no breakfast inside there is a desperate descent into despair.

We started the last two thousand feet without any luggage. I put my water bottle in the pocket of my duvet and went up the middle of the face kicking steps in the snow. We were following someone else's tracks but to our surprise they suddenly stopped after a few

THE VOID MANIFEST 191

hundred feet. Perhaps the climber had decided to move to the broken rocky ridge where the going was trickier but without snow. I decided to try the same ploy but as I shimmied sideways the water bottle fell out of my pocket. We both watched glumly as it did a cresta run back almost to the snow field. To make matters worse strong sun now played on the snow and started to affect my eyes. For the first time in my life I began to experience double vision and its message was I had reached my ceiling of safety. There was no way I was going to continue after this. I told VS I would wait for him. When I reached the rocky ridge I had the compensation of looking over into the Indus valley and beyond to the Karakoram. As I rested, my vision became normal and I could make out K2, the loveliest of mountains though at this distance its full beauty could only be guessed at.

After an hour I heard a yodel and a small black object waving announced the end of the affair. I set off back down the ridge to collect my water bottle noting how razor sharp were the schists and how friable they were to the touch. Here the outcrop of the Zanskar range marked the mighty suture resulting from colliding continents. My pleasure at sensing these ancient turmoils put my own into perspective.

21
The Coppery Kingdom

I became fascinated by Zanskar thanks to the *Lonely Planet* guide book. In particular I was turned on by the aplomb displayed by Gary Weare, an editor who managed to convey both the dangers of this challenging terrain and the feasibility of the ordinarily fit trekker getting round them. He matter of factly wrote about avoiding certain routes at certain seasons because of the impossibility of river crossings. And as a lure beyond the tough but inspiring terrain, Zanskar had a curious mystical tinge that made its Buddhism more rarefied. Ladakh, with its broad valleys at the receiving end of Lamaist influences emanating from Lhasa, perhaps allowed a thinning out of the Buddha's teaching. Zanskar, because of its location squashed between the crest of the Great Himalaya and the tangled but less elevated Zanskar range, was a cultural cul-de-sac whose Buddhism did not originate singly from Leh but derived from several sources including the pilgrim exaltation that surrounds the hub of the spiritual universe at Kailash Mansarover. In the middle ages Zanskar was part of the kingdom of Guge which extended from the definitive cultural watershed at the Pensi La (in the southeast) to the environs of Mount Kailash following the trend of the Zanskar range. The routes across this tangled crumple zone near the line of massive collision between the Indian and Asian plates are tortuously indirect. From the capital of Zanskar—which is the tiny village of Padum on a broad valley floor

THE COPPERY KINGDOM

under the sheer fall of the northern face of the Great Himalaya—the way to Leh is separated by a hundred-kilometres jumble of desiccated peaks and steep canyons that involves three high passes and nearly a hundred river crossings.

Zanskar is believed to get its name from the coppery tinge of its soil. Geography and culture travel together to explain why the region's enclosed cluster of monasteries came to acquire its aura of a scholarly retreat. Leh, though snowbound in winter, has lateral access along the length of the open Indus valley. In Zanskar (and across the Pensi La in the Muslim enclave of the Suru valley) the enclosed nature of the terrain makes travel unwise as avalanches are common. Life for six months of the year is effectively restricted to sitting around the family hearth or monastic cloister and surviving the savage conditions. The summer is spent in amassing supplies of brushwood or anything that will burn. This is stacked on the flat adobe roof along with drying crops of barley and apricots. In short, living in the lee of the Great Himalaya is twice as dangerous as living in the lee of the Zanskar range.

The stove is placed in the centre of the kitchen which becomes the family living room. Poorer people keep their livestock in proximity to share their heat. Wool is spun and woven and all the family clothes were handmade, hand dyed and hand tailored at least until the advent of adventure tourism. Elegantly shaped vessels, locally crafted in brass and copper and highly polished, line the kitchen. Also on view is the family treasure, a sewing machine which has been lugged all the way by pony from Manali. It is easier and cheaper to shop across the Great Himalaya than battle a way through to Leh.

Zanskar could be said to fulfil the Joshua Slocum prescription—its terrain exists to be trekked over. Everybody I had met said it was tough but rewarding. The only other destination that called forth this universal recommendation was the pilgrimage to Kailash. Zanskar it seemed evoked some of the uplifting sentiment aroused by the Kailash yatra and though not easily penetrated it involved neither permits nor border neuroses as with Mansarover.

A photographer friend in Mussoorie, Gurmeet Thukral, had

walked into Zanskar over the Pensi La with the writer Stephen Alter (before the motor road was built) and their palpable mood of having achieved something worthwhile made me yearn to set off for this elusive province. I soon did. I had just completed writing the commentary to go with Gurmeet's photographs of the Great range. From the proceeds I bought my second-hand motorbike and (like Gurmeet on his bike) set off the fun way to see how far I could get from one end of the Himalaya to the other.

Though I couldn't cover the whole span, it was enough to make me realise how fortunate I was to have seen so much. Eventually the trip reduced itself to a ride from Darjeeling to the Khardung La, a thoroughly satisfying traverse.

With my thoughts fixed on completing the course any side-traffickings had to depend on convenience. At Kargil I decided to turn off to explore the 250 kilometres new road to Padum but guessed from the start that I wasn't going to make it. The road was merely notional and the side streams so fierce that the bike was taking a severe battering. It made me fear that if I did reach Zanskar it might be the end of the trip. Parts of the bike began breaking off from the pounding. On that savage lonely road I would have had no help if it broke down altogether. Eventually I stopped at the settlement at Parkachik where the so-called surfaced road ended. For another hundred kilometres there was a kutcha track that wound up and over the Pensi La veering through riverbeds and skidding over patches of ice. Beyond Parkachik the great Peak of Nun loomed near and a hanging glacier of green ice tumbled from its base to beetle over the further bank of the Suru river. This was a titanic background to my puny bike. Luck was with me when I stopped for tea and found a German motorcyclist returning from Padum on a powerful BMW touring bike. His advice was that if I wished to reach the Khardung La in one piece I should turn around. He had experienced severe difficulties on his bigger machine reducing the round trip of five hundred kilometres (back to Kargil) a constant worry instead of a pleasure. He had found Padum primitive and isolated. There had been no Shangri La climax to his heroic ride, only the dismal realisation that even loveless and bleak Kargil seemed to offer more to a biker.

I was not in the least put off Zanskar by the foreigner's assessment. He was after all a motorbiking correspondent and more concerned with the nuts and bolts of passage than to discover subtle mystical overhang. For me Padum remained a desirable destination. Having managed to get halfway there by bike I was determined I would complete the trip one day.

Two years later in the monsoon I decided on the spur of the moment to give trekking to Padum a try. I wasn't sure about how to get there so adopted the cautious approach of taking one step at a time. If I couldn't get to Padum then I could try from Manali to get to Leh along what was then a road open only to the military. If I didn't get permission for that I would explore the Pangi valley from where passes into Zanskar led, albeit at a great height.

I set off from Mussoorie by bus and spent the first night in Mandi. At the beginning of July the weather in the plains was sticky and enervating and this continued as the bus crossed from Chandigarh into Himachal. I find the industrial development of these lower hills depressing and the drive through them boring. Mandi has character but is far too hot in summer for a traveller accustomed to the cooler air of Mussoorie.

I took the bus to Manali next day and rejoiced to pass through the one valley in the Himalaya where development was both controlled and successful. Kullu's distinctively dressed women may be the explanation for why this balance was achieved. In the evening I climbed up from the bazaar to John Banon's guest house to consult him on the best way to reach Padum. Major Banon was the local secretary of the Himalayan Club and ran in his family orchard a successful hotel for foreign climbers, way above the budget of Indian visitors like me. He told me to go to Darcha and haggle if I wanted the cheapest rates. The ponymen for Padum came to Manali but obviously charged extra for the trouble. The trekking agent would take his cut but guarantee reliable transport. In Darcha I would have to ask around and just hope some ponymen arrived without return bookings.

John Banon had a Kullu wife who brought me tea dressed in the colourful shawl the women of the valley weave and wear. Tragically the Banon family had lost a son on an expedition into Lahaul when his jeep crashed into the river. Rivers are the key to trekking in Zanskar and this is why ponies are so important. The local breed are good swimmers. Trekkers can only go solo between riverbanks. When you come to a river you have to sit and wait till another party turns up and then combining forces, help ferry the luggage across on horseback using a fixed rope to winch across the stranded trekkers.

John Banon having cautioned me that the bus to Darcha from Manali was always overcrowded, I returned to Kullu, where the bus started. I backtracked by the ridge route to Naggar and broke journey to see the Roerich art gallery. This Russian emigré was viewed with great suspicion by the British authorities. Were his forays into the mountains of genuine mystical and artistic intent or was he spying? The mystification deepened when he became the guru of an exotic American cult that claimed prophethood for their master.

The gallery is in a few rooms set aside in the family mansion up the hill from Naggar fort. The lady chowkidar was a bit reluctant to admit me but when she knew I was aware of Roerich's artistic status and not just a curious tourist she let me in. How reassuringly typical was the fierce loyalty in this Kullu village lady, as it was in Bhag Singh and other hill retainers.

In a way this visit to see Roerich's paintings was the highlight of my trek—what greater compliment could one give to Roerich's genius in capturing the essence of these middle kingdoms of the Himalaya where physical beauty intermingles with mystical. Perhaps the surest sign of Roerich's brilliance as an artist is that most of the works on view are done on the small black sheets of a pastel sketch book. Drawn on the march, these pastels are superlatively evocative of the colour, mood and texture of the landscape between the Pir Panjal and the Great Himalaya.

In the dark room the colours blue and purple stood out like transcendent statements from a visionary in tune with the magic of these mountains. No other art gallery in the world has hit my plexus so hard for the sheer exactitude of the truths conveyed about the Himalaya albeit, rendered in miniature, each a jewel of inner understanding. I have no doubt in my own mind that Roerich senior was a prophet granted special insights into the mind of divinity, and these insights are to be seen in his pastels not in his words.

His larger canvases too have the power to halt me in my tracks, as for example in Delhi's National Gallery of Modern Art. There is a power and authenticity in his vision of the Himalaya that seems like a gift given only to him. His son's paintings of the mountains are also powerful and sometimes overtly symbolic but Nicholas the senior has the rare skill of fusing symbol with reality to bring about the truest evocation of the inner wonder of the range.

Two other modern painters of the Himalaya come near Roerich in conveying the transcendental glory of the range and like Roerich they both involved themselves in expeditionary activity, exploring their subject close up to seek to understand the source of the mysteries they felt called upon to paint.

Serbjeet Singh and Ram Nath Pasricha are quite unlike in their personalities and painting styles. Ram Nath is a retiring man who has often been invited to accompany climbing expeditions as their official artist. His sketches, like Roerich's, are done on the spot and under great constraints. He has the gift of grasping the essence of a mountain scene and immortalising it with a few strokes.

Serbjeet is a hearty Sikh of private means who has a larger-than life approach to art. With his powerful outgoing personality, he seems the proper vehicle to convey the grandeur of scale of the Himalaya; his large and stunning canvases dramatise a portion of landscape, making for elemental encounters with it. One of Serbjeet's most remarkable talents is to visualise overviews: something few of us can begin to conceptualise. He has painted for a German publisher an overview of the Alps, an extraordinary Leonardo-like venture that frames the entire snowscape dominating Europe.

Serbjeet has other extraordinary facets and to his craggy personality cling colourful bits of modern Himalayan history. He filmed the remarkable tank battle on the Zoji La when Pakistan's challenge to control Ladakh was defeated by the audacious use of tanks by India's Seventh Cavalry. The Pakistanis thought the tanks were jeeps disguised as a ruse to scare them. After all tanks had never been deployed before or since at Zoji La's 11,500 feet altitude.

At the other end of the Himalaya Serbjeet had been commissioned to paint the disputed border with China in what is now Arunachal Pradesh. Even as Serbjeet painted the Bum La he saw Chinese troops swarming over it. Sadly for India Serbjeet was a civilian. Had he been a soldier he would have carried the fight back to the Chinese. Instead the top brass withdrew from the Se La without a fight and this feeble response led to a rout.

The morning after my visit to the Roerich museum I turned up for the Kullu bus and found it already packed. Some passengers had been camping in it all night.

I managed to find standing room but when we got to Manali and the crowd turned a squeeze into a jam I decided to join the overflow and clamber onto the roof. It was cold and uncomfortable circling up to the Rohtang pass still with plenty of snow on it but the transition from alpine to trans-Himalayan Scenery from this fantastic vantage point was exhilarating. On the way we were stopped by a policeman in a jeep. He abused the driver and the driver in turn abused us. Sheepishly we had to get down and start walking but without our luggage. This is a charade performed for legality's sake. After the jeep drove away the bus caught us up and we all climbed back onto the roof. These are the realities of life in the hills. Whatever the rules of the road say, they have little relevance in the interior with one bus a day squeezing in as many people on the roof as there are crammed inside. People on the roof accept the risk fatalistically and the bus crews make extra money for they do not issue tickets for the fare they receive from the overflow. For them overcrowding is a welcome bonus.

Over the Rohtang the clouds were still in abeyance and we had extraordinary views of the Chandrabhaga series of peaks in Lahaul, noble and elevated snow summits above a now suddenly barren landscape. The flip from dense viridian forests to sparse grey slopes both sudden and dramatic accounted for the old description of Kullu as 'the end of the inhabited world'. It seems that life suddenly stops as you cross the Pir Panjal and are confronted with the build up of arid ridges leading to the last uprise of the Great Himalaya. Zigzagging down the sheer northern face of the pass enabled us to make out in the valley bottoms some greenery and the occasional village. The trees turn out to be willow and poplar and the village houses to be of adobe instead of stone. On their flat roofs are the tell-tale signs of long gruelling Himalayan winters cut off from the rest of Himachal. Brushwood is stacked up to last for six months. For emergencies the government sends a helicopter to Keylong. The long-awaited tunnel into Lahaul from the southern base of the Rohtang seems to be going nowhere. The locals are cynical, saying the government started it as a gimmick to suggest they were serious about keeping links with Lahaul open all year.

Lahaul with its composite Hindu–Buddhist culture unlike Spiti and Zanskar has a comparatively healthy economy based on exotic cash crops like hops and kuth, a medicinal root. The most inviting feature however is the warmth and friendliness of the people. On the bus despite the crush no one complains and when we have to change to another bus in the Chandra valley because of an intervening landslide, everybody cheerfully humps their luggage on their back and walks a kilometre to where the other bus awaits. Some of the loads they were carrying were phenomenal since a visit to Manali means stocking up for the season. But the bigger the load the more the bearer seemed to laugh. It was extraordinary to see how lightly they took setbacks that in the plains would have had bus passengers red in the face with anger demanding their money back. The rigours of life in the trans-Himalaya have a liberating dimension. Where else in modern life do villagers make a joke of their privations?

In Keylong I put up in a modest hotel opposite the tourist bungalow, run by a jovial character called Jaspa. He was a successful hotelier because he analysed the tourist market and provided what people wanted. Jaspa catered to the trekker to and from the Shingo La. His was the first watering-hole for visitors who had set out a week before from Zanskar. Since the chances of finding lager in Zanskar was slight (the transport and shops are run by Shias and there is no army presence to justify a canteen) Jaspa's hotel doubled as the promised land. His food is also known to be good. So caring is Jaspa that his name has got round the travellers' grapevine. I was surprised to find a party of American Fulbright scholars on vacation here. They had come because of the fame of Lahaul's hospitality that vies with that of the Thakali community in Nepal.

The next morning I climbed up to the Khardung monastery across the Bhaga river but found it no different from other monasteries with guttering oil lamps and equally gutteral renderings of sacred texts. Leaving it quickly I came down and had my hair cut in the open air back in the bazaar with the barber pointing out as he snipped, the 'Old Lady of Keylong' formed by the snow on a peak in the direction of Darcha. I wanted to buy the lovely tunics worn by the Lahauli ladies but was told these are all made to order. This would have to wait till another visit. That afternoon I boarded the bus for Darcha and was bounced for forty kilometres along a kutcha road where the villages became poorer and the landscape bleaker. A few miles short of Darcha we had to get out and walk. The road had collapsed but luckily not the bridge to which it led. This bridge spans the first of many dangerous melt-water rivers.

Darcha was a colony of tents with two shops that sold provisions to trekkers gearing up for the Zanskar adventure. Across the bridge I was waved down by a self-important policeman and made to record my Indian passport details in his register of foreigners. The joke about these recurring security checks is that the nation's actual enemies, the Pakistanis and Chinese, can walk straight past—as they resemble villagers of the border regions, no one stops them. Foreigners of Indian descent—Candian British, American—all of whom I met on the Zanskar trail, were also exempt from security checking by virtue of their looks, testimony to the fact that appearances count for more than realities on the roof of the world.

Since I wasn't sure if I was going on the Zanskar trek I hadn't bought much in the way of food or equipment. In Keylong I acquired a stainless steel tureen that would double up as mug, plate, cooker and mirror. I also bought some khoya sweets since they travel well and provide instant energy. Basic rations I would only purchase if the Darcha deal came through. Luckily I don't eat much at altitude and a diet of alu paratha and Five Star bars would see me through.

22
Wild Rivers and a Rainbow

Preferring the stone shop to the flapping tents I was able to meet other candidates for the Zanskar test over supper. Topped up with chang the evening went splendidly. The shopkeeper who kept a register of trekking bookings told me a French couple were in search of a third member to share the cost of their three-horse expedition. They were already asleep in their own tent but would come to load their supplies in the morning. Their ponymen I met and liked and they said the deal was as good as fixed.

In the morning Andre and Martine showed up for breakfast. He was a dreamy Frenchman but an accomplished alpinist while Martine was both feminine and spunky. Together they were a happy solution to my problem. I now had to buy supplies at very inflated roadhead rates but could not complain as it had saved me lugging loads up and down the back of buses, a most wearing occupation in view of the milling crowds who shared space with the luggage on the roof.

There was one hitch to the plan. Andre and Martine wanted to use the less frequented Sarichan La approach to Zanskar which meant following the motor road over the Bara Lacha, only then proceeding west to join the main Shingo La route just before and above Khargyak, the first Zanskar village. I was not equipped for the exposure on this route with several nights on or near the crest of the Great Himalaya. On the other hand it was exciting to be doing a less-used route. Since the ponymen managed without a tent I thought I could take the risk.

In a way this route is preferable for those like me who had come by bus to Darcha. The Shingo La climb involves gruelling days of sweat to climb and cross its bleak and icy summit. We had the simpler task of plodding alongside our three loaded ponies, following the easy road gradient to the Bara Lacha La; the road was metalled in places but dug up again by the bulldozer which we passed the next day on its return to Darcha having opened the pass to the season's traffic.

The scenery as the Bhaga narrowed to its source was both bleak and sublime. The river was snagged in many places by monstrous snow bridges which we were told would survive till the next season's snowfall. That night was spent in the compound of the Patseo bungalow, the bungalow having been booked for a government road engineer whose jeep never showed up. Only the occasional Border Roads truck rumbled along the highway, its driver waving casually out. In the back amongst the road building equipment would be the occasional traveller glad for the lift since it could shorten their journey by days.

One of these trucks approached us honking from a blind bend. Our horses bolted and careered off the road above the river. The lead horse, a black mare, lost her footing but managed to stay upright. In the process however her load was shaken off and to my horror the rucksack I saw tumbling towards the river was my own. Then on the very brink it lodged in a clump of shrubbery. The horse's owner eased himself gingerly down to rescue the rucksack. The same black mare would come to grief the next day as we toiled up and over the Bara Lacha. Where the road swung into loops to gain height we kept to the old bridle path, in effect a shortcut now that snow began to lie underfoot. Near the top it got deeper until our shortcut became too exhausting to negotiate. Three feet of snow to slog through in the heat of the burning sun of mid-morning was too much and along with two of the horses we climbed by the longer route recently opened by the bulldozer. The black mare and her handler stuck to the snow slog and disappeared in a flurry of powder snow. We wound round the newly cleared bends skidding on the icy surface relieved the snow had been blizzarded up on both sides—to a height of fifteen feet—by yesterday's bulldozer. As we crossed the milestone marking the pass I saw the black mare strangely crouched in a kneeling posture almost as if saying her prayers. Thomay, her handler, announced she was dead with a broken neck. The mare had climbed a high bank of snow too near the edge of the road and fallen through a cornice. Because of the load she had stood no chance and plummeted to her death.

We were aghast at this terrible tragedy but the ponymen, less sentimental, got down to re-apportioning the loads. As Thomay was responsible for this navigational error he had to carry most of the horse's burden. The ponyman in charge was Gyalchen, a laid-back young man of great understanding. He took decisions almost bashfully but everyone respected him for the firm grip he kept on the expedition's progress. The third helper was actually a ponyman-turned-lama. On a return journey across the subcontinent from his monastery in south India to his village in Zanskar, he was glad for company.

In the event this young lama would be the beneficiary of a scholarship all three of us trekkers contributed to, in lieu of a replacement for the horse that had died. Later I would have the pleasure of providing another scholarship at the same monastery for Gyalchen. Every two or three years when they got leave to visit their homes these two lamas would call on me in Delhi bringing gifts with white scarves.

Along this punishing road over the crest we were surprised to find gangs of road labourers from the plains huddled in stone pens covered with torn plastic sheets. Most of them had been drafted in from Bihar and looked like underfed bonded labour. Unused to the cold and ill-equipped for it, they wrapped themselves in anything that came to hand—paper, cloth or plastic.

We spent a night in one of these pens on the bleak crest where the snow-cover under the blistering July sun yielded black scars as the rocks glistened in the melt of winter ice. There was no sense of exaltation whatever on topping out at this famous watershed at

16,000 ft. Perhaps the road lessened the impact or the altitude had got to us. Already you sense the plateau of Tibet is at hand and the actual crest of the Great Himalaya turns out to be a tame tapering into modest ridges. Laced with black rock the white flattened spread of mountainscape comes as a bit of an anticlimax. However the seasonal lakes are exquisite in July. They glisten a resplendent turquoise under the benevolent blue skies astounding travellers with the calming effect of their beauty. Even more astounding is their transient nature. Within two months they will vanish to confuse and disappoint later travellers.

The view from the Bara Lacha is more bleak than uplifting and seems hostile to life. Kuari in Garhwal and the Zoji La in Kashmir are also on the crest of the Great Himalaya, the latter providing perhaps the most spectacular study in sudden transition from the green of subalpine vegetation to the grey of trans-Himalayan aridity. Of the three I find Kuari the most inviting. At Keylong Sarai, another bleak campsite amidst black split rock and huddling road gangs, we spent the second night. Then we left the motor road and followed a marvellous Elysian meadow running for miles together like a celestial golf course into the Lingti plains. Thanks to the road gangs we had been able to make our supper more tasty with chillies and onion and now marched with the added luxury of chutney with our alu paratha. It had been made by an enterprising Nepali lady who had set up a flimsy shop to meet the simple needs of the labourers. What energy and initiative the Nepali shows in overcoming his poor economic circumstances. Throughout the Himalaya you find them in places few other hillmen would wish to visit let alone inhabit, whether as porters in Kumaun, dak bungalow chowkidars in Garhwal, dhaba owners in Himachal or hooch distillers in Arunachal. Their initiative has made them unpopular in some north-eastern states and their success has aroused so much envy that in Bhutan they have been victimised for seeking to assert their democratic rights.

In West Bengal's hill areas Nepalis long settled in India agitated for some autonomy in conducting their affairs and Darjeeling was granted a measure. Because of the size of India and its ethnic diver-

sity many do not know that the Nepali language is spoken by millions of Indians. Now it has been officially recognised but some years back even Prime Minister Morarji Desai went on record to state that Nepali was a foreign tongue. Such ignorance is understandable in a layman but in a prime minister it is an appalling admission of provincial thinking.

The lady who gave us food was the last Nepali we were to meet on the trail to Zanskar. Now we would only see the occasional Gaddi shepherd or a party of trekkers like ourselves. There would be no more shops for the next four days. There were horses grazing the rolling green plains and marmots chirruping from their dugouts. Mani walls pointed the way and most were large and betrayed a lot of artwork. We agreed not to filch any of these stones lest further misfortune dog our footsteps. But for outsiders unaccustomed to this form of devotion, to walk by such remarkable religious art scattered so randomly in these wide plains must be a sore temptation.

The scoured backdrop of leached fawn hills turned out on

WILD RIVERS AND A RAINBOW

closer inspection to host a surprising array of colours from bright orange stones to dark green clumps of a kind of gorse. Gullies of eroded rock now appeared and led towards a wide expanse of water. This was our first exposure to the dreaded rivers of Zanskar. All the streams along our route though not technically in Zanskar drained into the Zanskar river. The general name seemed to be Tsarap Lingti Chu and part of this system curled round to include the cliff-hanging Phugtal gompa. Lower down nearer to Padum this river would go by the name Lunak.

It was fascinating to contemplate on these watershed ridges how tortuous were nature's arrangements. Northwards the Zanskar river joins the west-flowing Indus and is carried to the Arabian Sea through Pakistan. Before it gets there it is joined by the waters flowing west from Ladakh into Tibet and then back again into Himachal. The Pare Chu becomes the Sutlej and before joining the Indus it is in turn swollen by the Chenab, none other than the Chandrabhaga which flows south of our receding footsteps. It is heavy irony that these life-giving rivers can so easily be the cause of death to the unwary forder in their upper reaches.

There have been countless cases of travellers scorning the caution of the locals since many of these streams do not come up much above the knee. But it is not the depth alone that has to be considered. These are glacial waters at a numbing temperature and just to wade for a prolonged time in them can result in casualties. Worse is the speed and strength at which they move and this varies according to the weather. Early in the day there is less melt and the rivers tend to be lower in level and ferocity. By afternoon they can be roaring torrents and not even the strongest party can find a way through. You have to sit it out till the next morning.

Before ten the flow was negotiable though our feet felt icy and numbed. The correct drill is to keep your footwear on to get a better grip but as I only had one pair of lightweight boots and hated the idea of walking thereafter in sploshing footwear (the rivers occurred every half hour on our path) I took mine off and trod gingerly barefoot. Without assistance this would have been suicidal. Usually Andre helped Martine while Thomay was allotted to provide me support. Because of the danger of icy exposure this meant Thomay virtually dragged me across. My rucksack had gone with the other luggage on the horses guided by Gyalchen and Tenzing the lama. Where the river got too deep in the middle the horses were left to make their own way over. This made a really splendid sight. What spirit these animals showed, swimming confidently even fully loaded and never missing a beat. Their example made me overcome my own fears about taking the plunge, but the water came up to my neck and Thomay had to fish me out. My passport though wrapped up in plastic still retains the watermark of the Tsarap Lingti Chu, a dubious souvenir.

Liaison officers with expeditions have been known to underestimate these rivers and perhaps endeavouring to show to their foreign climbing members what stuff they were made of would start fording situations which had been vetoed by the porters. The porters were usually right. The Himalaya calls forth a lot of macho behaviour on many levels but when common sense is abandoned the result can be fatal. There is a deceptive, almost enchanted quality to the transHimalayan rivers that lure with their even, grey, speeding beauty. Unlike the equally dangerous detritus-laden torrents of the southern face there are no obvious rocks here to snag the surge nor white water to signal dangers underwater. They flow slick, silent and urgent, their mesmerising smoothness concealing a silken, killing punch.

We came to the banks of another strong current caught between ravines in the late afternoon. The water was unfordable and still rising as we laid marking stones to gauge how much it would fall overnight. Here camp had to be made. The river gave us no choice. Andre and Martine erected their silver dome tent while I who was saved this chore for lack of a tent washed some clothes. So strong was the sun that these were dry by nightfall. I sat and typed a travel column for the Delhi *Statesman* but it would be at least three weeks before I could deliver it in the capital. There was plenty to get down and the mood had to be authentic. The only problem was the snapping paper caught by the wind winnowing through the ravine. The ponymen had gone off searching for a Gaddi's camp to try and find milk for our tea and meat for those who could stomach it at this altitude. Andre and Martine preferred their French dried foods and like most foreigners were neurotic about drinking water. The ponymen ate whatever came their way, falling back on tsampa when there was nothing more interesting. I was happy enough with the porters' diet of dal and potatoes done in the pressure cooker, which has become standard equipment throughout the Himalaya.

When I first came to Kausani the pressure cooker was not only new but expensive. Mirtola had invested in a Hawkins cooker from the start because they discovered it saved on fuel. Every foot in height means it takes longer for things to boil and items like dal were always apt at altitude to remain partly uncooked. The 'cooker press' as the porters call it, is truly a revolutionary invention for the hills and contributes greatly to easing the burden on firewood.

In the morning after breakfast we were sent off with the lama to follow the river upstream where some shepherds had reported a snow bridge. Gyalchen and Thomay would take the horses across at the campsite. The river had fallen dramatically during the night to only one-third of its width. After an hour or more of slogging up one side of the river we crossed and descended the other side over higher ground that eventually yielded a view down on our old campsite. The horses had crossed but were out of sight hidden by the drop of the hillside before us. Which way to go? I assumed up and west because above us could be seen at the top of a very steep scree slope several cairns that obviously indicated the meeting of routes.

The lama scrambled down the hill to get within earshot of Thomay and to our surprise he returned to say we must go east, up and over the hill where the horses would meet us on the far side. It was nine and the sun beginning to torment. But we fell to the chore of scrabbling up the scree and then descended to what looked like a very unused side of the mountain. There were no signs of tracks until we got down to another river and there we saw some footprints heading upstream. But there were no hoof marks. By now the horses should have, following the base of the hill, beaten us to it. We were getting a bit frazzled by the uncertainty of our movements. Tracking up and down loose mountainsides at 13,000 ft is not the most enjoyable of sports.

Eventually we came to the source of our untrodden stream where a drape of white ice announced finality. We were hemmed in by a frozen canyon and had to retrace our steps. Still no horses appeared and by now it was nearing midday. The only thing to do was climb back to the point where the lama had got his instructions from Thomay, in the hope that some message had been left there. Cursing and toiling back up the scree slope we were met halfway by a running figure. It was Gyalchen profusely apologetic and blaming the confusion on Thomay's instructions to Lama Tenzing. It was only later that I realised the confusion was unavoidable.

These ponymen accustomed to the Shingo La trail had never done the Sarichen La route, at least from the Darcha end. In order not to lose their French clients they had pretended they knew the way. We had all been sent off in different directions that morning to eliminate the false trails.

Our rage, intensified by the altitude, boiled and cascaded around the ears of our ponymen; but they never once reacted. From their point of view they hadn't lost the way: they had found it—thanks to our efforts! It was heartbreaking to trudge past the same cairns we had seen five hours earlier and head along a valley to the west, precisely the direction that I would have followed in the first place.

We now were approaching the base of the Sarichen pass and the snow was two feet deep. The only place to camp before this was at a site called Chumik Marpho on the lip of the frozen range that rings the erstwhile kingdom of Zanskar. Before us, piled up to a height of six feet and stretching for twenty were saddlebags of grain. Some shepherds from Rupshu (to the east) had been here before us and dumped the gunny bags awaiting the thaw and opening of the pass. The saddlebags meanwhile were being dive-bombed by dozens of snow pigeons who saw this stack of grain as a windfall from the Buddha. Every time they attacked the gunny bags their beaks tore holes to allow a few more grains to trickle out.

Worried by this sign that there was too much snow for animals to get over the pass, the ponymen went into a huddle to work out a plan. That night was the coldest on the journey. Clouds scudded overhead and some gusts of sleet pattered on the plastic survival bag I had erected as protection as I huddled in a pullu (stone pen) to write my notes. I kept glancing up at the sky and saw it changing rapidly every few minutes. This was classic Himalayan crest weather baffling in its unpredictability. One minute the sky would be a calm pale blue then within seconds it would darken to a navy blanket of rain cloud that was then tossed away as quickly as it came. Suddenly the sky was a dappled wren-egg blue and pink for a few minutes until this gave way to a ragged orange and brown curtain of drifting mist caught by the declining sun. Again it turned cold and blustery, the sky now a threatening battleship grey. Then capriciously it shook off this layer of mourning and flashed out rays of pure sunlight golden and warming. Finally as the ponymen huddled over the fire of twigs coaxing it to hasten our meal of khichri I looked up and was agape to find etched right across the evening's soft light a quivering rainbow. Its comprehensive protectiveness gave the warm feeling that the Buddha was looking after our passage. I ventured to conclude there would be no blizzard and we would reach Zanskar after all.

The night passed peacefully punctuated by the coppery notes of horse bells and the ponymen's farts rending the night air. After the fear of fighting for survival in a snowstorm I could cope with the percussive fallout of methane.

23
The Greatest Show on Earth

The experience of the vacillating weather on the roof of the world followed by the calming effect of the rainbow seemed to aptly reflect our earlier agitation and the meditative poise that followed. In spite of the freezing morning we struck camp early and while the ponymen went to round up the horses we tied up bundles of luggage in our frozen-hard plastic sheets. We piled these on top of the rucksacks to thaw out on the march. Every few kilometres the loads had to be rehitched and tightened. Some of the paths were so dangerously near the edge of defiles that the slightest sideways movement of a load could tilt the balance sending the horse over the void. In turn the horses when relieved of their weights at longer halts would gambol in the dust and vigorously celebrate their return to freedom. At night they were let free to roam for grazing but never strayed far. Later when our path took us past the precious barley fields of Zanskar's staple diet the horses had to be hobbled. Even this did not stop them from trespassing on occasion. Gyalchen stumped up a heavy fine of 750 rupees to a farmer convinced only our horses could have done the damage to his field. I was amazed at the courtesy with which this transaction was performed. South of the crest the hillman (even more so his shrewish wife) will make a huge song and dance over crop damage by a neighbour's cattle and abuse of the most lurid kind is randomly hurled by both sides. Provocative hand gestures are also made to stoke the charged debate and at the end both parties are drained by the intensity of the emotions released. Gyalchen listened quietly to the man's measured complaint, went with him to check the evidence and returned to fork out the amount. Not an angry word was exchanged and Gyalchen's restrained behaviour in not arguing over the amount of the fine (though it was discussed) struck me as remarkable evidence of how far removed the Zanskari is from the north Indian for whom haggling energetically is such an everyday fact of life it can be deemed a companion sport.

We climbed along a distinct path that disappeared under a rounded snow slope rising a thousand feet above us. This was the crux of the route. The horses began to flounder and thrash and the higher we strove the more their loads got snagged. Eventually they came to a halt exhausted, within a few hundred feet of the top. Now we would have to carry the loads to lighten the skidding horses. As the old man of the party I was assigned with Martine to get the stove going for tea. We were in the middle of a very slushy snowfield but luckily had got the steepest part of the climb behind us. It was one p.m. and the sun had turned the early morning hard snow into mush.

The lama was sent to the crest to reconnoitre and when he waved back to signify some cairns had been spotted—indicating this was the real pass—we plodded up to join him. What we saw made us whistle in dismay. Never have I seen a grander cirque of icy impenetrability. It seemed as though the great frozen ring stretched for a kilometre, sealing off entry into the Middle Kingdom. Down there, over half a dozen snow-laden ridges lay the green valley of Zanskar but how to get down? This explained all those saddlebags of grain at Chumik Marpho. The Sarichen La was still in the grip of winter and the traders had dumped their loads at a junction where the alternative (but higher) pass into Zanskar, the Phirtse La, could be accessed.

The shepherds went into another huddle and a few minutes later Gyalchen issued crisp orders. It was now well past two and we had to reach the first village by nightfall. That meant we had to fit two days' marching into one afternoon. Only essentials would be carried in our daybags. Lightness was crucial since our descent would be a race against the declining sun. All the luggage including the horses' gear would be stashed on the pass. Gyalchen's brother would be sent the next day to collect it, using the family yaks.

By the time we had tea, opened the loads and got our survival gear sorted, it was nearing three. We had five hours at the most to get off the pass and negotiate the canyons that led down to Kargyak. Our leader initially would be the lama. The other ponymen would lead the horses round the rim and get down by any gap in its ice face that they could locate. They promised to catch us up in no time and set off with the two horses. It was grand to be overlooking our goal but annoying not to be able to study the route. However in all my encounters with really high passes I have come to expect panic situations. Never do you get the leisure to luxuriate in your achievement. Either the weather threatens or the clock. The lama trotted confidently over the icy curtain and began a long tricky glissade. We gulped and digging in our heels followed him at a more gingerly pace. Then to our horror—that quickly turned to amusement—the lama disappeared. He was in a crevasse that claimed him up to his shoulders. He was laughing and waving his arms but it was a nasty moment. When we got down to him his monastic tonsure didn't help in the extrication process.

Now Andre took the lead. He was a regular visitor to the Alps and could read the snow surface. I stayed at the back glissading in my own style and thoroughly enjoying the experience of descending. All the worries of the morning and the grim plod through the snow disappeared in the relief of getting off the mountain at high speed. We started our slides gracefully then lost balance and ended up on our backsides. Even a few cartwheels in the snow did not dampen our exhilaration at catching up on our schedule. It was a challenge we warmed to.

When the snow at last thinned and rocky scree made the going more tricky our muscles were already attuned to the steepness of the descent. The pace didn't slacken: we now simply danced our way down with little side steps or took the less slippery detours. The frenzy of our galloping mode began to tell on Martine who had never imagined that a trek in the Himalaya could turn so suddenly into an endurance course for commandos. Luckily the horses now appeared, skidding down the scree, happier on this surface than on the treacherous ice. Gyalchen promptly put Martine on a horse but this was only helpful to the extent of saving her leg muscles. The pony was bareback and she had to use all her energy just to cling on as it swerved on its descent pulled by the trotting Gyalchen who as always led from the front.

Not a word was spoken. Everyone was enclosed in his private resolution to beat the clock. The scenery began to soften though the canyon remained narrow and steep. We had hit a faint path leading ultimately to the village and that augured safety at the end of our efforts. But the increasing flow and cold of the melt water that drummed down the canyon began to slow us down. In places it had submerged the accompanying path and we had to wade through knee deep, skidding on the slick polished boulders, our eyes always on the time. Lower still when the water got waist deep we had to rein in the horses and sit bareback on them to do short fording gallops. You leant forward, put your head alongside the pony's neck, then held on grimly as the ponyman charged forward into the flood. You went straight into the water, head first, then were thrown back by the explosive cold of the water as the pony plunged across. Breath knocked out of you, the pony reared back on its haunches for the struggle out onto the other side. It was all over in seconds if one had the time to analyse it. We hadn't. Focused on reaching the village before dark we had eyes only for the path downwards to our goal. Every second of fading daylight counted.

Just as the sun was beaming out its last rays we came to a clearer patch of mountainside where the canyon opened out briefly. This is where the ponymen decided they would graze the horses for the night. It would be too dangerous to take them down the last section, narrow, steep and slippery, in the half-light. Several streams funnelled into the defile making a mighty clash of frothing white water. This was the worst time of day to be entering the maelstrom. The water raced so high in places it scoured our line of advance. We would be wading the last section in bad light with our energy reserves at their lowest.

As I cast around my gaze, I looked west to where another canyon branched. Red angry rock faces that rose several hundred feet were separated by a space of possibly thirty feet. As our party munched on dry biscuits and caught its breath for the last act in our desperate rushed descent we heard a rattle of falling stone. I looked up to see where it originated. There in the glow of the sun's final beams I saw the most ethereal sight I have ever set eyes on. We were paralysed with wonder at the ballet enacted before our eyes. A party of maybe six or more ibex began cavorting back and forth across the red canyon walls in amazing defiance of gravity. I couldn't believe this was physically possible. Each one effortlessly leaped up from a standing bunched-up position and launched itself into space. In a graceful ascending arc it gained height and was catapulted across the canyon face. The moment their hoofs touched the further wall they pirouetted and took off again instantaneously to reverse the elegant curve and touch the other side. In this continuous, casual zigzag ascent of the canyon walls was poetry of the most sublime sort, as though demonstrating the miraculous nature of life's ordering.

It was the uncanny juxtaposition of concentrated energy at each take-off with the effortless ease of flight that seemed extra-ordinary. This magical interlude in our descent somehow held a message from a more profound dimension than the physical. This was not just the surefootedness of mountain goats being demonstrated but a definition of the true meaning of yoga: skill in action. Panini obviously had never seen a mountain goat otherwise he might have mentioned the analogy. We in turn felt that this stupendous vision of grace in nature had been vouchsafed us in recognition of our fierce resolution to beat the odds and reach our target.

Few travellers arrived at this time of evening and possibly the ibex were as surprised to see us as we were to see them. The ponymen just smiled when they saw the animals zigzagging in their death-defying leaps. They too were cragsmen used to skipping out of danger and accustomed to using bursts of energy to escape tight corners. Gyalchen's decision to send us flying down this series of gorges was in a minor key a similar kind of zigzag to what we were now witnessing above our heads.

THE GREATEST SHOW ON EARTH 217

The ringing of hoofs echoed from the rock faces and for a moment I thought these animals must be drunk from the exuberance of their leaps. Like accomplished artists in an idle practice session the ibex were going through their paces to keep them in trim for when a real enemy was on their tail. Because of Zanskar's Buddhist traditions and the fact that this area has no military presence they were clearly not afraid of men or horses. Their rainbow bursts back and forth were accompanied by snorts of satisfaction as though a young pianist had been through his scales and got everything right.

Birds in the high mountains rarely fly energetically except for the frantic snow pigeon. Their characteristic behaviour on or above the treeline is to skulk as partridges do or laze like the chough. These mountain gazelles demonstrated that mankind's depiction of an electric spark as a zigzag bolt may have been inspired by the nimble ricochet of the ascending ibex. We saw no sparks because the rock of the Zanskar range is so friable but it would be easy to imagine on granite or igneous surfaces a flash of momentary fire where the clinking hoofs touched hard rock then soared away to the opposite side of the cliff to score another metallic imprint.

Time now to heft our daysacks and plunge into the cascading defile. Martine was tired and had to be assisted by one of the ponymen. The sight of the ibex had filled us all with a kind of invincible elixir and now no challenge could be too great. Down we grappled into the black defile, its walls polished in summer by the roar of melt water and worn by the feet of centuries of travellers. It was night now and we had to grope and flounder up to our waists in narrow sections where the water could not escape and boiled back onto our path. At the best of times this could only be called a catwalk and in the fury of the day's volume of melt it now had gone under. Without a guide this would have been a suicidal mission but the ponymen knew every bend in the route, when to cross and how to find less dangerous ground on the other bank. At the bad patches they would stretch a rope over and we were unceremoniously bundled into the cascading torrent. No time for niceties in the pecking order of client and porter. The man at the dry end held the rope tightly till you were almost across then he winched you home with a desperate tug. We were running now just to keep warm. Our clothes were drenched and our teeth chattered, yet strangely we were in control of our situation. Like the coiled energy locked in the winged heels of the ibex we called on hidden reserves of stamina to handle the punishment meted out by the river. Gargling from a slip midstream you would find yourself manhandled upright over the torrent to safety. No question of thanks or even recognition of whose helping hand it was. Fiercely focused since our three o'clock departure off the pass, it was now nearing eight and we were stumbling down the falling stream in pitch darkness. No one had thought of packing a torch.

I heard Gyalchen assuring Martine we were nearly through. The clunk of boots on rock and the slippery slap of wet running feet suddenly ceased and there was the reassuring thump of level mother earth under our feet. Through the dark I could just about make out the ripple of growing things and a path that snaked between these squares of even growth. Magically I heard a woman's voice call out interrogatively, the wife of one of the ponymen. Gyalchen's shouted reply immediately made her voice go up a key to that of relief and welcome.

It was follow-my-leader for we couldn't see a thing. Led by the local lady we filed through the fields and came to a stone wall that shone from the white boulders it was built of. Then we turned inside to an adobe wall that was the side of a low house. Instead of a door there was a tunnel and down this we stumbled still following the lady in front blindly, getting dry from the scorching pace we had set. The tunnel wound around past bleating goats and stocks of brushwood and then popped up before a junction with steps. We climbed out to emerge into the classic scene of a trans-Himalayan nomad's hearth. Sitting with woollen robe open to reveal a bare shoulder was the family patriarch with ladle raised to stir the butter tea simmering in a huge kettle on the central hob. Around him were gathered family members of various ages all gazing at the newcomers with amused tolerance, for this was how so many visitors made it to Zanskar—more dead than alive! Their

THE GREATEST SHOW ON EARTH 219

job was to revive the casualties of the way and nobody minded when I found a corner and just crashed out. The fug in that enclosed room was delicious after the scour of freezing water we had been victim to for the last part of the descent.

I was too far gone to eat, or drink the butter tea that was passed round endlessly. Eventually Gyalchen gave me a glass of cocoa which had been saved from an earlier expedition passing through. But there was no sugar. Sugar was still a treasured commodity in interior Zanskar and we would not find it on the trail till we were a day out of Padum. The short length of motor road from Padum had opened ten years earlier so what I witnessed was the end of the time-honoured system of barter. Also I saw the sea change in the diet of the people. Now sacks of government-subsidised rice were trucked in to Padum for families confined for millennia to the unvarying taste of ground barley. Sugar was most sought after and soon the Zanskari would vie with his neighbours south of the crest in ladling in spoonfuls of this energy giver, forsaking 'gur gur chai' for the leafier variety. In 1988 gur-gur chai was the only tea available in Kargyak. I lay stretched out in front of the great wooden cylindrical churn with its brass bindings, a symbol of the unified Buddhist culture that stretches all the way from Kargyak on the far side of the western crest to Tawang at the eastern end of the range but sitting south of the divide. Interestingly Tawang in restricted Arunachal was then still free of tourist influences whereas in Ladakh (but not till that time in Zanskar) tickets were being issued for visitors to look over the monasteries. In Tawang the lamas were genuinely surprised when I offered them a ten rupee note. It never occurred to them that a cash economy views everything including the sacred as a purchasable commodity.

24
Cliff-Hanging Gompa

I lay the night and the whole of the next day in the same spot stretched out in my sleeping bag. The family continued its routine of gathering for tea drinking bouts and always before drinking enquired if I would join them. I imagined how a family of British householders would have reacted if someone on a cold and stormy night had barged into their living room and spread out his bedding. There would have been an uproar and the police would have been called in to deal with the gatecrasher. Eventually with all the legal formalities completed the interloper would have been transferred to a lunatic asylum.

This is why I find Britain such a boringly predictable society: there is no space for madness in ordinary life. India on the other hand allows our loony instincts room for expression to add to the sum of creative possibilities.

I have never acquired a taste for butter tea and had to be content with ordinary chai without sugar. Gyalchen claimed that the expedition sugar (rescued by his brother's yaks the following day) had got wet in the snow—but we all knew what that really meant. Obviously there is a practical reason why hill people relish three tablespoonfuls of sugar in a small glass of tea. It gives a feeling of instant energy just as drawing on a beedi does. The hill person's plain diet is eaten usually in two large meals morning and evening. In between his routine is punctuated by tea and tobacco. Everywhere the tea-shop is considered a crucial part of the social landscape. It

doubles up as a place where you can buy beedis and on recognised routes it turns into a hotel that puts up overnight travellers. The use of the word 'hotel' in the Himalayan context is a travesty of the English original. The accommodation amounts to a string bed and a greasy cotton quilt under a thatched roof. 'Hotel' to the hill mind signifies a daring alternative to the traditional hostelry, the dharmshala. These charitable institutions run by religious trusts provide a plain unfurnished room almost free and expect the traveller to be orthodox enough to insist on preparing his own food. The hotel by contrast will provide forbidden fare like eggs, fish and meat and best of all, daru—home-distilled whisky. This explains why so many of the interior dhabas are manned by Nepali ladies for they are popular hostesses by day and master distillers by night. Thanks to Victorian morality that intensified traditional brahminical distaste no caste Hindu will flaunt his taste for liquor in public. In Nepal by contrast (and echoing the taste of ancient India for intoxicating drinks) both male and female Hindus enjoy alcoholic beverages. The same is true for the Buddhist regions of the high Himalaya where chang is socially acceptable, and in the tribal tracts of the northeast where no stigma attaches to the enjoyment of locally produced spirits.

The problem in India is not that the general population is averse to alcohol; on the contrary, since alcohol is proscribed by polite society in public people tend to drink more than is good for them in private. This may be a fallout from the hold of the joint family where juniors have no opportunity to develop individual tastes. Their secret drinking may be a form of subliminal revenge against the system since shame attaches to a family that has a 'sharabi' on its roster, at least in theory. In practice it can be a subliminal sign of modernity in families well-off enough to be unconcerned with what others think of them.

The only stranger I met at Kargyak was the village primary schoolteacher sent by the Jammu and Kashmir government. Incredibly he was a Muslim who spoke Urdu and knew no Zanskari. This meant both he and the Buddhist children were free most of the day after signing the attendance register. He would get his pay and the children would be added to the government literacy statistics. Local lamas saw to it that the children got a grounding in the Tibetan texts that I had seen my ponymen so earnestly consulting on our walk in.

India's problems are always said to derive from the poor level of education offered to the masses. To compound this is the lack of realism in legislators far removed from the situation on the ground. You could ask any leading politician a hundred questions about the country they always claim to speak for and all their answers would be wrong. In New Delhi's list of preoccupations Zanskar is somewhere near the end and Kargyak drops to the bottom altogether. The minister in Delhi will declare grandly that even such backward villages have government schools, unaware that the school exists on paper only. Throughout the length of the Himalaya similar situations exist and the most common is the absenteeism of teachers who find the hill terrain too taxing. (Just two kilometres down the hill from Landour I had found that the village primary schoolteacher attends duties only when he comes to collect his pay.)

Fit again after a day's rest but leaner from the retreat down the canyon we set out along the open running valley that would lead to Padum. The walk was both beautiful and perilous. At places the river was wide but soon the ranges closed in to make us climb and take outflanking measures. In places the soil was so crumbly that at each footstep the path collapsed under our feet into the river. This meant you had to sprint up certain volatile alleys to reach a secure surface. The ponies were nonchalant in their outstepping of the collapsing hillside. Their lightness of foot was inbred and they accommodated the dangerous stretches of overhang as confidently as they had breasted the treacherous currents.

The occasional bridge had to be swung over and here we were too late by a handful of years to experience the characteristic feature of earlier treks in Zanskar, the crossing of precarious bridges made of interwoven twigs. Because of the paucity of materials the villagers had to rely on the pliant stalks of the pollarded willow along with any other brushwood species that yielded lengths of flexible material. The weaving of a twig bridge is an extension of the making of baskets, a well-developed craft throughout the Himalaya, with a rich lore of regional variation. In the northeast frontier states where bamboo is heavily relied on for many household functions (including the building of the house itself) you find grass bridges (bamboo is technically a grass) of extraordinary length. These graceful seasonal bridges are built with community effort, a custom all over the range. In Lata for example when tree-trunk bridges over the Rishi Ganga rotted they were replaced by villagers who sent their goats to graze above Dharansi. To man-handle a full-sized deodar armed only with axes you need at least a hundred men.

Worse than the flimsiness of the traditional Zanskar bridges was their sag and sway. Most were meant for one-way traffic and were unusable by horses. I saw an example of a twig bridge standing near the turn off for Phugtal gompa but it was deep in the gorge and the effort to climb down and try out its elasticity did not appeal. I was content to photograph it and accept that had I come a decade earlier I would have been forced to use this swaying contraption. Now wooden bridges were being built by the public works department and these luckily are of a fairly simple and aesthetic design. These bridges would open up valuable communication between villages as well as allow horse loads to reach needy communities. If you did not live in the three converging valleys that radiated out from Padum you were very much left to your own devices. Higher up you had the compensation of apricot orchards to vitalise your days: this crop is often credited with giving long life to interior villagers. However the few high altitude villages I did come across on my trek did not yield any obvious proof of this contention.

On the trail we saw the occasional farmer in maroon robe astride a prancing pony with tinkling harness returning to his village from Padum, or some wizened old inhabitant tottering between hamlets with his praying wheel at full spin. The river now was a distinctly hostile entity flowing with a swift silent bore of unvarying light grey defining the landscape with its incisive presence. Here and there a few plots of barley were on view but these oases were the exception in the chalky calm of the desiccated ranges we passed over, enlivened only by the occasional wild pink rose bush. We spent that night with Thomay's family in Testa. His old father and elder brother were both strong and hearty as were the womenfolk of the household.

I chose to sleep on the flat roof of the house after being closely scrutinised by all the neighbourhood who had gathered to examine the foreign guests. Martine came in for most scrutiny since women everywhere are considered the more interesting species. She submitted to the inspection gracefully in spite of her tiredness. The trip had proved to be far more wearing than she had bargained for. Already she and Andre had decided to scrap their onward trek from Padum to Lamayuru, a strenuous five-day extension.

French trekkers were drawn in large numbers to Zanskar because of Michel Peissel's book, *The Hidden Kingdom*. This French academic irritated a lot of English and Indian readers with his Gallic flamboyance that made out he was the first modern explorer to have rediscovered the magic of this lost valley. Perhaps the resentment arose from the British colonial feeling that theirs had been the first white feet in these parts. Who was this Frenchman to suggest otherwise? In fact Peissel writes enthusiastically and well and succeeds in capturing the vivid landscape wherever he goes. Indian readers get wild when he defines the way out of Zanskar as 'the road to India', an anachronism borrowed from colonial writers who would always refer to (British) India as being distinct from Kashmir (of which Zanskar is now an administrative part).

The Maharaja of the vast state of Kashmir enjoyed the reputation of a ruler with an iron fist but his territories were so scattered that local (nominally Muslim) warlords did what they pleased for most of the time. This was a situation similar to that obtaining in Tibet where the ultimate power was the Emperor of China. Only when seriously roused did the emperor bother to send an expeditionary force to quell distant tributary powers. When a Dogra general tried to expand the possessions of Kashmir in 1841 to include the Kailash region the Chinese drove out the invaders as comprehensively as they had cut the Nepalis to size in Kathmandu as reprisals for the Gurkha invasion of Tibet some fifty years earlier.

Much has been made of the Dogra general Zorawar Singh's military gifts but his early victories were hardly a test of generalship. The Chinese and the weather combined to defeat him in Tibet where his daring in committing Dogra troops far from their base in winter now seems foolhardy. Zorawar Singh's name has also been invoked in Garhwal to help explain the mystery of the three hundred corpses in the Rup Kund tarn at the base of Trisul. Since the general's samadhi lies across the Lipu Lekh pass in Tibet and the survivors of his army presumably straggled back to India over the Uttarakhand passes some have theorised that this remnant accounts for the bodies in the lake at Rup Kund.

The theory does not make sense. The preserved bodies bear no weapons and only shepherds and pilgrims have any use for the route to the base of Trisul. Though the bones of the dead have been carbon dated to the fourteenth century to settle the issue, Zorawar Singh continues to command a romantic following. According to Swami Pranavananda the general was held in superstitious regard by his Tibetan opponents. After killing him with a bullet made of gold his body was hacked to pieces and his testicles preserved in Simbiling gompa near Taklakot.

The absence of weapons at Rup Kund is a reminder of why the Himalayan kingdoms rarely produced marauding armies with imperial prospects. The reason the exception to this rule—Prithvi Narayan Shah of Gorkha—was successful was due in part to the altitude of the Kathmandu valley where he made his name. Any situation higher and it is a problem to temper steel: metal blades cannot achieve a high temperature given the high altitude decline in oxygen that makes it difficult stoking a charcoal fire. It is interesting to note that the characteristic weapon of the Gurkhas, the kukri, always has alongside it two smaller blades to keep it whetted.

The usefulness of the kukri (that becomes the dao in the Eastern Himalaya) is related to the increasing density of bamboo growth following the south-east trend of the Himalaya.

In Arunachal unlike Nepal men do not wear the dao for macho effect. It is a basic piece of equipment without which they cannot penetrate the jungle. So dense are the bamboo clumps in Arunachal that you literally have to hack a way through. I was astonished to find that bamboo of more than an inch diameter can be found near the top of the Se La pass at 14,000 ft. Women like men are forced to wear a dao at their waist when foraging in the jungle.

Gyalchen had a relation living in the gompa at Phugtal, a lama of ten years standing, and I was keen to sample the night-time mood of the place. Everything I had heard about this monastery made it seem like a candidate for the location of Madam Blavatsky's *Masters of Wisdom* where, penned on the walls of the building, were tantalising fragments of the inspiration for her *Secret Doctrine*. Nowadays it is fashionable to pooh-pooh Blavatsky and write off her spiritual investigations as bogus. Certainly her book the *Veil of Isis* which I was recommended to read in Mirtola is tedious in style and tiresome in content. But so too is Gurdjieff's *All and Everything*. The likely place to search for inner wisdom I learned is not the slick best-sellers favoured by polite society. By their very uncouthness Blavatsky and Gurdjieff were trying to separate the true seeker from the casual enquirer.

The gorge on the way to the gompa was copper in the slanting sun sandwiching with its sheer sides the steely grey river that surged silently below our undulating path. A new timber bridge had been built to carry trekkers across the dangerous flow and once over this elegant structure we had our first view of the gompa. Leading up to it were a series of white somewhat battered chortens. Framed between a bank of pink roses the marker chortens led the eye up to an amazing eyrie crowning not a hill but a tumble of Tibetan-style monastic quarters. This white spill of ecclesiastical architecture in turn poured out from the black mouth of a large cavern. And atop the cavern was a lone cedar tree, a bizarre capping for a bare gorge of unending grey tones.

We toiled up looking at crows seemingly levitating in the updraught of air from the swift river slicing underfoot. As always the path teetered on the brink and now to keep it company was the slew of lama dwellings stacked one on top of the other, each set back slightly to counter the slope of the chalky hillside.

The interior, as in most monasteries, was cold, dark and draughty and redolent with the smell of rancid butter. This is something acolytes of the Mahayana path seem to learn to live with. This fatty odour is found the length of the Buddhist Himalaya from Arunachal to Spiti. Zanskar is a rich butter-producing valley and its flavour is sought after outside the province. In winter, men from Padum will brave the frozen Zanskar river and after a perilous week of skating and wading along the gorge with loads of butter on their back will find it snapped up in Leh's market.

Gyalchen's relation was a handsome but matter-of-fact young man who showed us to a room for the night. It was plain and cold but at least not draughty. This young lama was very intent that the Dalai Lama—due any day to arrive in Padum—should visit Phugtal. To overcome protests that the monastery was too out of the way for His Holiness he had organised a group of lamas to build a helipad on the roof of the cave. Sadly the Dalai Lama would have too many calls on his time and was unable to avail of this facility.

For me the monastery was disappointing in the sense that nothing of the Blavatsky mystique emerged. I have been to so many similar gompas that everything seemed predictable from the grunting chants of ancient ritualists to the boyish giggles from the kitchen where innocent attempts at affectionate exchange might have occasioned the mirth. Sex in the transHimalaya tends to be less guilt-laden than in other parts of the range though for form's sake no public acknowledgement of this reality is encouraged. As in orthodox Hinduism, subjects like homosexuality are regarded as signs of unenlightenment. Ironically Andrew Harvey, the most lyrical writer on Ladakhi Buddhism, was forced to part ways with his (Hindu) guru over her narrow and timid understanding of love's wayward possibilities.

The Phugtal gompa is where Alexander Csoma de Koros, the Hungarian linguist, lived for a year. He set out from Europe in 1818 to enquire into the roots of his native tongue and found his way to Leh where he was helped by that remarkable explorer-entrepreneur Moorcraft. He lived for several years in Zanskar, learning the language. This enabled the dedicated de Koros to compile the first dictionary of the Tibetan language in English. His dictionary still appears in the catalogue of Delhi publishers of Tibetiana. He first lived in Zangla then in Phugtal from 1825 to 1826. From 1827 to 1830 he moved to Karcham in the Sutlej valley. After his dictionary he was accepted as the librarian of the Royal Asiatic Society in Calcutta. Eager to visit Tibet the ageing Hungarian got as far as Darjeeling where worn out by the privations of his ascetic years he passed away in 1842. I had seen his gravestone—beautifully maintained—when I visited Darjeeling in 1986. Alongside the Zanskar monastery in a shrine is preserved the slate on which the linguist carved his name and the dates of his stay.

25
The King Over the Water

The next two nights were spent at camping sites near Pepala and Muni. Our horsemen were deliberately spinning out our rate of progress to inflate the bill, but it was true fodder was scarce so at midday the animals needed a long time to find any grass to graze. Pepala marked the onset of tourist culture. A village youth had set up a tented dhaba by the riverside and for five rupees parties could pitch their own tent alongside. Sugar was available in the tea and the meal was likewise more interesting than higher up the valley where tsampa was the only item on the menu.

The next day we reached Muni and as a wonderful climax there was a small lake nearby where we could strip off our sweat-caked shirts and bathe. A jeepable road from Padum extended as far as this point and inevitably there was a large mingling of trekkers round the cluster of dhabas. Those gearing up for a crossing of the Shingo La buttonholed those who had done it and asked for tips. There aren't any of course except to start early and watch the weather closely.

That night I found the perfect camping place. I climbed away from the scrum of trekkers camped around the tiny monastic building to a field of green swaying barley at whose edge grew luxurious clumps of wild geranium, of all flowers in the Himalaya my favourite. The range and resilience of this species is astonishing. In Mirtola on the cold northern side of the hill it flourishes and yields a wonderfully delicate mauve flower after the rains. In Mussoorie the wonder increases in winter when the superbly reticulated leaf turns a brilliant red. Never have I seen such a perfectly proportioned leaf. Typically if a miracle of life is underfoot people refuse to recognise its uniqueness. Gardeners in Mussoorie view jungly geranium as a weed. Strangely they will offer undue respect to the bright red potted variety whose leaf is not a patch on the beauty of the wild plant.

At Muni the geraniums grew in banks of purple and I settled down for the night amongst their sensational assemblage. For a traveller it is easy to remember good camping sites. You stay in so many different places that only the very good—or very bad—stand out. For a budget traveller the bad nights tend to exceed the good but it is a noticeable fact that even bad nights spent perforce under the stars are less depressing than those confined to a grotty hut or dank cavern.

Some miserable occasions become funny in retrospect. On my trek to Stok Kangri with Wienerschnitzel we slept in a cattle pen that bedded down a variety of grazing species. During the night every breed of animal identified itself by the volume of its fart and the quantity of its piss. One could have composed a concerto for wind instruments entitled 'Variations on an Evacuatory Theme'.

Like so many expeditionists at altitude my body finds it hard enough to breathe, let alone sleep. Usually sleep overcomes exhaustion at dawn and just as deep slumber finally settles over the tired trekker it is time for that early start to beat the predicted bad weather or high running river.

The soothing swish of the barley and the sway of the geranium made me sleep fairly well at Muni and I woke up only once when a pony sneaked away to forage in a neighbouring field and was chased out by a watchman. The trail now was along a jeepable 'highway' and we reached Padum by noon. In fact we almost bypassed it for we had followed a path that skirted the village and made straight for the vast open valley ahead.

For anyone with Shangri La inclinations Padum is a sore letdown. It is small, scruffy, primitive and overpriced. The hotels are worse than basic and I have stayed in some high altitude caves that offer more protection from the wind than these bare cells. Worst of all is the quality of drinking water. Because the valley sits right under the crest of the Great range the water hurtles down for some 9000 ft full of sediment and soil. It takes weeks for the sediment to settle and still there remains a peaty brownness to the water. Small wonder that the very first, least likely and most welcome advertisement greeting the traveller in Padum is for Pepsi Cola.

I found lodgings in a small guest house set amidst the newly harvested fields. Andre and Martine elected to camp near the tourist bungalow where passable food was to be found. The horsemen had relations in Padum and stayed in their shops. We passed on any excess baggage and lightened our loads for returning by bus. It was strange to see the government bus after a week of hoofing it over the Himalaya. A Sikh driver sat next to the bus and I asked when it would return to Kargil. That depended, he said, on when he could gather a full complement of passengers. He was quite used to sitting for up to a week waiting for the bus to fill. Sympathy for the plight of these shivering government employees however tends to evaporate when closer acquaintance is made with their mode of operation. These far out postings with no checks are sought after by the more entrepreneurial of the transport staff since they can make a tidy pile on tourist pickings and the local carting of heavy luggage. Unless the passenger insists, no tickets are issued.

Padum's bazaar was a tiny tumbledown place of grey stone houses that had been tacked on to the medieval crumble of the original village. The river curves behind the village but is hidden by higher ground under which the bazaar shelters. Government development schemes with eyesore alien architecture and tottering official notice boards add to the visual carnage. After the transcendent beauty of the chalky white gorges Padum seemed to be the bottom end.

I viewed the local sights over the next three days, and visited Karsha, a prominent monastery, which meant crossing the river and climbing the hill at the end of the long broad valley. Padum itself has a fine carved outcrop depicting a line of Bodhisattvas but it is a bit of a scrabble to reach it, right above the curving river. Karsha was a day's trip there and back and though it had its appeal it was just another monastery as far as I was concerned: friendly monks (much less demanding of baksheesh than their Ladakhi counterparts), a fine library of manuscripts and excellent art on the monastery walls. But this was true for many of the monasteries I saw along the length of the Himalaya. In fact the sameness is remarkable when you consider the distance from Hemis in Ladakh to Tawang in Arunachal. However these extremes viewed from Tibet (with access along the banks of the Indus–Brahmaputra) somewhat shrink the perspective. Building a transHimalayan highway along the foothills of India is an engineering nightmare because of the run-off of dozens of huge rivers. Building it on the roof of the world is comparatively plain sailing since you command the watersheds of the rivers that do the damage in the plains of India.

Padum was filling up with villagers dressed in their Sunday best for the visit of the Dalai Lama. The valley boasted of a new gompa—whose baked earth walls had not yet been painted—to host His Holiness for the public initiation ceremony of Kalachakra whereby the entire province would be blessed. Along with the Tibetan entourage came Government of India emissaries. I gathered with a group of local Zanskaris and a cluster of foreign trekkers to welcome the jeep cavalcade of the colonel who was to supervise the arrangements. The Zanskaris were all red-faced from the sun and wind in their hard lives; the foreigners too bore these marks of the unrelenting sun and wind by virtue of their trek over the Shingo La. When the colonel got out of his vehicle followed by his plump wife and daughters dressed in saris, there was a gasp of disbelief. Visitors from a distant planet would probably have looked less strange on the Zanskar landscape than these people from the plains. The punishing road journey had made them pale and disgruntled and the smiling faces of the reception committee were greeted with weary grimaces from the arrivals. It seemed the classical colonial situation: the alien representatives of a distant authority had appeared, and the profound contrast in physical types, mental attitudes and civilisational behaviour made the scene embarrassing to behold.

The Dalai Lama's visit was dampened by gusts of rain. Deep grey clouds loured over the Padum valley to render the collage of beautiful costumes on display a soggy mess. But nobody seemed to notice the rain so avid was their gaze fixed on the Dalai Lama. The more fashionable ladies flashed folding umbrellas while the US-returned lamas of His Holiness's entourage sported colourful anoraks and Rayban sunglasses.

It was a magical moment for the people of Zanskar. Gyalchen's reverence for the Tibetan religious texts which he read round the campfire each evening after the meal was now receiving its due reward. For three days the maroon robes and home-dyed shawls eddied about the valley where hundreds of tents had been set up. The daily audience given by His Holiness drew rapt attention. This was without question the most religious mass gathering I have ever attended and knocked Billy Graham revivalist meetings into the shade.

Needless to say the unsavoury aspects of religion reared their seedy heads too with credulous villagers ripped off. Lamas with raffle books offered consumer gadgets and flaunted two-in-one radio–cassettes to lure the faithful. The pious public relations officer of the Dalai Lama turned away an Indian journalist on the grounds that His Holiness was too busy to give interviews. Minutes later, when an American journalist claiming to be from the *National Geographic* sought a similar interview I was amused to see him whisked straight in. I had seen this happen before, in Dharmshala, though the surrender to the dollar by the coterie surrounding the Dalai Lama was a little less abject there.

THE KING OVER THE WATER

My Zanskar journeys had not ended. In 1995 I fulfilled a dream, flying over the Zanskar gorge with the object of making a film down its course from Padum. We were to raft the white water with cameras and crew. When originally approached by the director Gayatri Singh, a young lady who happened to be my neighbour in Mussoorie, I suggested starting at the headwaters on the Bara Lacha La and following the various incarnations of the river to its meeting with the Stod at Karsha where the name Zanskar is given to it. Oddly the river only flows through Zanskar for some thirty kilometres, entering Ladakh at the gorge beyond Zangla. The river flows for another hundred kilometres through the narrow towering canyon to emerge at the surrealistic sangam near Nyemo only thirty-five kilometres from Leh. The translucent coppery beauty of the gorge remains one of the most overpowering images of my first ride to Leh from Srinagar. I vowed I would enter this magical gorge one day and explore its austere magic.

Neither the weather nor the local political situation in Padum permitted a start to our rafting expedition. We had driven from Leh in two Suzuki Gypsies plus a Tata truck carrying the rafting gear and crew. With the politics of the plains spilling over to poison the traditional secular traditions of Ladakh, the Muslim Purigpas of Kargil had been separated administratively from the Buddhist Lehpas of upper Ladakh. This meant that our Gypsy utility vehicles hired in Leh were not allowed to run beyond Kargil. We had to change jeeps.

Kargil is a dump at the best of times and without doubt the least lively point in the entire length of the Indian Himalaya—that is until the Pakistani army only two kilometres away starts shelling it! But the valley that follows the river Suru immediately under the crest of the Great Himalaya is both spectacular and fairly prosperous. Though outwardly you find the loveless face of the Ayatollah's brand of Islam, beneath the burqa the ladies apply lipstick. The menfolk are famous as cooks (and mechanics) and the great modern fad in Europe of 'Balti Takeaways' arose from this unprepossessing culture.

We passed the cultural divider of Rangdum gompa built on a beacon-like rise in the floodplains marking the origins of the Suru.

Above is the Pensi La leading over to the hidden province of Zanskar. This pass marks a great fulcrum of world religion. Look eastwards and the writ of Buddhism runs for 3000 kilometres to the Pacific. Glance west and the doctrine of Islam holds sway for the same distance as far as the Mediterranean. Southwards all the works will be of Hindu fashioning until the subcontinent meets the ocean another 3000 kilometres away.

The physical view from the pass is likewise dramatic. An extraordinary curling glacier unwinds to announce Zanskar's steep valleys cut off from the rest of India by the crest of the Great Himalaya.

One of Zanskar's former kings now lives in Padum and while waiting for the snow to stop we went to call on him. The miserable huddle of tumbledown stone houses that signify the capital are primitive even in good weather but now in the slush and sleet of unseasonal rain it was like visiting a refugee colony. The king, reduced to very modest circumstances is better known as the kindly person who runs the village primary school. His house is just one among the huddle of buildings all badly leaking since their flat mud roofs were designed for sun or snow but nothing in between. The sleet had destroyed the whole barley crop, which laid out in stooks to dry on the roof, was now rotting in the rain. Touchingly on the planked outer door of the monarch's house someone had printed 'KING' using a finger dipped in turmeric.

Meeting the former king we do not broach the sensitive subject of the locals' drastic decision to hold three foreign (French) trekkers 'hostage' in the dak bungalow. The locals wish to bring their displeasure at the way tourism is run in Zanskar to the notice of the authorities. A few hotheads have argued that the sure way to grab the headlines is to borrow the techniques of neighbouring Kashmir. That way you are sure to get exposure on TV news channels internationally.

Most Zanskaris while they share the resentment at rich Kashmiri tour operators making all the profits and the fact that foreigners do not spend a penny in Padum (since they camp in tents provided by the tour operator) feel to take hostages will be counterproductive.

It seems wiser counsels prevailed for as we were rafting through the gorge two helicopters winged overhead on their way to rescue the French visitors from the confines of the dak bungalow. Amusingly by the time we got to Leh the tourist authorities had begun to deny the whole thing and pretend that no hostages had been taken.

I was in full sympathy with the grievances of the Padum residents against the profiteering Kashmiris who come in with mule trains of supplies for their foreign clients. Padum was the underdog. It had no infrastructure and only in this lost-world environment would a scruffy tumbledown village like this ever achieve the status of a provincial capital. The truth is that many visitors walk past Padum in disbelief. They cannot bring themselves to feel this cluster of houses signifies anything important. Only Kaza in a similar situation in Spiti rates with Padum as a hard-to-believe provincial headquarters.

Our raft trip through the gorge was as dramatic as hoped for but only for the sailors. Owing to a bad back I could not row and was told to sit in front and hold on to a rope. Ahead of me standing in the prow was Kabir Khan our adventurous cameraman who believed in taking the elements head on. As the meeting rivers below the monastery at Karsha buffeted our craft I noted Kabir bending down to get a close-up of the rapids. Then he disappeared overboard in slow motion and took the rope with him. I foolishly was still hanging on to it so followed him into the water. My flailing feet in turn knocked another paddler into the river. Luckily we were all properly dressed for a ducking and no untoward rocks put our crash helmets to the test. Jigme Dorje, our tough and capable admiral, hauled us out and put us ashore to change into dry clothes. The bad news was that the video camera had been affected and we had no spare. The good news was that the bad weather had cleared and we would now have strong sun in which to dry our clothes.

The sail through the gorge usually takes three to four days leisurely enjoying the truly sensational colours of the canyon rocks that rear up sheer from the racing water. To salvage her film our director had somehow to reach civilisation to book a relief camera by air. The only option lay ahead in Leh so we set off early next morning rafting to Chiling then walking to Nyemo and going to Leh by truck.

On our return, a few miles short of Chiling the road was blocked and we had to walk. As we skirted the river we saw rounding a bend ahead the curious sight of a loaded pack-horse bulging from two tin trunks strapped to its sides. Even stranger was the person who accompanied it, a scholarly foreigner with granny glasses looking like a prospector for gold. Cautious pleasantries were exchanged followed by a 'Dr Livingstone I presume' revelation. It was Gary Weare, who had inspired me to visit Zanskar by his writings in the *Lonely Planet* guide.

What a million to one chance to bump into this Australian editor whose letter had by coincidence fetched up on my desk only a few days before I set out. To sober my expectations when I sought the promised reward—he had offered a bottle of Glenfiddich to quote from my Nanda Devi book—Gary confessed that the rigours of the trail from Lamayuru over the Dung Dung La had caused him to prematurely finish his stock. True to his word he would later have a bottle delivered to me in Delhi.

But all was not lost on the liquor front. Back in Chiling to watch the last traditional craftsmen fashion copper pots and musical instruments, we adjourned to the home of the most prosperous farmer. In the golden lantern light the faces of the company glowed as if in a Rembrandt painting. We toasted our luck with unending beakers of chang and raised a special cheer for the world's most modest monarch at the other end of the Zanskar gorge, our very own 'king over the water'.

26
The Taste of Vintage Chang

After the fulfilment of dreams comes the pleasure of recapitulation. The vow I had taken in the Asiatic Society library in Calcutta in 1959 to explore Nanda Devi Sanctuary had come to fruition in 1980. Twice more in successive years I gained entry to the Sanctuary to continue my adoration of the Goddess's beauties. Then the Sanctuary was closed to protect its fragile ecology.

Treks around the southern arc outside the Sanctuary took me to Rup Kund, Hom Kund, Delisera, Sevai, Kuari, Auli, Nauti, Krur and Nauli to follow up leads on the physical and religious persona of the Goddess. Travelling through the Pindari eastern flank of the Sanctuary curtain I felt the urge to try and cross the ice-fall that culminates at Traill's Pass. This was wishful thinking of an almost suicidal order revealing how passion for the Devi can blind a walker to his limitations. Even more disturbing for the conventional thought processes of the ordinary citizen, the mountain lover intoxicated by the danger of the challenge before him feels (if he is a bachelor with few prospects of ever becoming secretary-general of the United Nations) that should his plan misfire there could be no more glorious place in which to offer his last breath.

This is a form of madness but since some men do it for less worthy causes like political chauvinism and sectarian fervour, the mountaineer should be judged least culpable since he has answered the call of an overwhelming authentic lure. Possibly when the science of the soul is as developed as the science of the mind it will be recognised that our bodily hunger for food and sex is matched by the soul's desire for communion with eternity.

In 1995, after ten years, I travelled to Joshimath having read that mountaineering expeditions were being allowed to approach Changabang from the north outside the Sanctuary curtain along the Bagini glacier. I had long wanted to see beyond the Inner Line barrier at Surai Tota and visit the village of Dunagiri famous in the lore of the *Ramayana*. It is here that Lord Hanuman carried off the whole neighbouring mountaintop to guarantee the required medicinal herb would be available to cure the wounded brother of Lord Rama.

Dunagiri was like Lata, a village that moved down in winter, but unlike Lata which only moved downhill 3000 ft to the Dhauli Ganga, the residents of Dunagiri had to drop almost 10,000 ft to their winter quarters in Chamoli. The other Dunagiri near Dwarahat in Kumaun is emphatically an easily accessible understudy to the giant peak in Garhwal that towers almost menacingly in front of the village set high near the snout of the Bagini glacier. The Garhwal village boasts of a tiny shrine whereas in Kumaun at the foot of the 9500 ft Butkot peak stands a distinguished old temple. Butkot in the middle ranges is an imposing enough presence but still a midget when compared to the 23,184 ft stature of the real peak.

I caught the Shatabdi from Delhi to Haridwar. This fast train has revolutionised access to the hills of Uttaranchal. Ironically it had only come after public agitation for a hill state and was in the nature of a sop to the students of Dehra Dun who regularly held up road traffic to the hills to demand better facilities and statehood. The irony lies in the fact this is a luxury train that only businessmen (or subsidised government officers)—certainly not students—can afford. But it means the traveller can be in Haridwar by midday and reach Srinagar easily the same evening.

It was instructive to see how the hill paravs had changed over a decade of expanding tourist inflow. Now even the smallest of wayside shopkeepers boasted of a refrigerator that sold Pepsi. Most useful was the employment of young men as taxi operators to interior villages. The local bank 'hypothecates' the diesel jeep and villagers are jammed aboard ten times above the legal norm in order to repay the loan. Just a few years ago if you missed the once-daily bus to your village you had to wait till next day, or walk. Now you can by means of judicious hopping between villages reach your destination the same day provided you are not fussy about being rammed up hard against insalubrious fellow passengers not only smelling of sheep and goats but sometimes accompanied by them in the well of the jeep.

One young driver told me his hard luck story of how he had paid a lakh of rupees to a tout who guaranteed him a job in the Gulf. After a year earning good money (half of which found its way back to the tout) the Dubai police found the hillman's work permit had been forged and he was expelled from the country. Here was a typical case of an innocent Pahari who lacked the gumption to secure his own future. The same evening in the bungalow where I stayed I met a successful forest contractor who had spent ten years in America, made his pile and had come home to capitalise on his shrewd business instincts. The difference between the rich contractor and the poor Pahari was that the former was a Punjabi who could not easily be taken for a ride. Quite possibly the tout who took the Pahari for a ride was a relation of the contractor.

In Srinagar it is noticeable that the most bustling dhabas are run by pushy Punjabis. Hill proprietors will be distinguished by the down-at-heel appearance of their establishments. They will also—ridiculously in view of the lack of hygiene—boast of their shuddha status and might even provide a menu printed in Sanskrit. This brahminical posturing that guarantees they will only attract an unpaying clientele reflects a widespread urge in modern caste-bound hill society to escape into narcissism instead of adjusting to the challenge of keeping up with the less orthodox Punjabi. The latter has the common sense to realise that his restaurant exists to make money while the orthodox proprietor believes the existence of his establishment will somehow further the cause of dharma.

When I went to check in at the Joshimath tourist bungalow I was pleasantly surprised to find M.I. Khan, a tourist officer I knew from Mussoorie, behind the desk. This was a propitious start for Khan is the best tourist officer I have met in India. For a government servant he is unique. He loves his job, has tourist maps printed at his own expense and goes trekking enthusiastically. When I told him of my plans he immediately said he would join me.

This had to be the grace of the Goddess. Technically the approach to the village is said to lie within the confines of the Nanda Devi Biosphere Reserve and a permit would be required from the forest department to pass through the valley that leads to Dunagiri. Better still Khan was going to employ Raju a young Lata guide as our porter. I knew Raju's father who belonged to the older generation of Lata porters. Besides, Raju had relations living in Dunagiri and since we weren't carrying a tent that would guarantee us a place to stay.

I saw how today's porter in contrast to those of the earlier generation was wonderfully well up in expedition knowhow. Raju and his brother ran a trekking agency from Nanda Devi Hotel in Joshimath and this brought back memories of the one and only Yashu who ten years earlier had informally held this job and was in great demand for his knowledge of local lore.

As it happened I bumped into Yashu on the trail. He was leading a small party of American trekkers around the outside of the Sanctuary by what seemed a most bizarre route, zooming up and down between villages. Yashu was always an original and I thought no more about it till later we met one of his American clients who told us the reason for this yo-yoing route. The guide needed to keep himself topped up on village grog. Yashu was prey to that common hill complaint of loving 'daru' not too wisely but too well. It was a touching meeting for he is a lovable person and a true devotee of the Devi.

On one occasion when I turned up during Yashu's tenure at the Nanda Devi Hotel he introduced me to Kishore Parekh, a famous photo-journalist from Delhi who was planning to trek the next day to the Valley of Flowers and Hemkund Sahib. We exchanged pleasantries as Yashu served tea, then went our several ways. After a couple of weeks I returned from my trek and just by chance enquired how the famous photographer had fared. Yashu told me he had died of a heart attack upon reaching his goal. In the old days this would have been considered auspicious but in a more hurried age it seemed a terrible blow as cruel as it was unexpected.

It was just as well I went in the company of Mr Khan because the policeman on duty at Jumma beyond the old inner line post claimed he knew nothing about the revised rules that allowed visitors to turn off the road here and proceed eastwards up the Bagini khad. A little chai-pani soothed and enlightened the policeman and we were allowed to cross the bridge. The climb through steep conifer jungle had caused Atkinson's *Gazetteer* to wax poetic. 'The scenery retaining all its grandeur also becomes exquisitely lovely. Villages of the true Swiss character are seen. . . . Surrounded by cedar trees and overhung by crags of the most stupendous character wooded up to the snow which shines on their summits.' A good bridle path looking down into plunging torrents or up to a briefly glimpsed peak startlingly white against the strong blue sky, wound purposefully towards the village above this enchanted forest. As we climbed higher the terrain became more tangled and in places the path had been obliterated by landslides of titanic proportions. We had to jump over huge rocks dislodged by the drilling spout of water that poured off the lip of the plateau that we now sweated to attain.

At last we crested the spill of rockfall and were astonished to see the sheer size of Dunagiri village spread out below the moraine of the glacier now seeded with grass. It was one of the biggest villages I have ever set eyes on in the hills. There were dozens of houses mostly of wood, all blackened by the elements and the smoke of the permanent fires lit inside for warmth at this chilling height. Across the melt stream of the glacier up whose course we forced a path were the extensive fields, all harvested and betraying the hewn stubble of buckwheat (popularly known as *oogle*). Some cattle grazed but few families were in residence. They had gone down with their harvest and would not return until May next year.

We were invited to stay at Raju's aunt's house and this turned out to be an unexpected treat. At night after a meal of rotis and alu we bedded down on carpets woven by the ladies of the house from their own sheep, then after a few whispered consultations with Raju I was asked if I would like some chang—Khan did not drink. Accustomed to the Mussoorie variety that comes by the kettleful I said yes, thinking it would be impolite to say otherwise. The old lady seemed to forget what she had offered and bent down to unlock a large wooden box containing the family heirlooms. To my surprise, however, she eased out from it a clay jar with a sealed cap. She carefully poured out a measure in a small tumbler, handed it to me and announced its vintage. I put it to my lips. I was astounded at the delicacy of the kick. It was like being gifted a rare single malt after being plucked out of the North Sea. The woman waited for this flash of enlightenment to cross my face then her own creased with pleasure. Here in the ultimate back of beyond the locals had learned how to make a drink fit for the gods.

The morning was cold but clear and after a couple of rotis from the night before heated up we were off at six to try and reach our objective before midday when the clouds would intervene to obscure the curtain ridge on which Changabang sat. We were too near the vast brooding base of Dunagiri to see the summit and had to be content with making out the peaks on the horizon—Tirsuli and Hardeol—beyond which lay the Milam glacier over impossibly tangled terrain. At first there was a good village path but as the contours rose and the grazing became less plentiful we were forced to find our own route, stumbling up steeply rising ground that had once been glacial detritus but now was seeded shale. Across the way Changabang rose in a smooth granite sweep almost bronze in the morning light, a rare mountain whose full beauty can only be guessed at from this rear view. Across the curtain inside the Sanctuary mountaineers have been known to sit and contemplate its ecstatic lines for hours together. Nothing matches the sheer breathless soar of this peak from that inner vantage point and there the colour of the granite is silver grey. Or so I am told. Try as I might I never got to see this angle, at least from close up. I did once glimpse Changabang's extraordinary spire as I climbed out of the inner Sanctuary en route to Nanda Kharak, a pass discovered by shepherds high on the Devistan ridge. But from that distance Changabang resembles a distant missile aimed at heaven. My only close-up view inside the Sanctuary had been from the head of the Changabang glacier. But from this angle the mountain is disappointingly bland in outline. It is extraordinary how this most beautiful peak in the Himalaya is plain from all angles except from Dunagiri base camp, the single point from which the full beauty of 'the Shining Peak' is revealed. But at least from Bagini, where we were, the mountain is more appealing than seen from Changabang glacier. Clearly it was at Dunagiri base camp that the peak got its name, because the peak adjoining it and on the same ridge is called Kalanka, signifying a blot on the landscape. Move to another angle however and Kalanka is hardly a blot.

From our 'backside' vantage point this neighbouring peak looked fairly distinguished. Changabang and Kalanka resembled sisters and shared a common bronze base. Their smooth granite towers almost suggest twins though neither would win any prizes in a beauty contest. Kalanka holds its own here settling scores about her name.

Looking back, the Dunagiri massif was now coming into focus but still the huge bulk of its base obscured the grandeur of its peak. By eleven o'clock we were starting to feel glacier lassitude and our party was beginning to sound negative about its chances of stealing a close-up view before the clouds descended. I voted we should keep slogging till midday and only then admit defeat. We were hungry and it is hard work toiling up moraine. So far we had avoided snow and slush however, and I told Khan to look on the bright side. To have got this far at this altitude without getting our feet wet was something of a record.

Unfortunately only Khan was carrying a camera. I had set out on the spur of the moment and hadn't brought mine along. Now it hurts to think what great slides I would have got of these splendid peaks all lined up in perfect weather. For me the exploration was made more interesting for having been inside the Sanctuary:

I knew exactly (in spite of the different outer shapes) which mountain belonged where. I was determined to reach the ridge and went at the route so ferociously that I left even Raju floundering.

Just before twelve we were faced with a steep slope with scree so loose it covered our trekking shoes. The sun was beating down and we were high enough now to have a cold wind soughing round our ears as well as a swell of clouds inexorably building up to blot out the peaks. Khan almost threw in the towel and suggested we go no further. The sharp ridge we hoped to attain was hopelessly unstable and for every step up you slid two down and forever your shoes were filled with rubble. Somehow I forged up the last remaining slip. The clouds were still tantalisingly short of their blockade. I yodelled down to Khan telling him he would regret not having taken this angle with his camera for the rest of his life. The view was stunning. This concern for posterity was enough to egg him on and exactly on schedule we all rejoiced atop our objective.

I wistfully considered making my way down to the roots of Changabang to spend the night in the proximity of this ravishing mountain. But it was only a prompting since I had neither food, clothes nor tent to survive the night. Over the years I have had masochistic moments and while they are rich in retrospective amusement value I would never, given the choice, undertake them again. They were experiments that had to be made and I am grateful to have survived them. Tired from our struggle our return was much slower than expected. By six when the light was beginning to fail we were so exhausted we lost the trail and found ourselves on the wrong side of the stream that led to the village. Luckily a search party had set out to find us. Once again thanks to Khan's status as tourist officer we had been let off the hook. Being benighted on the Bagini would have been a cruel end to a most rewarding day. Flickering lantern lights across the stream announced our rescuers and we were soon home and dry. Too dry perhaps because the old lady did not offer a second dram of her magic potion.

On the way back to Joshimath I called in to see my old porters in Lata. I was delighted to see Natha Singh's nephew Shobha

Singh, whom I had photographed as a little child. He had grown into a sensitive student who knew all about the environmental problems that had led to the closure of the Sanctuary. Since my account of the Sanctuary had contributed to hastening its closure, I was relieved to find that the younger generation understood why I had argued the way I did. Naturally the older porters viewed me with less enthusiasm because the closures had affected their cash income in a big way. Today I would feel much less sure about going public with my opinions on such matters. When I had supported the closure I imagined areas outside the Sanctuary would be opened up to prevent the porters from losing their wages. I even wrote to Mr Sarin to this effect. But the government sadly did the mindless thing and closed the entire area, unconcerned about the suffering this would cause to hundreds of households in the Dhauli valley. I feel ashamed to go back to Lata now, after the villagers' livelihood has been cut off.

In Joshimath I sampled the new ropeway to Auli and took the trolley (as it's called) all the way to the top. Then I climbed further up to get a view of Nanda Devi from the buggial. The mountain looks most impressive from the cable car though the ride is expensive. I decided to walk all the way down to Joshimath and this was a fascinating exercise in noting the different layers of climate and growth. As always the hillman had made a path straight down the middle and it was much quicker to drop down this pakdandi than ride in a jeep.

From Joshimath I caught a bus to Srinagar and after a meal took another bus to Tehri en route to Mussoorie. On the way we climbed past the rice paddies of Maletha and I noticed in a field a colourful new statue of the local medieval hero Madho Singh Bhandari (not to be confused with the Kumaun Madho Singh, a famous teashop owner who serviced pilgrims to Kailash). It overlooks both the fields he irrigated and the means he created to irrigate them, a small canal cleverly constructed to follow the contours of the hillside. Hence the local refrain

Ek Singh Madho Singh, ek Singh gai ka
Ek Singh Madho Singh aur Singh kahi ka.

Madho Singh had fought skirmishes on the border with Tibet two centuries before Gabbar Singh of the Garhwal Rifles won the Victoria Cross in France for similar acts of bravery. The memorial to Gabbar Singh came next, appropriately at the crossroads where one route leads to the plains and the other back to Mussoorie.

27
East of the Devi

Travel writers by advertising the rarer corners of the Himalaya cannot escape the charge that they risk cheapening the experience they hold most dear (though where in his *Valley of Flowers* does Frank Smythe recommend visitors trample the beauty underfoot?). Responsible trekking involves keeping our eyes open to every aspect of environmental health and treading with a respect for the ecosystem and the cultural traditions that have grown out of it. Trekker and mountain are both growing together and a sense of this living relationship is what Himalayan travel ideally ought to inspire.

In 1998 I learned that the trek to Milam had been derestricted and getting an Inner Line permit in Munsyari was now a formality. Since I had long wanted to check the eastern view of Nanda Devi I set out on 15th June by bus from Mussoorie. It would have been much quicker to go via the plains but the heat would be unbearable not to mention the squeeze of passengers. (India's population was nearing the billion mark and if anyone needed proof of the fact—just board a bus in Uttar Pradesh.) I decided to go by the hill road and put up with the slow rate of progress.

From Tehri I caught a connection to Srinagar that passed Maletha with the familiar figure of Madho Singh wielding not a weapon but the spade with which he dug his famous canal. After a filling lunch in my favourite Punjabi dhaba I caught a third bus that got me to Karnaprayag by nightfall. Unprepossessing though it is, Karnaprayag enjoys sentinel status, guarding entry to the Great Himalaya: once across the Pindar you have left the Lesser range and are now in the major league. The upper bazaar in Karnaprayag is the parav's redeeming feature though most pilgrims passing through below are unaware of its existence. I climbed up to try and locate Bhuvan, son of the late Dev Ram Nautiyal the secretary of the Nanda Devi Raj Jat.

I wanted to apologise to Bhuvan for getting his name wrong. This is the risk travel writers face when they make notes en route hoping to avoid mistakes later when they try and recall names. Tired from long droning hill journeys my habit is to have a peg each evening to revive the creative principle. When the peg is too stiff spelling mistakes are apt to be committed and a scrawled 'Bhuvan' runs the risk of appearing 'Bimal' to sober eyes when several months later you type up the manuscript.

In the morning, no bus was going to Gwaldam, the last parav in Garhwal, so I hopped aboard a local taxi that would take me halfway. Then I caught another to Tharali. As I sat in a tea shack munching pakoras I heard the sound of a bus and was agreeably surprised to see a government vehicle going all the way to Delhi. I only found standing room but as I wasn't going very far (compared to the other long-distance passengers) this hardly mattered. I thought of alighting at Garur and then going east to Bageshwar but since the bus was climbing to Kausani I decided to visit Lakshmi Ashram, the source of my inspiration for Nanda Devi since the peak rides regally before the ashram.

A samadhi to Sarala Devi had been erected at the ashram and I wondered how this stickler for modesty would have reacted to finding her remains honoured by a minor shrine. To prove Sarala was a great if not easy soul to live with, she had the unique privilege in the modern world of being cremated in her own garden with wood from her own apple trees. She would have approved of the economy of burning diseased branches to render into ashes a body no longer capable of work. At least they would provide potash for further apple growth!

Next morning I caught a taxi down to Garur passing through the lush rice paddies and from that tumbledown parav (that always reminds me of a set for a spaghetti cowboy film) I took a bus to Bageshwar. Although hot at 2000 ft Bageshwar has a sangam that offers the possibility of a breeze. Its bazaar has some character if you are impervious to the flies. After a meal and an hour's wait a bus drove in going all the way to Munsyari. This was a stroke of luck because changing buses further in the interior would mean another night halt. As it was, the Munsyari bus didn't get us there till seven p.m. so bad was the road.

It was a grinding journey climbing from 2000 ft to crest a pass above 10,000 ft. On the way we passed Kotmuniya where Sarala Behn had spent her last years in solitude. She had a cottage called 'Him Darshan' built exactly on the ridge dividing Almora from Pithoragarh districts. The Gandhians, because they had entered the early governments of Uttar Pradesh, knew all the tricks when it came to acquiring government bounty. Boundary ridges which were disputed were taken over by the British and called 'Kaiser-e-Hind' properties. They were used to reward loyal villagers or old soldiers who had served with distinction. Sarala definitely qualified because she was a true freedom fighter.

From Chaukori with its great view of the extraordinary axe-blade summit of Nanda Kot we wound down past Dan Singh Maldar's tea gardens and halted in the Berinag bazaar. The ancient tea factory architecture could still be discerned and even some former sahib morality. An old notice in blue enamel with white lettering above a shop selling newspapers warned 'It is a sin to read without paying'. This flew in the face of local custom where a little surreptitious skimming of the headlines was considered *de rigueur* for the well-informed bazaar regular. Should he want to read more and lack the means to buy the publication a compromise could be reached whereby he could hire the magazine at a discount and return it after the fashion of a lending library.

To my delight, I was able to find for sale some old packs of Berinag tea, once highly sought by London tea blenders for its kippery flavour. The packing is just the same as it was in the 1930s and printed on one side of the box is the advertisement 'Berenag Tea Revives You'. At the top is the claim 'Fresh From Garden' and below, the garden itself is depicted. Beneath three snow peaks runs the long factory building at Chaukori complete with red tin roof. Picking the tea bushes are three ladies all with black bobbed hair. The girl in the foreground looks convent-educated and carries on her back the long narrow wicker basket peculiar to Kumaun. (Garhwal and Himachal favour the short and wide kandi made of split bamboo.) What is intriguing is the girl's dress. Her salwar kameez is more Chinese than Indian and sports a mandarin collar. It is well known that the tea gardens of Uttarakhand were started with Chinese knowhow and Chowfins, the famous family of Pauri, was renowned for its expertise as tea planters.

Berinag Tea was owned by D.S. Bist & Sons and this appears on the other side of the label along with instructions on how to achieve the best brew: 'Allow one tea spoonful to each cup and proportionally to the pot and infuse for eight to ten minutes.' Though delicious in flavour Berinag is low in colour and this accounts for the delay in infusion. A final instruction would only be heeded by local drinkers 'Fresh milk should be added for best results.' To the connoisseur it would be sacrilege to contaminate such a rare flavour with any animal substance.

The road continues down to the junction at Thal then turns north for the arduous ascent to the pass that leads to Munsyari. The transition from the Lesser range to the Greater is visible in the sheer brute rise of a white rocky rampart above the kinder scenery left below. In Munsyari I decided to spend the night in the new tourist bungalow and noted that as in other places in Kumaun the design had been made back-to-front. Instead of putting the dramatic view of Panch Chhuli at the front for visitors to rejoice in as they enter and leave, the entrance has been placed at the side and so hard against the hill you can hardly squeeze in. Because of the squeeze to get in through the main entrance everybody enters through the kitchen! The saving grace in such official bungling is that the level of lunacy achieved is so sublime it almost qualifies as entertainment. Similar baffling design conundrums can be witnessed at other places in Kumaun where the snow view instead of being emphasised is kept in the background, blocked by the barn-like structures that pass today as bungalows. These buildings are not so much designed for the public as for freeloading servants of the people and here outside Munsyari's back-to-front bungalow were parked several politicians' cars with party flags on the mudguard.

The manager turned out to be useful in arranging a reliable if diminutive porter who turned up next morning and took me to the tehsildar's office. We had to wait an hour for his signature on the permit to allow me to visit Milam (and back) within a week. There was some confusion over whether a camera could be carried or used. Further confusion ensued at the Bogdwar police checkpost: apparently, while foreigners can take photos Indians need special permission. The problem was compounded by the police in Milam who confiscated my cheap camera overnight and returned it with solemn ceremony next morning. As I had already filmed the approach to Milam on my way up the valley (and again filmed it on departure) I don't know what security purposes keeping cameras overnight are sought to further.

The walk in is dramatic. After the initial steep descent to Madgaon we entered the hot valley of the Gori Ganga. Never have I seen a more angry torrent. The mud-coloured water roars down like an express train and several steaming cataracts mark the lower course. But from the humid bamboo thickets we had to climb to Malla Lilam as the bridle path along the river has not only collapsed but been washed away comprehensively for miles without a trace.

That night we stayed in a village house and slept upstairs in the bare loft after a homely meal of roti and potatoes. The porter was a quiet sort of young man, a regular on this route. Everyone liked him but I noticed when it came to food he was always served last. Here were Kumaun's caste concerns to the fore as always. It is deeply woven into the fabric of society and has religious overtones.

critical comments only produce a neurotic range of evasive or negative responses. So you watch the charade and realise that it is from the mindlessness of such discredited systems that the lunacy witnessed in the back-to-front works of officialdom takes some of its inspiration.

Because of the broken river path we had to climb a vertical 3000 ft next morning and shared the ascent with endless flocks of sheep and goats on their way to the grazing meadows higher up the Johar valley. The flies and heat were killing. Someone suggested this route is called 'Nain Singh Marg' since it was worked out by the famous Pandit spy when the river was in flood. It doesn't say much for Nain Singh's ability to find and keep a steady gradient—but then he was a Pahari and instinctively chose the *diretissima* route. Most of the way it just went up and up and once on top it then went down and down. From the top we see the parav of 'Railgarhi' (so called I imagine because it resembles a railway carriage) quite literally under our feet, a steep spiral through fine forest but at the same killing gradient.

We had lunch there and moved on to Bogdwar to spend the night. The Nalapani temple marks the actual centre of the great divide: the crest of the Great Himalaya not passed over by land but bored through by water. A vast smooth blackened cliff face rises absolutely sheer above a narrow catwalk that signifies—when the snow is not melting—a path. It is a graphic demonstration of the towering strength of the granite thrusting out from the earth's molten core. The magical act of crossing the crest of the Great range is performed here at less than 9000 ft. There is a foot of choppy water swirling over the path but by clinging to the rock face we managed to wade through the icy flood. Coming back we would have to get our timing right.

All my treks have sought to savour the precise moment when you can experience the gnawing force that has given rise to the Himalaya. Most who view the still, dreamy panorama of floating snow peaks find it difficult to imagine the seething cauldron bubbling at the roots of this serene composition. Even when confronted by a hot spring spitting out molten sulphur—as at Tapovan under the Kuari—visitors are reluctant to make the ineluctable connection between Nanda Devi's soaring snow-white graces and this witch's brew that has conjured them up. Similarly most of us prefer to visualise Shiva in his aloof, detached yogic form rather than applaud him as Nataraj the fiery dancer whose agitated movement represents the tumescent affirmation of life's miraculous energy.

Here at Nalapani the rush and sweep of choppy glacial water funnelling impetuously through the towering rock walls forces on the traveller awareness of nature's ongoing conflict. The evidence of colliding continents may not be obvious but the growling war of attrition between rock and water is audible. The racing torrent successfully wears away the incremental upthrust and the sheer black walls of this looming canyon testify to the astonishing thrust and parry of fire and water.

The satisfaction I feel on gazing up at this blind face of awesome elemental interplay is the reward of forty years of probing walks. This moment defines for me the reality that the Himalaya's greatness lies as much in its geomorphic roots as in its aesthetic culmination. Change and movement is the chief characteristic of the range not inert stability. In heraldic terms the Himalaya is more rampant than couchant, or as the I Ching might put it—'there is fire at the foot of the mountain'.

This moment also defines the accuracy of the popular perception that the crest of the Great Himalaya marks the extent of Bharat. Once across Kalidas's 'measuring rod' at Nalapani you are effectively amidst a different kind of terrain. Immediately the temperature drops and the mood of the rushing river is muffled by a series of massive snow bridges. We climb through deliciously emerald, springy alpine meadows to reach Martoli. After the hellish humidity of Lilam it is like being admitted to paradise. The heart lifts with pleasure at the untrammelled spread of scented loveliness that climaxes in the upsweep of snowy summits.

Martoli's beauty however wore a desolate air. The dancing meadows with brilliant buttercups lining the tumbling springs, and enlivened by the overwhelming aroma of thyme sprinkled in pink abandon: surely this deserved a thriving population. But the beautifully crafted village was empty. Seldom on my travels have I seen such masterly stonework. Every course of stone was so expertly laid that no blade however fine could be inserted between them. The stone is of the local lichen-toned grey and the natty slate roofs capped elegant small windows and wood-pillared doorways each with Ganesh carved as the centrepiece but done in the erotic mode of the unorthodox.

Nanda Mai's temple came as a disappointment. Situated a kilometre away from the village in order to command a view down the Lawan valley to the ramparts of the Sanctuary's east curtain, it is a low ramshackle structure of slate-capped stone that lacks either dignity or authority. In the village we put up in a house converted to 'Nanda Devi Hotel' and the young man who owned it laughed when we discounted his make believe that the peak we could see from his door was Nanda Devi. It was in fact Nanda Khat, an understudy of the Goddess, who rises above the approach to the Pindari glacier. Almost all visitors to Martoli are taken in by this tale of convenience. The fact is you cannot see Nanda Devi from the village, though from Nanda Mai temple you can glimpse a portion of the east peak. To view Nanda Devi you must make the next march beyond Burfu (nowadays the most inhabited of the villages in the Johar valley) to Bilju. At Burfu a new and bland Hindu temple has come up in place of the Buddhist shrine to signify how the locals have turned their backs on the cultural ties that went with the Tibetan trade connection. But the signs of this trade, in the beautifully constructed houses of Martoli, Burfu and Milam, are too manifest for it to be fully forgotten. A small but exquisitely sculpted dharmshala (possibly built for visiting dignitaries) stands on the trail outside Burfu. It is worthy of heritage status but unlikely to be reclaimed since it reminds the locals of a past they would now rather forget.

Carpet weaving is still very much a viable village craft and I was tempted all along the trail to pick up a rug as a long-lasting memento. However Ram told me his family had a good selection and that I could save myself the weight of carrying one by buying from him. When we got back to Munsyari it was to find that his designs were all modern and trendy whereas I wanted traditional Buddhist mandalas. Their absence was a further reminder of what the villagers chose to turn away from.

These empty villages—Milam was no different—only sustain one crop, small plots of jumbu, the wild shallot, and other herbs that have some market value. Jumbu is sought after in lower Kumaun as the only onion, especially tasty in dal, that the hill brahmin may eat without losing caste.

The walk along the upper Johar valley is like meandering through a celestial golfcourse. Above Burfu serious snow peaks declare themselves and the icy approaches glisten in the morning sun to announce how grisly it would be to set foot on them. Ahead Tirsuli and Hardeol make superbly artistic statements of mountain grandeur locking within their tangled fastnesses the thrown away key of a route over to the Bagini glacier. Close up however the Milam glacier disappoints. As there are restrictions on movement by the border police I do not go beyond the first three kilometres. Coming back I have tea in the house of one of the Pandit spies' descendants. He turns out to be rather stupid and insolent and I muse on how quickly family reputations can dissipate. A hundred years ago border trade flourished in this valley. Laden caravans and jingling pack-goats brought fortunes to the Bhotias who risked their necks over these exposed passes into Tibet. Suddenly in 1962 it all stopped and villages like Martoli ceased to have any meaning.

At the crack of dawn next morning I reclaim my camera and set off at a gallop to try and get a shot of Nanda Devi's twin peaks from the village of Bilju that looks westwards up the Pachi glacier. My porter grumbles at the early start and the pace I set but is quite happy to have his photo taken against the Devi's uplift. Years later when I attend a mountaineering seminar in Mumbai a trekker comes up to me with a coloured photo of this very view. My porter had been employed a year after my trek by this Mumbaikar and recalled to him on passing Bilju how a sahib from Mussoorie had made him race down from Milam at five in the morning to catch this view of the Devi. The porter remembered because the *pagal angrez* was also called 'Bill-ji'!